Conversations with Paul Bowles

Literary Conversations Series

Peggy Whitman Prenshaw
General Editor

Conversations
with Paul Bowles

Edited by
Gena Dagel Caponi

University Press of Mississippi
Jackson

Library of Congress Cataloging-in-Publication Data

Bowles, Paul, 1910–
    Conversations with Paul Bowles / edited by Gena Dagel Caponi.
      p. cm. — (Literary conversations series)
    Includes index.
    ISBN 0-87805-649-1 (cloth : alk. paper). — ISBN 0-87805-650-5
(pbk. : alk. paper)
    1. Bowles, Paul, 1910– —Interviews. 2. Authors, American—20th
century—Interviews. 3. Composers—United States—Interviews.
I. Caponi, Gena Dagel. II. Title. III. Series.
PS3552.O874Z463 1993
813′.54—dc20   93-25038
                                               CIP

British Library Cataloging-in-Publication data available

Books by Paul Bowles

Two Poems. New York: The Modern Editions Press, 1933.

The Sheltering Sky. London: John Lehmann, 1949; New York: New Directions, 1949; New York: The Ecco Press, 1978; London: Peter Owen, 1981; New York: Vintage International, 1990; New York: Paladin, 1990.

A Little Stone. London: John Lehmann, 1950.

The Delicate Prey. New York: Random House, 1950; New York: The Ecco Press, 1972, 1980, 1984, 1985.

The Lost Trail of the Sahara. By R. Frison-Roche, translated by Paul Bowles. New York: Prentice-Hall, 1951.

Let It Come Down. London: John Lehmann, 1952; New York: Random House, 1952; Santa Barbara: Black Sparrow, 1980; London: Peter Owen, 1984; London: Arena, 1985; London: Abacus, 1990.

The Spider's House. New York: Random House, 1955; London: Macdonald & Co., 1957; Santa Barbara: Black Sparrow, 1982; London: Peter Owen, 1985; London: Abacus Books, 1991.

Yallah. Photographs by Peter W. Haeberlin, with text by Paul Bowles. Zurich: Manesse, 1956; New York: McDowell, Obolensky, Inc., 1957.

No Exit. By Jean-Paul Sartre, adapted by Paul Bowles. New York: Samuel French, Inc., 1958.

The Hours after Noon. London: Heinemann, 1959.

A Hundred Camels in the Courtyard. San Francisco: City Lights Books, 1962, 1986.

Their Heads Are Green and Their Hands Are Blue. London: Peter Owen, 1963; New York: Random House, 1963; New York: The Ecco Press, 1984; London: Abacus, 1990.

A Life Full of Holes. By Driss ben Hamed Charhadi, translated by Paul Bowles. New York: Grove Press, Inc., 1964; London: Weidenfeld & Nicolson, 1964.

Up Above the World. New York: Simon and Schuster, 1966; London: Peter Owen, 1967; New York: Pocket Books, 1968; New York: The Ecco Press, 1982; London: Peter Owen, 1982; London: Arena, 1984; London: Abacus Books, 1991.

Love with a Few Hairs. By Mohammed Mrabet, taped and translated by Paul Bowles. London: Peter Owen, 1967; New York: George Braziller, 1968; San Francisco: City Lights Books, 1986; London: Arena, 1986.

The Time of Friendship. New York: Holt, Rinehart and Winston, 1967.

Pages from Cold Point. London: Peter Owen, 1968; New York: Zenith, 1983; London: Arena, 1986; London: Abacus, 1990, 1991.

Scenes. Los Angeles: Black Sparrow Press, 1968.

The Lemon. By Mohammed Mrabet, translated and edited by Paul Bowles. London: Peter Owen, 1969; New York: McGraw-Hill, 1972; San Francisco: City Lights Books, 1986.

M'Hashish. By Mohammed Mrabet, taped and translated by Paul Bowles. San Francisco: City Lights Books, 1969.

Thicket of Spring. Los Angeles: Black Sparrow Press, 1972.

Without Stopping. New York: G. P. Putnam's Sons, 1972; London: Peter Owen, 1972; New York: The Ecco Press, 1985, 1991; London: Hamish Hamilton, 1989.

For Bread Alone. By Mohamed Choukri, translated and with an introduction by Paul Bowles. London: Peter Owen, 1974; London: Grafton, 1987.

The Boy Who Set the Fire. By Mohammed Mrabet, taped and translated by Paul Bowles. Los Angeles: Black Sparrow Press, 1974; San Francisco: City Lights Books, 1988, 1989.

Jean Genet in Tangier. By Mohamed Choukri, translated by Paul Bowles. New York: The Ecco Press, 1974, 1990.

Hadidan Aharam. By Mohammed Mrabet, translated by Paul Bowles. Los Angeles: Black Sparrow Press, 1975.

The Oblivion Seekers. By Isabelle Eberhardt, translated by Paul Bowles. San Francisco: City Lights, 1975; London: Peter Owen, 1987.

Three Tales. New York: Frank Hallman, 1975; New York: School of Visual Arts, 1983.

Look & Move On. By Mohammed Mrabet, taped and translated by Paul Bowles. Santa Barbara: Black Sparrow Press, 1976; London: Peter Owen, 1989.

Harmless Poisons, Blameless Sins. By Mohammed Mrabet, taped and translated by Paul Bowles. Santa Barbara: Black Sparrow Press, 1976.

Next to Nothing. Kathmandu, Nepal: Starstreams 5, 1976.

The Big Mirror. Santa Barbara: Black Sparrow Press, 1977.

Things Gone and Things Still Here. Santa Barbara: Black Sparrow Press, 1977.

Tennessee Williams In Tangier. By Mohamed Choukri, translated by Paul Bowles. Santa Barbara: Cadmus, 1979.

Collected Stories 1939–1976. Santa Barbara: Black Sparrow Press, 1979, 1989.

Five Eyes. By Abdeslam Boulaich, Mohamed Choukri, Larbi Layachi, Mohammed Mrabet, Ahmed Yacoubi, edited and translated by Paul Bowles. Santa Barbara: Black Sparrow Press, 1979.

The Beach Café & the Voice. By Mohammed Mrabet, taped and translated by Paul Bowles. Santa Barbara: Black Sparrow Press, 1980.

The Husband. 1980. Publisher unknown.

Midnight Mass. Santa Barbara: Black Sparrow Press, 1981, 1983, 1989; London: Peter Owen, 1985; New York: Harper and Row, 1991.

Next to Nothing: Collected Poems 1926–1977. Santa Barbara: Black Sparrow Press, 1981.

In the Red Room. Los Angeles: Sylvester & Orphanos, 1981.

Points in Time. London: Peter Owen, 1982; New York: The Ecco Press, 1984, 1986.

The Path Doubles Back. By Rodrigo Rey Rosa, translated by Paul Bowles. New York: Red Ozier Press, 1982.

The Chest. By Mohammed Mrabet, translated by Paul Bowles. Bolinas, California: Tombouctou Books, 1983.

Selected Songs. Santa Fe, New Mexico: Soundings Press, 1984.

International Poem. 1985. Publisher unknown.

She Woke Me Up So I Killed Her. Translations by Paul Bowles. San Francisco: Cadmus Editions, 1985.

The Beggar's Knife. By Rodrigo Rey Rosa, translated by Paul Bowles. San Francisco: City Lights Books, 1985; London: Peter Owen, 1988.

Marriage with Papers. By Mohammed Mrabet, translated by Paul Bowles. Bolinas, California: Tombouctou Books, 1986.

For Bread Alone. London: Grafton, 1987.

Call at Corazón and Other Stories. London: Peter Owen, 1988; London: Abacus, 1989.

Unwelcome Words: Seven Stories. Bolinas, California: Tombouctou Books, 1988.

A Distant Episode: The Selected Stories. New York: The Ecco Press, 1988, 1989.

Al Maghrib: Photographs. Edinburgh: Polygon, 1989; Third Eye, 1989.

A Thousand Days for Mokhtar. London: Peter Owen, 1989; London: Abacus, 1990.

Two Years Beside the Strait. London: Peter Owen, 1990.

Days, Tangier Journal: 1987–1989. New York: The Ecco Press, 1991, 1992.

Too Far From Home: The Selected Writings of Paul Bowles. New York: The Ecco Press, 1992.

The Letters of Paul Bowles. New York: Farrar, Strauss, Giroux, 1993.

Contents

Introduction

In view of the chronology of Paul Bowles's life, it seems remarkable
that any interviews with him exist at all. Few writers have been more
nomadic or less accessible. Bowles dropped out of college his freshman
year at the University of Virginia for a trip to Paris. He then spent most
of the next four years (1929–1933) traveling through Europe and North
Africa. Even when working fairly steadily as a composer in New York
City from 1933 to 1947, Bowles continued to move about, sometimes to
travel to Mexico, Cuba, or Central America, sometimes simply to move
to a better or cheaper location within or near the city. During only one
two-and-one-half year period (1944–47) did Bowles keep the same
address longer than six months. It was only after settling in Tangier in
1947 that Bowles began to be interviewed (though still not with regu-
larity) by the increasing number of students, writers, and journalists
who tracked him down.

Paul Bowles first went to Tangier on a lark in 1931; he returned after
World War II in order to write a novel. He had not intended to emigrate
to Morocco, but one day found that he had done exactly that. In 1947 he
wrote to Charles-Henri Ford: "Certainly I never meant to stay in Tangier
again, but for no reason at all I have remained on and on, perhaps
because one can get everything one wants here and the life is cheap as
dirt, and travel is so damned difficult . . . and mainly the great fact that
I haven't the energy to pack up and go anywhere else."[1] By 1963, he
wrote to William Burroughs, "the only way to live in Morocco now is
to remember constantly that the world outside is still more repulsive."[2]
Twenty years later he concluded, "Tangier is now the last word in
shabbiness; it has become European only in the sense that the Moroccans have become European. The population consists of partially West-
ernized Moroccans and the tourists who arrive in tens of thousands."[3]

For those who know Bowles only through his exotic tales of deceit,
dislocation, and intrigue—set in Mexico, Central America, North
Africa, or India—meeting him often comes as a surprise. Gracious,
witty, and entertaining, he is gentle, soft-spoken, and patient (even with

the most offensive and demanding guests). He is white-haired and blue-eyed, not exactly frail but slim. At home he dresses casually, in a conservative American fashion. Daniel Halpern commented on this discrepancy between Paul Bowles the person and Paul Bowles the author, to which Bowles replied, "Why is it that Americans expect an artist's work to be a clear reflection of his life? They never seem to want to believe that the two can be independent of each other and go their separate ways." Bowles has done his best to isolate himself from his readers and from western life, even though his antennae stretch around the globe and he has acquaintances in every part of the world. He has no telephone and blames poor mail delivery for his refusing to answer letters he would rather not have received, letters that number more than fifteen a day, generally from strangers. He is protective of his privacy. "The man who wrote the books didn't exist. No writer exists. He exists in his books, and that's all," he told Catherine Warnow and Regina Weinreich. He avoids subjects that are painful to him, such as questions about his wife's illness. He refuses to answer prying personal questions, and when pressed simply invents an answer appropriate to his feelings at the time. He categorically avoids questions that begin with "why?". By now he has been asked the same questions about himself and his work so many times that he is able to give consistent information, each answer a replication of the previous one. In his 1972 autobiography *Without Stopping*, Bowles recalled Jorge Luis Borges's story about memory: Borges's father once laid a coin on a tabletop and called it "the image," laid another coin on top and said that was the memory of the image, and then continued laying coins on top of coins, building a series of memories of memories, each more distant from the original image. Bowles's relating the tale was prophetic: since writing his autobiography, interviewers have been questioning him about that, too, forcing him to add to an already tall stack of coins.

Bowles can be an arbitrary interview subject. He has said many times that he empties his mind each time he begins writing, and one feels he starts each interview the same way. While many of his personal anecdotes seem static, answers to questions about his state of mind and ideas about his work change from one interview to the next. One is left with answers that are consistent and deliberately stale, as if to stall further biographical questions, or answers that intrigue and seem invented just for the occasion. In one interview, he will say Gide was his favorite writer as a young man; in another, Lautréamont. He claims he wrote 95 percent of his work in bed; that he wrote almost an entire novel while walking; that he agonizes over each word; that he never revises; that he revises while he types his manuscript from longhand; that he doesn't use a typewriter because he finds it too cumbersome; that he writes without conscious awareness of what he is doing. "There's a truth for everyone, and no one truth carries away all the others," he tells Michael Rogers.

In a letter to someone wondering about the twists and turns in Bowles's life and career, Bowles's friend and mentor Virgil Thomson said, "Please try not to view his life as a planned career. He had more spontaneity than that, and he was always resistant to pressure, both from others and from his own convictions about 'duty' or calculations about 'advantage.' He is as 'free' a man as I have ever known, even when accepting an obligation, which he does strictly on his own, never under pressure."[4]

Bowles's most consistent trait is his insistence on precision in the use of language. He obligates interviewers to mean exactly what they say, or to say exactly what they mean; he will use this requirement to evade the leading implications of an interviewer's question and to avoid being pinned down. However, such fastidiousness awards interviewers the opportunity of securing a correct answer, if they ask the right question. Jeffrey Bailey suggested, "I guess it's understandable that living outside your indigenous culture became almost a compulsion with you," and Bowles clarified, "Not almost; it was a *real* compulsion."

The interviews in this volume fall into five groups, each corresponding to a different stage of Bowles's fame or celebrity. The first two, by Harvey Breit and Jay Harrison, date from 1952 and 1953, following publication of Bowles's first two novels and first short story collection. More than anything else, these interviews document New Yorkers' memory of Bowles as a composer, and there are many questions about his transition from writing music to writing fiction. In an airmail letter to Harvey Breit, Bowles candidly discusses the cathartic function of writing fiction and suggests that as a writer he takes a musical approach to his work, being conscious "of the sound of the phrase and sentence." The Harrison interview also reviews Bowles's career as a composer of chamber music, opera, and incidental music for Broadway, the most public aspects of Bowles's career.

The 1960s were a decade of personal difficulty and public neglect for

Bowles, as he spent them nursing his seriously ill wife, the writer Jane Bowles. Lacking long stretches of time to concentrate on a novel, he turned again to short stories and to transcribing and translating stories from the Moghrebi (a Moroccan dialect). From these years we have two long conversations with personal friends and one interview focusing on his friendship with Tennessee Williams. The Ira Cohen interview, the longest in this collection, took place at a low point in Bowles's public visibility and popularity; it shows Bowles at his least defensive and least rehearsed. Bowles loves to talk about Morocco, Moroccan music, and Moroccan beliefs, but doesn't always get a chance to do so, and in this interview the wide range of his Moroccan experience comes through. Here also Bowles describes for the first time his 1931 summer stay with Gertrude Stein at Bilignin ("She was sort of a very loving grandmother").

The Mike Steen interview, from *A Look at Tennessee Williams*, has a lot to say not only about Williams, but about the way he and Bowles worked together on *The Glass Menagerie, Sweet Bird of Youth, Summer and Smoke, The Milk Train Doesn't Stop Here Anymore,* the film *Senso,* and several songs. Williams and Bowles also traveled together, and Bowles's descriptions of Williams as a poor traveler and worse linguist remind the reader how much Bowles values facility in language and adaptability in travel.

Oliver Evans induces Bowles to review his life and career, his habits as a writer, and his ideas concerning the role of the artist in and out of the United States. Here for the last time Bowles discusses his writing from a composer's point of view: "I think in terms of syncopation, counterpoint, simultaneous motifs, solo and tutti passages. It helps to make things more precise in my mind."

The next set of interviews follows the 1972 publication of Bowles's autobiography *Without Stopping.* Two come from the post-1960s drug culture—*Rolling Stone* and *Stone Age* interviews—and approach Bowles as exotic guru to the Beat generation and the world's foremost *kif* expert; the *Rolling Stone* interview even includes a recipe for Moroccan Majoun (it is said that Bowles gave Alice B. Toklas her recipe for marijuana brownies). Michael Rogers had the unusual opportunity of accompanying Bowles to some picturesque spots near Tangier and recorded some of Bowles's ethnographic history of the city, particularly of the brotherhoods and what Bowles calls a "mass psychosis" surrounding a spirit woman named Aicha Qandicha.

The interview with Daniel Halpern is one of the first to confine itself almost exclusively to Bowles as a writer of fiction, a prelude to the next period of Bowles's life: rediscovery following the 1979 Black Sparrow publication of his *Collected Stories* and establishment of Bowles as a major American talent. Of this large group of interviews, Jeffrey Bailey's interview in *The Paris Review* and Jay McInerny's *Vanity Fair* story suggest serious mainstream interest in Bowles's writing; the appearance of other interviews from *TriQuarterly, oboe, Bomb,* and *Gargoyle* is proof of Bowles's continued underground following.

Two previously unpublished interviews also date from this period. Catherine Warnow and Regina Weinreich spent several days in 1988 filming conversations with Bowles for their documentary work, "Paul Bowles: the Complete Outsider," from which this interview is extracted. Earlier that same year Allen Hibbard talked with Bowles exclusively about his short stories, paying particular attention to recent short works.

Bowles's greatest celebrity coincided with Bernardo Bertolucci's movie of Bowles's first novel, *The Sheltering Sky* (1990). Interviews from Spain represent Bowles's widespread international following, and Stephen Davis's *Boston Globe* Sunday magazine essay indicates Bowles's new status as a film icon. Unfortunately, Bowles's health has since been unstable, and he has declined many recent requests for interviews.

In one of his interviews with Paul Bowles, Stephen Davis came upon the notion of Bowles as Mercury, a satisfying description from many angles. Bowles is indeed Mercurial: a messenger, world-traveler, transporter of communications from one realm to the next. He is, as well, mercurial. If he has refused to let geography or convention pin him down, he is not about to let an interview lock him into a particular position on any subject, least of all, himself.

In his recent book *Days, Tangier Journal: 1987–1989,* Paul Bowles remarked on his decreased mobility, due to a blocked artery. He is no longer able to climb along the rocky shore of the Merkala beach outside Tangier, where his sure-footedness once inspired friends to compare him to a goat, the zodiac sign under which he was born. "Pointless to pretend that time makes no difference," he wrote.[5] Time makes one difference: the subject ages—yet how clear the vision remains. "You must watch your universe as it cracks above your head," he told Harvey Breit in 1952. Never has he strayed from that opinion, although he maintained, in 1990, "Everything happened as it had to happen." One will find few explanations in this volume as to why things happened as they did. Bowles refuses to speculate. He will, however, converse; he will continue the discussion his works have begun. The interviews in this volume should be taken as conversational snapshots made during the past forty years of Bowles's career, a series of illustrations to accompany a body of work which the author, no doubt, considers in need of no further comment.

As in other volumes in the Literary Conversations series, these interviews appear uncut, largely unedited, and in the order in which they were conducted. Throughout, book titles have been italicized and typographical and factual errors have been silently corrected. The interview with Ira Cohen was found in the Rare Book and Manuscript Library at Columbia University in fragments: its 56 pages of half, quarter, or eighth portions of 8½″ by 11″ sheets have been edited for continuity and sense.

I am grateful to the writers and publishers who granted permission to reprint interviews, as well as to Mark Longley for help in translating two Spanish interviews, to Jane Elkind Bowers for her editing and listening skills, and to Jeffrey Miller for his invaluable contribution to Bowles scholarship, *Paul Bowles: A Descriptive Bibliography* (Santa Barbara: Black Sparrow Press, 1986). Seetha Srinivasan, at the University Press of Mississippi, most kindly encouraged the development of this volume and has attended to its progress with great patience and skill. My parents have supported almost everything I've ever done, and I am especially grateful to them for their help over this past year. I thank Brenda and Reed Smith, Mary and Steve Bell, Jackie Dudley, John McLeod, and Matt Martinez for friendship and diversion. Conversations with Jennie Skerl, Melissa Hield, Cindy Brandimarte, Lisa Jones, and Joel Dinerstein helped me think things through and made work possible. So did Becky Fife's and Debbie Sanchez's child-caring, Val and Marion Caponi's grandparenting, Pete Caponi's singular surprising wisdom, Maff Caponi's smiles, and Tom Caponi's endurance. I thank Tom, as well, for having grace and strength enough to understand

my year in Spain and spirit enough to share two memorable trips
to Morocco.

GDC
March 1993

NOTES

1. PB to Charles-Henri Ford, 19 November 1947, Harry Ransom Humanities Research
Center (HRHRC), University of Texas, Austin.

2. Quoted in Ted Morgan, *Literary Outlaw* (New York: Henry Holt, 1988) p. 393.

3. PB to Buffie Johnson, 8 April 1982, HRHRC.

4. Virgil Thomson to Mr. Patterson, 17 November 1970, Jackson Music Library, Yale
University.

5. Paul Bowles, *Days, Tangier Journal: 1987–1989* (New York: The Ecco Press, 1991)
p. 86.

Chronology

1910   Paul Frederic Bowles is born in Jamaica, Long Island, on 30 December, only child of Rena Winnewisser Bowles and Claude Dietz Bowles, a dentist.

1924   In January, PB begins high school.

1925   While visiting his Aunt Mary Robbins Meade in Watkins Glen, New York, PB begins a series of crime stories based on a character called the "Snake Woman."

1928   In the spring, PB publishes his surrealist poem "Spire Song" in the international literary magazine *transition* (12). In the next issue, he publishes "Entity," a prose piece. In the fall, he enters college at the University of Virginia in Charlottesville.

1929   PB leaves school without telling his parents and sails for Paris. In the fall he returns to New York, where he works at Dutton's Bookstore. He introduces himself to *New Music* editor and composer Henry Cowell, who writes a letter of introduction to composer Aaron Copland. He begins study with Copland, meanwhile publishing several poems in various small magazines.

1930   At his parents' insistence, PB returns to the University of Virginia, where Copland visits him. He continues to publish poetry and his first published piece of fiction, "A White Goat's Shadow," for Princeton's *Argo* (I:2). He completes the semester and joins Copland at the artists' retreat Yaddo, in Saratoga, New York.

1931   In March, PB sails again for Paris. He meets Gertrude

Stein, Jean Cocteau, Ezra Pound, and André Gide. He joins
Copland in Berlin, travels throughout Europe, visits Stein at
her summer home, and at her suggestion, departs with
Copland for his first trip to Morocco. In December,
Copland introduces PB's Sonata for Oboe and Clarinet in
London at a concert of new American music at Aeolian
Hall.

1932   In the spring, PB visits Tangier and Fez before returning to
Europe. He writes a cantata on his own text from St. John
Perse's *Anabase*, and the Piano Sonatina. In May, Copland
introduces PB's "Six Songs" at Yaddo. In December, after a
stay of some months in Europe, he returns to North Africa,
where he writes his cantata *Par le Détroit*.

1933   In January, PB meets George Turner, with whom he travels
across the Sahara and after whom he names Tunner in *The
Sheltering Sky*. In June, he returns to New York.

1934   John Kirkpatrick performs PB's Piano Sonatina at a League
of Composers concert. PB writes *Memnon*, a cycle of six
songs set to a Cocteau text, scores Harry Dunham's film
Bride of Samoa, and then in June returns to North Africa.

1935   In April, Henry Cowell publishes five PB compositions in
New Music (8:3). PB spends the fall working on the ballet
Yankee Clipper, for Lincoln Kirstein.

1936   On 2 April, the Federal Music Project presents an all-
Bowles concert. In July, PB helps form the Committee on
Republican Spain and writes the score for *Who Fights This
Battle?* to raise money for the Madrid government. Virgil
Thomson introduces PB to Orson Welles, for whom he
writes the scores to *Horse Eats Hat* and *Doctor Faustus*. He
also composes a score for a film on the Southern Tenant
Farmers' Union, *America's Disinherited*, using traditional
folk songs as thematic material.

1937   With his future wife Jane Auer, PB travels by bus to
        Mexico City. The American Ballet Caravan premiers his
        ballet *Yankee Clipper* in Philadelphia in June. PB spends the
        summer working on the never-completed opera *Denmark
        Vesey,* to a libretto by Charles-Henri Ford.

1938   On 22 February, PB and Jane Auer marry and then leave for
        Central America and France. At the request of Orson
        Welles, PB returns from Europe to write music for *Too
        Much Johnson,* which Welles never produces.

1939   PB applies for and receives relief in order to get on the
        WPA rolls as a composer, collecting $23.86 weekly. Using
        the apartment of Clifford Odets as a studio, he composes the
        score to William Saroyan's *My Heart's in the Highlands.*
        He writes the score to Saroyan's *Love's Old Sweet Song* and
        then leaves for New Mexico to write the music for a Soil
        Erosion Service film on the Rio Grande Valley, *Roots in the
        Soil.*

1940   After finishing the film score, PB hurries to Mexico,
        visiting Acapulco and settling in Taxco. In the fall, the
        Theatre Guild calls him back to New York to write the score
        for *Twelfth Night.* He plans to stay only for six weeks but
        then is engaged to write the scores for *Liberty Jones* and
        Lillian Hellman's *Watch on the Rhine.* The Bowleses spend
        the winter living with George Davis, Benjamin Britten,
        Peter Pears, Oliver Smith, and W. H. Auden, on Middaugh
        Street in Brooklyn Heights, where PB writes *Pastorela* for
        the American Ballet Caravan.

1941   In March, PB receives a Guggenheim Foundation grant to
        write an opera. He travels to Taxco and Acapulco to work
        with García Lorca's *Así Que Pasen Cinco Años,* which he
        translates and adapts for his libretto.

1942   PB returns to Watkins Glen, New York, in the summer, and
        in the fall, to New York City where he orchestrates his

opera, *The Wind Remains*. In November, he begins writing music criticism for the *Herald Tribune*. He is called by the Selective Service but refused for service.

1943　　*The Wind Remains* premiers at the Museum of Modern Art on 30 March, under the direction of Leonard Bernstein, with choreography by Merce Cunningham. *'Tis Pity She's a Whore* premiers (18 May), with incidental music by PB. Peggy Guggenheim inaugurates her *Art of This Century* recordings with PB's Flute Sonata, with a cover illustration by Max Ernst. *South Pacific* (29 December) premiers in New York, with music by PB.

1944　　PB's ballet *Colloque Sentimental* for the Ballet de Monte Carlo premiers, as does *Jacobowsky and the Colonel* (14 March), for which he wrote the score.

1945　　*The Glass Menagerie* opens in New York on 31 March, with music by PB. PB edits a South American issue for Charles-Henri Ford and Parker Tyler's surrealist magazine *View* (V:2). Inspired by texts of the Arapesh and Tara-humara, PB begins writing fiction and publishes "The Scorpion" in *View* (V:5). With Oliver Smith, he travels to Central America and returns to write the score for *Ondine*.

1946　　PB's translation of Jean-Paul Sartre's *Huis Clos, No Exit,* directed by John Huston, wins the Drama Critics' Circle Award for the best foreign play of the year. He writes his Concerto for Two Pianos, Winds, and Percussion and completes scores for *Twilight Bar, The Dancer, Cyrano de Bergerac* (8 October premiere), *Land's End* (11 December premiere). *Harper's Bazaar* publishes "The Echo," and *View* publishes his story "By The Water."

1947　　When *Partisan Review* publishes his story "A Distant Episode," PB decides to pursue a career as a writer. He publishes "Under the Sky" in *Horizon* and "Call at Corazón" in *Harper's Bazaar*. He also completes the score

for *On Whitman Avenue*. In May he begins planning his
novel *The Sheltering Sky*, and after dreaming of Tangier,
books passage and departs. The film *Dreams That Money
Can Buy*, for which PB wrote the music, wins an award in
July at the Venice Film Festival. In September, the O.
Henry Awards includes "The Echo" in *Prize Stories of
1947*.

1948   "You Are Not I" appears in the January issue of
Mademoiselle, "Under the Sky" in the March issue of
Partisan Review, and "At Paso Rojo" in the September
issue of *Mademoiselle*. After nearly a year of a nomadic life
in North Africa, PB completes his first novel in Fez. In
July, he sends the novel to Doubleday, which refuses it.
John Lehmann in London and James Laughlin at New
Directions subsequently publish the book. During June and
July, PB and singer Libby Holman travel through the Anti-
Atlas mountains in North Africa and Holman suggests PB
write an opera for her. In September, "A Distant Episode"
appears in Houghton Mifflin's *Best American Short Stories
1948*. Receiving a request from Tennessee Williams to write
the score for *Summer and Smoke* (New York premiere, 6
October), PB returns to New York. In December he goes
back to Tangier, accompanied by Williams and Frank
Merlo. *New Directions 10 in Prose and Poetry* publishes "A
Distant Episode" in December.

1949   The February issue of *Mademoiselle* includes PB's story
"Pastor Dowe at Tacaté." In the spring, PB crosses to Paris,
to hear Arthur Gold and Robert Fizdale perform his
concerto. Truman Capote and Gore Vidal follow him to
Tangier. "Under the Sky" appears in *Best American Short
Stories 1949* in July, and the O. Henry Awards *Prize Stories
of 1949* includes "Pastor Dowe at Tacaté." In November,
when *The Sheltering Sky* is published in London, PB travels
there to help publicize it. From London he sails for Ceylon
where he works on his second novel, *Let It Come Down*.
His story "Pages from Cold Point" is published twice: first

in *Wake* (8), and then in *New Directions in Prose and Poetry #11*.

1950   *The Sheltering Sky* stays on the *New York Times* Best Seller List from 1 January through 12 March. PB travels in Ceylon and southern India through the spring and then moves into a house in the medina of Tangier, which he shares with artist Brion Gysin. In the summer, PB and Libby Holman travel for a month through Andalusia, discussing the opera *Yerma*. The July publication of *Best American Short Stories 1950* includes "Pastor Dowe at Tacaté." In August PB and Gysin move to Fez, where PB continues work on his novel and renews a friendship with Moroccan Ahmed Yacoubi. "How Many Midnights" is published in the April issue of *World Review*; *Mademoiselle* publishes "Señor Ong and Señor Ha" in July; "By the Water" is included in *Penguin New Writing*; and "Doña Faustina" appears in *New Directions in Prose & Poetry #12*. The July issue of *Holiday* includes a PB essay on Fez.

1951   PB buys his first car, a black Jaguar, and with his chauffer Temsamany and Brion Gysin, takes a three-to-four-month trip through the desert from Morocco to Algeria. In the fall he takes Ahmed Yacoubi with him to Spain to meet Jane, who is returning from Paris. In December, he and Ahmed Yacoubi leave for India.

1952   *Let It Come Down* is published. PB spends most of the year traveling with Ahmed Yacoubi, first in India and Ceylon, and then through Italy and Spain, before returning to Tangier in the fall. Upon learning of a small island, Taprobane, off the coast of Ceylon, he decides to purchase it. When PB goes to New York to write the music for Jane's play *In the Summer House,* he takes Ahmed with him.

1953   Several collections include contributions by PB: *Stories, British and American* prints "Under the Sky"; *The New Partisan Reader 1945–1953* includes "A Distant Episode";

New Directions in Prose & Poetry #14 includes "The
Soup," "The Art of Poetry," "Prose Poem," and "The Thin
Man's Game," all by Paul Colinet and translated by PB; *21
Variations on a Theme* includes "Pages From Cold Point."
PB returns to Tangier alone, leaving Jane and Ahmed at
Libby Holman's estate in Connecticut. That summer he
spends six weeks in Rome, writing dialogue with Tennessee
Williams for Luchino Visconti's film *Senso.* In September,
Holiday sends him to Istanbul for a month to write an
article. When he returns, Temsamany meets him in Naples,
and he drives to Rome, Florence, Monte Parioli, and
Portofino, where he stays with Truman Capote. He spends
November through January in Tangier.

1954   PB is in bed three weeks with typhoid. His *A Picnic
Cantata* is featured in New York (23 March). He journeys
to Fez in May and then begins his third novel, *The Spider's
House.* In December he, Jane, Ahmed, and Temsamany sail
to Taprobane. *The London Magazine* publishes "If I Should
Open My Mouth."

1955   Jane and Temsamany return to Tangier while PB remains on
Taprobane. Random House publishes *The Spider's House* in
November.

1956   PB begins recording and transcribing Moghrebi tales by
Ahmed Yacoubi. He publishes several travel essays in
Holiday and *The Nation*; and "The Hours After Noon,"
"From Notes Taken in Ceylon," and "The Man and the
Woman," by Ahmed Ben Driss el Yacoubi, translated by
PB, appear in *Zero Anthology No. 8 of Literature and Art.*
Ten Years of Holiday includes PB's "The Secret Sahara."

1957   In March, the collection *Abroad: Travel Stories* includes
"Call at Corazón." Jane suffers a stroke on 4 April. PB
receives the news in Gran Canaria and returns to Tangier to
nurse her. *The Nation* and *Holiday* publish several pieces by
PB on India, Ceylon, and Africa, and *Harper's Bazaar*

publishes "The Frozen Fields" (July 1957). In July, Jane sees neurologists in London but discovers little regarding her condition. Unrest in Tangier escalates. The book *Holiday in France* includes PB's "Artists in Paris."

1958   In February the Bowleses leave Tangier for Portugal, where they hope to be safer. In April, Jane flies to New York. PB follows in June for rehearsals of his opera *Yerma* (29 July premiere in Denver). In September, *The Best American Short Stories 1958* includes "The Frozen Fields." While Jane receives treatment in New York, PB works on the score to a play for José Ferrer, *Edwin Booth,* which opens in November. In mid-December he returns to Tangier.

1959   In late February, PB receives a request to write the score for Tennessee Williams's *Sweet Bird of Youth* (10 March premiere). He receives a Rockefeller Foundation grant to record music of Morocco and travels through the country.

1960   PB publishes stories "He of the Assembly" (*Big Table*), "Merkala Beach" (*The London Magazine,* published in *100 Camels in the Courtyard* as "The Story of Lahcen and Idir"), and "Madeira" (*Holiday*). *40 Best Stories From Mademoiselle 1935–1960* includes "Pastor Dowe at Tac-até."

1961   Allen Ginsberg, Peter Orlovsky, Gregory Corso, Alan Ansen come to Tangier to visit PB and William Burroughs during the summer. PB translates several stories of Yacoubi. *A Casebook on the Beat* includes "Burroughs in Tangier," and *Artists' & Writers Cookbook* prints PB's recipe for *majoun.*

1962   PB continues translating stories of Moroccans. Tennessee Williams arrives for a visit. In September, PB goes to New York to write the music for Williams's *The Milk Train Doesn't Stop Here Anymore.* In November, *The World of Mankind* prints PB's "The Moslems."

1963   In November, PB begins writing his fourth novel, *Up Above the World*. He continues translating native stories and publishes two essays on Tangier. The anthology *The Expanded Moment* contains "The Frozen Fields."

1964   *The Worlds of Fiction* collection, published in March, includes "A Distant Episode." *Stories From the London Magazine* in August includes "The Time of Friendship," and *A New Directions Reader* selects "A Distant Episode." By mid-November, PB has finished *Up Above the World*.

1965   PB visits the United States, including a trip to Santa Fe, New Mexico. Little-Brown signs a contract with him to write a book on Bangkok. Meanwhile, he continues translating a book-length story by Moroccan Mohammed Mrabet. *The Uncommon Reader* includes "The Frozen Fields." PB writes music for a production of *Electra* for The American School in Tangier.

1966   In August, PB begins a seven-week journey to Bangkok. After receiving a letter from Jane's doctor in December, PB realizes he must return to Tangier without having completed the research for his book. "A Distant Episode" appears in *The World of Modern Fiction*; "Under the Sky" appears in the collection *The Short Story, Classic & Contemporary*; and "The Story of Lahcen and Idir" appears in *The Marijuana Papers*. PB writes the music for the American School's production of *Oedipus the King*.

1967   PB leaves Bangkok in January. In April he takes Jane to a rest home in Malaga, Spain. His first book with Mrabet, *Love with a Few Hairs*, is published. *The Book of Grass* publishes "Kif—Prologue and Compendium of Terms," as well as "He of the Assembly." The American School performs *The Garden* with music by PB.

1968   PB spends the fall teaching at San Fernando Valley State College and composes music for a play by James Bridges,

Bachelor Furnished, and for *Wet and Dry* by Leonard Melfi. "Pages from Cold Point" appears in *American Short Stories Since 1945*.

1969   In April, at Jane's request, but against the advice of her doctors, PB brings her home. She returns to Malaga after only a short visit in Tangier, her last. *The Short Story: Fiction in Transition* includes "The Scorpion." "A Distant Episode" appears in *The Survival Years* and in *Art of the Short Story*. PB writes the music for the American School production of *The Bacchae*.

1970   Daniel Halpern begins the magazine *Antaeus* in Tangier, with PB as founding editor. *Students' Choice* includes "Pages from Cold Point"; *Stories From the Transatlantic Review* includes "The Hyena"; and *Fifty Years of the American Short Story* publishes "The Echo."

1971   *The World of The Short Story* publishes PB's "The Fourth Day Out from Santa Cruz" and "The Young Man Who Lived Alone," by Mohammed Mrabet, taped and translated by PB.

1972   The Ecco Press inaugurates its series "Neglected Books of the 20th Century" with PB's *The Delicate Prey,* soon followed by several other of PB's works.

1973   Jane Bowles dies in Malaga on 3 May. *Live and Learn: Stories About Students and Their Teachers* includes "The Time of Friendship."

1974   *International Short Novels: A Contemporary Anthology* includes "Love with a Few Hairs," by Mohammed Mrabet, translated by PB. Lawrence Stewart's *Paul Bowles, The Illumination of North Africa* appears, the first critical book on PB's writing.

1978   The American School in Tangier commissions PB to write music for their production of Euripides's *Orestes* and of Camus's *Caligula*.

1979   *The Best American Short Stories of 1979* includes "The Eye."

1980   PB begins teaching writing in the School of the Visual Arts in Tangier. He also begins working on *Points in Time*, a "lyrical history" of Morocco.

1981   Leonard Melfi's play *Birdhouse* uses music by PB.

1982   Peter Owen publishes *Points in Time*. Joyce Carol Oates's anthology *Night Walks* includes "The Eye."

1984   Soundings Press publishes a collection of PB's compositions for voice and piano in *Selected Songs*.

1985   Black Sparrow Press publishes *Midnight Mass*, a collection of short stories written since 1976.

1987   *Antaeus* (58) publishes PB's story "In Absentia."

1988   Tombouctou Press publishes the collection *Unwelcome Words: Seven Stories*.

1989   Vintage Books pays "in the six figures" to reprint *The Sheltering Sky*.

1990   Bernardo Bertolucci's movie of PB's novel *The Sheltering Sky* premiers. PB writes and publishes a journal, *Days, Tangier Journal: 1987–1989*.

Conversations with Paul Bowles

Talk with Paul Bowles

Harvey Breit/1952

From *The New York Times Book Review* LVII:10 (9 March 1952).
Copyright © 1952 by The New York Times Company. Reprinted by
permission.

Just before Paul Bowles' new novel, *Let It Come Down,* came out, it
suddenly seemed apparent that this astonishingly able writer was barely
known by his countrymen: he had been out of the country so often,
particularly in recent years. Obviously, one had to fly to Tangier, or
some remote Arab village, to run into him. That, after brief consideration, was decided against; an airmail letter was decided on. It caught
Mr. Bowles on the point of departure—from Tangier to Bombay. In
between packing, Mr. Bowles considerately answered a number of
questions, pertinent and impertinent both.

Before that, there's a bit of biography to be gotten over: Born 1910.
Published in *Transition* while a high school moppet. Fled the University
of Virginia in first year, thence to Paris while parents and faculty sought
him. Job in foreign exchange at the Bankers Trust, Place Vendôme.
Published in all the little mags, mainly verse. Returned U.S. and U. of
V., where he finished out freshman year. To Germany and music composition under Aaron Copland. This in 1931, the summer of visits to
Gertrude Stein, who gave him lead on Tangier. From 1932 on, traveling
and tacking: Morocco, West Indies, Spain, Sahara, Tunisia, Colombia,
on and on. In 1936 first theatre score: Orson Welles' production *Horse
Eats Hat.* Music for, among others, Saroyan's *Love's Old Sweet Song*;
the Theatre Guild's *Twelfth Night*; Ferrer's *Cyrano*; Williams *The Glass
Menagerie.*

"The question of music and prose, it's a tricky one to answer," writes
Mr. Bowles. "If I had ever known I was going to write the latter seriously, I should have taken another name. I wrote a short story, and then
another, and then others, and very quickly I found myself writing a
novel, by which time of course it was too late to pretend to be another
person. I must admit, however, that I still think it would be fun to have
a *nom de plume.* Yet perhaps it would be bad psychologically: one

might feel less implicated, less responsible toward one's self. I don't know.

"Music and Prose: For one thing, I had always felt extremely circumscribed in music. It seemed to me there were a great many things I wanted to say that were too precise to express in musical terms. Writing music was not enough of a cathartic. Nor, perhaps, would writing words be if I should do it exclusively. The two together work very well. As to the influence, I think there is a considerable one. I am extremely conscious of the sound of the word, the phrase and the sentence. Not so much the paragraph; it's probably nonsense to speak of the sound of the paragraph anyway. The truth is that I've never thought of any of this until this moment. Since this is an interview I suppose it won't matter if I occasionally produce a bit of nonsense. One usually does in conversation, but then one cleverly covers it up with word or gesture.

"In *The Sheltering Sky* I did think of the three parts as separate 'movements' but I can see that was an error. A novel is not a symphony or a sonata. If it's anything that can be compared to music, it's a melody.

"I have no political ideas to speak of. I don't think we're likely to get to know the Moslems very well, and I suspect that if we should we'd find them less sympathetic than we do at present. And I believe the same applies to their getting to know us. At the moment they admire us for our technique; I don't think they could find more than that compatible. Their culture is essentially barbarous, their mentality that of a purely predatory people. It seems to me that their political aspirations, while emotionally understandable, are absurd, and any realization of them will have a disastrous effect on the rest of the world.

"The critics who refer to what I have written as 'decadent' would be likely to be the same people who take it for granted that the U.S. has the highest moral standard in the world, and that the 'outlook' of its inhabitants is automatically 'healthier' than elsewhere. I don't think either of those hypotheses needs discussion. The xenophobe will always find the alien unhealthy; even the rustic does the urbanite. I'm afraid of you, thus I must find you inferior. Unhealthiness is one of a hundred ways of being inferior. It's the obvious one in my case, because I am writing about disease. Why? Because I am writing about today . . . not about what happens today, but about today itself.

"You ask what decadence is. I should think in art and literature nothing is decadent but incompetence and commercialism. If I stress the various facets of unhappiness, it is because I believe unhappiness should be studied very carefully; this is certainly no time for anyone to pretend to be happy, or to put his unhappiness away in the dark. (And anyone who is not unhappy now must be a monster, a saint or an idiot.) You must watch your universe as it cracks above your head."

Composer at Home Abroad

Jay S. Harrison/1953

From *The New York Herald Tribune* IV:5 (17 May 1953). Copyright © 1953, New York Herald Tribune Inc. All rights reserved. Reprinted by permission.

Composer-author Paul Bowles recently arrived in town, furtively took to the hinterlands and then spent the remainder of his time roaming hither and yon and making it impossible, by and large, to contact him through any means known to mortal man. We met him finally, however, and not a moment too soon. For when last seen, Mr. Bowles was preparing once again to depart for exotic places.

The term "exotic," in fact, not only defines Mr. Bowles' preferences in matters of habitat, fiction and song; it might also serve to describe the course of his life. Certainly his accomplishments are not of the usual variety, nor have his successes been casual. Proof? Well—the record speaks for itself.

But better still, hear it now in Mr. Bowles' own words:

"Where do I go from here? I don't know. Turkey—perhaps Tangier or some other part of Morocco. What am I up to? I've just signed a contract with Random House for three more books, and at present I'm writing an opera for Libby Holman based on my translation of Garcia Lorca's *Yerma*. It's been a long time in the making and it's not really an opera. It's a *zarzuela,* a Spanish musical play, and it will have to be choreographed.

"As far as personal background goes, I think music and writing have been intertwined since I was six. At four I wrote a story titled 'The Fox and the Wolf,' and between seven and eight I turned out an opera 'in nine chapters.' You can see from that how closely tied the two were. I really remember my early history quite vividly. As a child I was given a babygrand piano by my parents—it was all very suburban. But instead of playing my Czerny exercises, I composed little pieces; and my father, who wanted to see me practice, in a rage sent the piano back. If that hadn't happened, I think eventually I'd have given up music. But I stuck to it now out of spite. Then I began writing short stories and at twelve got another piano and began to study theory."

At this point Mr. Bowles stopped short. "Are you honestly interested in all this?" he asked. A vigorous nod convinced him. "All right then. Where was I? Oh, yes. Between high school and college I went to art school. I didn't like it much, though at one time I did consider becoming an artist. The University of Virginia came next and it lasted a half year because without telling a soul I ran away to Paris. Not only that. Once I got to Paris I kept running away from *it*. Like a hobo I traveled around Italy, Switzerland, Germany. It was the happiest time of my life. I had no luggage, no worries. All I did was write music at old pianos— impressions, vignettes of the places I had been to and seen. Then I returned to the States and met Henry Cowell. He looked at my music, told me it out-Frenched the French and sent me to study with Aaron Copland. With Aaron I had a lesson every day, and my whole musical and intellectual background was formed by him.

"Then he sent me to Nadia Boulanger, but that didn't work out at all. Aaron also was in Paris at the time and I studied with him again and toured the Continent chasing after music festivals. (I've always had an itchy foot, you know.) Then, at the advice of Gertrude Stein, who had sort of adopted me, I went to Tangier. From 1931 to 1934 I kept going back into North Africa and through the Sahara. Those were the days. I even got to see South America, and of course I fell in love with the tropics.

"Meanwhile I was involved only with music. Gertrude told me to stop writing—she hated my poetry. In fact she said it wasn't even bad poetry, it simply wasn't poetry. For fifteen years, then, music was my occupation and I only returned to writing through music criticism. I worked as a critic on your paper and did pieces for *Modern Music*; but before that I began to write music for some Orson Welles shows, and ballets for Lincoln Kirstein and de Cuevas. Also, after I was awarded a Guggenheim, I did an opera, 'The Wind Remains,' which Lenny Bernstein conducted at the Museum of Modern Art.

"The rest you know pretty well. At one time or another I've written my books, *The Sheltering Sky* and *The Delicate Prey,* and now and then I compose scores for Tennessee Williams' plays. A lot of it was done in Morocco or the Sahara. Those, you see, are my homes."

Mr. Bowles paused for breath while this reporter shook his hand to relieve writer's cramp. "For me, at least," he continued, "writing and music are an ideal combination. The writing helps me, and anything that helps me helps my music. Music takes care of the inexpressible, the purely emotional things that cannot be translated. And writing takes care of what one thinks about the world—with the emphasis on 'thinks.'

"As a composer I find that I don't like 'big' music. I mean I won't subscribe to the theory that a symphony is necessarily more important than a string quartet or song. Today, there isn't much room for little pieces, I suppose, but that doesn't make them any less valuable. And as far as my working schedule is concerned, I feel happier when I'm writing on commission than when I'm not. When you've got a commission you *have* to work. You cannot idle. And right now, I confess, before I leave the States, I have plenty of work to do."

It was over. Time is treasure to a man whose interests are profitably divided. We shook hands and parted, but not before the thought occurred that with Mr. Bowles it would have been eminently more appropriate to salaam.

Interview with Paul Bowles

Ira Cohen/1965

An unpublished interview from the Paul Bowles Papers, Rare Book
and Manuscript Library, Columbia University, New York. By permission of the Rare Book and Manuscript Library, Columbia University. Edited by Gena Dagel Caponi.

Note: this manuscript consists of 56 pages of half, quarter, or
eighth portions of 8½″ by 11″ sheets. Many questions are
missing, and the interview itself is fragmentary.

Ira Cohen: You had come to Morocco when for the first time?

Paul Bowles: 1931.

IC: That was after that conversation with Gertrude Stein. Was it
really based on that that you came or was it just coincidental?

PB: No. It's completely because of that that I came.

IC: The sense of being able to be changed by Gertrude Stein—that I
suppose had very much to do with her personality, not only her writing.

PB: Much more her conversation, yes. Her writing is almost meaningless without the conversation as a key. It's like footnotes to the
writing, really. Particularly with regard to the approach that you
take.

She wasn't particularly interested in music. She thought it was an
inferior art. She once sent me a cartoon out of the *New Yorker,* I
remember, two women sitting on the beach looking at a little boy
digging in the sand, and one woman said to the other, "We're very
disappointed in Arthur's horoscope. We thought he'd turn out to be a
painter or at least a musician." She was very proud of that. She was
always trying to put me in my place.

She had an ear for dissonance, consonance. But I don't think she had
an ear for pitch, and I think that's the basis of liking music. She had
eyes, but she had no ears. She couldn't tell a tune, whether it was going
forwards or backwards.

IC: Didn't you write a piece of music once for her or for some piece
of hers?

9

PB: There were several. Yes, a sort of letter. I made a song out of it, which was made into a record. Schirmer published it. "Letter to Freddie."

IC: Why "Letter to Freddie?" Is that a nickname that she . . .

PB: A nickname she called me. It's my middle name, Frederic. She said, "Oh, your name isn't Paul."

IC: "You're a Freddie," she said.

PB: That's right. "You're no Paul." She had certain ideas about the aura that goes around the name of Paul and it was too steadfast for me. Freddie's much more like me, she said.

She'd say, "Ah, Freddie. Freddie, Freddie." She would do that all the time and I would just grin and giggle. I was playing a part. She wanted me to be this naughty little boy. She wanted me to dress in short pants which she called "Faunties."

IC: How old were you then?

PB: Oh, I was twenty. No, but she saw me as twelve, that's the point, and that was her whole kick with me, I know. She was sort of a very loving grandmother.

I did two other songs of hers which I've published called "Scenes from the Door." And I did some other songs later, subsequently, in the thirties. But that's all.

IC: Had you met Cocteau before this?

PB: I had, yes, that same spring.

IC: Did you feel in any way strongly affected by him as an artistic personality?

PB: No, no. He was always to me the epitome of celebritydom. He was *the* celebrity but his actual work never affected me very deeply.

IC: So Stein said "Go to Morocco," just like that?

PB: Go to Tangier. She said, "Go to Tangier," and Aaron Copland, the composer, and I came here. We went to the Minzah [Hotel], and we stayed about two weeks, and I was very eager to get out, because I thought it was too touristy. It was very nice in those days, not like now. But I wanted to get out, so I kept wandering up the mountain. Found a marvelous house, so up we went.

She sent people off on very strange goose chases. She told me to come to Tangier and she knew that certain people were already here, and what she wanted to see was what would happen when I hit there, you see.

IC: Who was here when you came?

PB: The surrealist painter, Kristians Tonny was here, and she knew that I would contact him, and the writer that everyone's forgotten now but who was very popular at that time, named Claude McKay, who wrote a book called *Home to Harlem*. He was living here like a Maharajah. It was incredible. He had a house full of slaves and he just clapped his hands and in they came. It was marvelous. Dancing girls.

IC: You mention sometimes people like Djuna Barnes here in the thirties. Was that at this time, or some time afterwards?

PB: It was about two years after. She came here, let's see. I got back from the long trip in the Sahara. I went to Tunis and I got back in the spring of '33. She had just come to Tangier. That's right. It was two years later.

IC: Didn't you share a house with Djuna Barnes? Where was that?

PB: Well, it's before you get to Michael Scott's, where you begin going down the hill suddenly. It was a little house there, cost fifty francs a month, two dollars. Very nice. Lots of rooms. Charles-Henri Ford lived in it with her. I said, "All right, you can have the house. You don't have to pay a penny." They were short on funds or something. She had just come from Peggy Guggenheim's in Devonshire and she had fifty dollars. Nobody had any money in those days. And I had this little house for two dollars a month, and she thought it would be nice to live without paying anything, since it was costing me so little. I lived in a hotel in town, but I had a piano in the house and I wanted to get in by 1:30 every day to work. I was writing a cantata. I never could get in. I'd go there and pound and pound. Pretty soon I'd hear Charlie Ford inside, saying, "Oh Paul, you come so early."

IC: Have you ever worked straight out of a dream state?

PB: Oh, in music many times, but only once in fiction, in a story called "You Are Not I." It begins "You are not I. Nobody but me could possibly be. I know who I am, who I've been ever since the train went off the track in the valley." It begins with a trainwreck.

IC: And that was a direct recording of a dream then?

PB: It was the result of a dream. I didn't know what it was, but I remember thinking, "I've got to get all this down." It wasn't like a dream, it was like an idea. It came in a second between waking and sleeping, or sleeping and waking. I happened to know that I had a notebook of some sort there. I had been writing before I went to bed and I just reached down and picked it up without turning on the light. It was dark in the room.

IC: You had the mask on, I suppose, while writing, which would have kept out any light.

PB: I think I pushed it up because I always do when I sit up. I don't like the feeling of being blindfolded. There is always a certain amount of light in a dark room. I began to write with my eyes shut, of course.

IC: Did you have any trouble staying on the paper?

PB: I wrote quite big and kept turning the pages, covered many pages with big carefully scrawled handwriting so that I could read it, and then I just went on and on without moving until I was very tired, and stopped and went back to sleep.

IC: Did you ever revise the story afterwards or did you keep it as it was?

PB: I kept it almost as it was; I changed one sentence.

IC: I always liked that story for its dreamlike quality. I remember particularly one part of the story when the woman pushes a stone into someone's mouth. Was that a stone she picked up at the trainwreck or what?

PB: Oh yes, I know, she's in the entrance hall of her sister's house and she's supposed to transform her sister into herself and vice versa and she tries to put a stone into her sister's mouth.

IC: The stone was in her mouth, wasn't it?

PB: Yes, I guess she had to have had it in her mouth. But she only put stones in the mouths of dead people. That was amusing because several years after that I remember reading an account of tribal customs in Melanesia, I think, and that was one of the customs. I had never heard of it—putting stones in the mouths of dead people. It's amusing—one knows things without knowing it.

IC: Haven't you taken ideas for your compositions from sounds you hear?

PB: That's true. Once in my hotel room in Taza, I had nothing to do, couldn't sleep, and had taken something against the fever and felt really crazy. So I just starting dripping water in the sink at different speeds. It was a very good tap. I got my idea for my two piano concerto in 1946 from the same idea, in the bathtub. The water was dripping in, and suddenly, it kept dripping the same way and it made a melody. I got the whole first part of the first movement from the water that morning. I immediately wrote it down. It has to do with the acoustics of the basin and the acoustics of the bathroom in which the basin was. Have you ever noticed that certain notes when you're in a bathtub will come out three times as strong as other notes? If you hold that one note, even very slightly, it fills the whole room or as you go down a bit, it doesn't do it. You go up a bit, and it doesn't do it. You've got to be right on that spot. Well, it was lucky that way. The water dripping seemed to have overtones, echoes, pitch echoes, inside the room.

You often get things, from the squeaking of a door, the singing of a bird, or a certain rhythm of a truck on a highway backfiring. Anything can be the stimulus. If you can do that with a symphony orchestra, how much more can you do it with electronics and just with ordinary tape recorders.

IC: You generally work at night, don't you?

PB: Yes, recently for the last six or seven years.

IC: Is that why you wear an eyeshade when you sleep, to keep the sunlight out during the day?

PB: Yes, although I wore it before. I've worn a mask for sleeping ever since I had typhoid, that was in 1932. That was because in the hospital there in Paris the windows were big and the light came in, and with typhoid you get photophobia. I had a nurse who kept coming in every day saying, "How's your photophobia?" She was one of those joking buxom women. I didn't know what she meant until she explained it to me, and then I said, "Yes, it's true. The light bothers me very much. As soon as it gets light I'm wide awake." She got me a black mask and earstops.

IC: I somehow always think of you as a scorpion, with a cat some-where around in the background, a parrot maybe on its shoulder.

PB: I used to carry the green parrot around on my shoulder. I carried him all over the Sahara. They're very good to travel with. They're happy, they're not miserable traveling. You try to travel with a cat, and it's miserable. Parrots don't mind moving. They really attach them-selves to a person, and the place they're in be damned.

IC: When you talk to a parrot is there some special tone or pitch you use to cue into that parrot language?

PB: I try to imitate them, yes. Naturally that's the only thing you can do, I suppose, mimic them in order for them to mimic you later. You try to make the exact sounds they make, because each one's different.

Not one of them is like another. They have different voices, speak in different pitches. Each individual parrot is different from each other one.

My gray parrot lives in the kitchen in Jane's apartment downstairs. It's better for her to be with people and they worship the bird, talk to it all day, give it things. As they cut up food they give it pieces. That's the way it should live. I would neglect it here. It's much better for it to be there. It likes to come up. It doesn't get worried at all when I bring it up.

IC: Does it relate to you as a person separately when you come in?

PB: It won't let anyone touch it at all except Cherifa and me.

IC: I know it pecked a real piece out of my finger one day.

PB: Well, it bites everybody.

IC: When it comes up here does it get into a certain conversation that it's used to having with you?

PB: I don't find it as amusing really as the green one I had, which really got into conversations with me. It was more like songs, or dialogue that both sides learn, and we would put it on, and he would always take my cue and go on from there.

IC: Could you give me a sample of it? I know you could do a perfect mimicking of it.

PB: As a matter of fact, I have it taped somewhere. If I ever find it, I'll put it aside and you can hear it. It's music after all. You play a tune and try to imitate the instrument it's being played on. Imitating a parrot's voice is playing over a melody.

IC: Have you ever heard tapes of bird songs slowed down? Does it really come out like a composed piece of ordered music?

PB: Absolutely. Very accurately.

IC: Is there any way of transposing a slowed-down bird song into some music that could be played?

PB: You mean actually reorchestrating it for musical instruments? Sure.

IC: Do you know any piece that's ever been done like that?

PB: It must have been done. Without the use of the tape recorder. If you slow down bird song far enough, it sounds like lions roaring. It makes one assume that their sense of time must be quite different, so to them it must sound like what it sounds like to us slowed down. Obviously the spectrum of their aural sensibility must be very different from ours, because some of the tones we can't even hear. So their time sense obviously is also different, since it goes so fast it may quite possibly be that to each other they sound like people talking or lions roaring.

IC: That's really the basis of all music, this kind of communication, like bees, crickets, birds. What is the first instrument?

PB: It's supposed to be the drum, the palm of the hand, and the voice.

IC: Those are all the closest to direct communication.

PB: Good music is still based on that. The hand-clapping and the voice.

IC: But that's just in so-called "primitive music," isn't it?

PB: Even symphonic music is still based on the same idea. It should be. Although it gets extremely refined. Instruments imitate the human voice, most of them, at least the first ones. I suppose the only instruments that don't imitate the human voice in one way or another are the stroke instruments, and they're really ramifications of the drum. The piano is closer to the drum than to the human voice.

IC: Brion [Gysin] has been living upstairs from someone who has been giving Arab boys piano lessons. Brion considers this the most blasphemous thing.

PB: It's not so blasphemous, but it's very bad, because it gives all the young people the idea that music must be read, and they must know solfege in order to be musicians. First-rate intuitive musicians have become twelfth-rate learned musicians. No taste and no real ability. Very hampering.

IC: Brion said he thought it was an impure cross between a string instrument and a percussion instrument, and that it was not one or the other.

PB: The piano has been incorporated pretty much into Moroccan music, and even into the Andalous music. It's terrible. It ruins the sound of the orchestra.

IC: What's the most primitive instrument that they still use here in Morocco? Do they ever use anything like a flute made out of a bone?

PB: Yes, but not here in Morocco. Instruments with one string. You see the Tiznit musicians in the Djemaa El Fna in Marrakech playing them. One cat gut that makes a very rasping sound. That box of leather that the Gnaoua play. It's not a *guinbri*. A *guinbri* is Moroccan. And the *gogo* is a completely different shape. It's a beautiful looking instrument. Rectangular. The *guinbri* is generally oval. It can even be made out of a big turtle, but generally they are made of wood. But the *gogo* is leather on all sides, and looks like a shoe box and a long bar with resonators on the end.

IC: The Jilala use just *bendirs*. It's amazing how much music can be made with those two simple basic instruments, and how beautiful.

PB: They're masters on both. They could make good music on anything.

IC: Do you think they would consider the flute and the drum the most basic instruments?

PB: I suppose they are. The reed flute and the drum. A simple *bendir,* one skin stretched over a frame.

IC: You've seen Aissaoua and Jilala and Gnaoua. What do the Terkawa do? I have the feeling that it's the purest, that it's mostly just singing. Perhaps jumping straight up in the air on the word "Allah" is their main thing, but I'm not sure. They certainly have the most beautiful Zawie in Tangier.

PB: It's right under my house, the Zawie de Terkawa. They had their own Muezin, and they would come right up on the terrace, but I never saw any kind of dance or heard any drums. It was very quiet except for the calling to prayer, which went on for quite a while and was all in music.

IC: They seem to be the most pure, the most abstract, and least primitive of these brotherhoods.

PB: You never know how many there are of anybody. I don't know myself exactly how rigid those distinctions are, if people can be considered as members of more than one group, if they can somehow make the rhythm of more than one group. There is one person in the Jilala whom I know has played with the Gnaoua. The Jilala do a special Gnaoua thing which is part of their own regular performance. It's not like the way the Gnaoua dance, but it is a Gnaoua song, or it's about the Gnaoua. One never knows what one is seeing. I've seen crazy things, of course, and I've never at the moment been certain what was happening.

IC: Do you believe in its efficacy, spiritually or medicinally or in any other way? Or do you think it's just a superstition.

PB: Oh, no, it's therapy. It seems to be necessary.

IC: What do you think *Djinn* is, and what is *Djinnung*?

PB: There seems to be a whole construction, a whole cosmos of *Djin-nung*. It's very hard to know what a *Djinn* is, because many of them are in human form. Therefore, it means that a whole group of people of the country are considered to be of another kind. They're called *Djinnung*, but they're certainly real enough.

IC: Don't they consider that *Djinnung* inhabit houses or special sites?

PB: They think of them as magic, of course. They can appear and disappear at will, transform themselves.

IC: Where did you say that you might find a *Djinn*?

PB: Anywhere. I don't think there's any one place. Most likely where there is running water and foliage, and it's likely to be at night.

IC: The *Hammra* also has water connected with it.

PB: Running water seems to mean female to them. I guess it does to most cultures.

IC: They also think of themselves as being invested with some *Djinn*, that some spirit has taken them over. Do they have their own *Djinns*? When someone feels that someone who is acting crazy should be exorcised?

PB: Then they say, "Yes, they've gotten inside him." This could mean so many different things. It can mean a neurosis, for instance.

IC: Do you feel that there are real *Djinns*? It's like asking if you believe in ghosts. Do you believe in the existence of these . . .

PB: No, no. I believe in the existence of them as projected by common belief.

IC: Have you ever seen one yourself?

PB: Obviously they don't exist outside the minds of people who believe in them. If they all believe in them, then they do exist. For them they exist, or it's as though they existed and therefore they exist. I can't believe in their objective existence, obviously.

IC: Do you feel that if someone lives in a house, he invests that house with his personality and his attitudes and feelings in a very intense way, like the way people would shy away from a house that a murderer had lived in? That the person's spirit does somehow linger in the corners of the house?

PB: They do say that, and it may easily be true. It would be absurd to say that it couldn't happen. When the chauffeur told me there was a *Djinn* in my car, I didn't pay attention. Then he came in white-faced and had wrecked it. He said the *Djinn* had driven it off the bridge in

Fez. It was a Jaguar. It started out black, lined with red leather, and
ended up all sand colored. I had a new top made for it in Rome, a nice
paint job, so it looked even better. It was all sand, the whole car.

IC: It's marvelous to drive around Morocco in a nice fast car. You
must have done a lot of traveling.

PB: Over in Europe too, but particularly here, and in Algeria. We
used to go down the Timbuktu road. It was wonderful, but no more.
You can't even get in down through there. Now there's more traffic and
everything has changed. It would be very expensive to insure such a car
now.

IC: You've lived in Morocco and Mexico mostly, haven't you?
Besides America, and Ceylon, of course.

PB: That's right. Ceylon is lush, colorful, warm. There was always
plenty of good food around.

IC: Did you own the whole island [Taprobane] yourself?

PB: I bought it. It was about $5,000. About two acres, very small.
Taprobane. Originally it was where they threw all the cobras—they're
Buddhists and wouldn't kill them. It was just a big pile of rocks. By the
time I got there there was a very big house on it. That was built by a
Frenchman. He evidently was a kind of megalomaniac and built himself
this fantasy on top of the island. The central room was thirty feet high
and circular. It was furnished and everything. At low tide you could
walk across to the mainland, and at high tide you could swim across.
There was a long wooden jetty. I spent six months there every winter
for seven years.

IC: Did you learn the language or have any contact with the Ceylon-
ese? Do you learn anything about perfumes or incenses?

PB: I didn't learn the language. The most interesting thing I found
was devil dancing.

IC: Is it anything like the trance dancing they do here in Morocco?

PB: It's different. You call the devil dancers and they put on a
show. It's really folk theater. It's one act after the other, but it's also
therapeutic. One number is sort of preparing the patient as it were
for the main act, which is the exorcising of the spirits. That's very
thrilling to watch. The last of the lot is in costume, and they scream
and groan and rush at the person. He's had a stroke or is mad or is
melancholic.

IC: It's very much like the function of a great deal of the Moroccan trance dancing. They use masks and what kind of instruments?

PB: They don't have any music at all except drums. And screaming. But you never hear any music. I think the Dutch must really have wiped it out. I never recorded anything. There wasn't much to record. Maybe animal sounds and jungle sounds. But I haven't been out there since 1957, and at that time there was no good portable equipment.

IC: Did the islanders mind your being on the island, or buying the island?

PB: Well, I remember in '55 the official Communist newspaper published a great blast against me, saying that I was employed by the central intelligence department and had a wireless sending station on the island and was sending messages. A complete invention. They suggested that the people of the region should come over and destroy the house and probably kill us. They didn't say that, but it was an incitation to violence, and I had to go to the embassy and talk to the ambassador about it.

IC: Was there any religious pressure about your living on the island as a foreigner? The British are very tolerant, I suppose.

PB: A lot are Roman Catholics. I should think about thirty thousand of them.

IC: Is that what made you finally decide to get off the island?

PB: No. I think the main thing was that I felt there was danger of their simply requisitioning it, taking it away, because other articles appeared saying it should be made into a national monument. Delegations kept coming saying, "You are very lucky to be living here in this national monument. We are very nice people to allow you to go on living here." This sort of thing gave me the idea to sell it for whatever I could get for it.

IC: What happened to all those cobras that were there?

PB: I never saw a snake. I suppose they transported them to some other island.

IC: It seems like a lot of snakes to go and pick up even for a devoted Buddhist monk.

PB: It does seem like a lot of work, but then out there at that time they might have devoted a year to it. And they have people who call them, you know, beating on a drum and singing.

IC: What's the principle of that? It's not like the mimicry you were talking about before in birds.

PB: The snakes are deaf anyway. They have no hearing apparatus. They're reacting to the vibration of the drum. It tickles them or something. They don't actually hear the sound, but they feel the air, which sort of massages them. I've been told out there that the flute has no effect whatever on them, but the drum is all powerful with the snake. For some reason it doesn't strike, although it would if anyone came near it. The person with the drum goes over quite near it and beats the drum in a certain way, and the snake lolls its head and begins going toward the drum. This person keeps backing up, and the snake follows the drum, like the pied piper.

IC: You've known Tennessee Williams for a long time, haven't you?

PB: Twenty-five years. I met him twenty-five years ago last summer, in Acapulco. He came around and knocked on the door one day, introduced himself, handed me a little letter from Lawrence Langner, and said he had done a play. *The Battle of Angels.* I don't think I knew about it then. It had been bought by the Theatre Guild, and Miriam Hopkins was playing the lead. I said, "Yes, yes, yes, very nice." And I was sort of impressed, but I didn't know him at all. We didn't get to know him terribly well. He came around and we got drunk together, Janie and he and I. We'd go to the beach and so on, and then he left and went back, I guess, to America. Very shortly after that I got a cable from the Theatre Guild asking me to come back and do a show with Helen Hayes and Maurice Evans—*Twelfth Night.*

IC: You did the music for it.

PB: Yes, I went back and did it. It was right after that that his *Battle of Angels* went off. There was a scandal about it. It never left Boston. Miriam Hopkins was misbehaving, and the reviews said it was a shocking play, loathsome, decadent. So it never got to Broadway at all. It was rewritten and presented under the title of *Orpheus Descending,* which was then made into a movie with Marlon Brando called *The Fugitive Kind.* Terrible movie.

IC: Movies seldom to justice to plays. Don't you think movies should be created out of their own materials, out of cinematic ideas, not out of a play, or even a book, for that matter?

PB: Of course. Making a movie out of a play is about like manufacturing an automobile with a place for the harness of a horse out front.

IC: What about that movie that you once worked on, *Senso*?

PB: That was made from a short story written by Boeto. That wasn't an organic work at all. Visconti had asked Tennessee to work on this film. Tennessee didn't have time. He was doing something else, so he cabled me and said would I like to do it. They paid $500 a week, and twelve years ago that sum looked very good to me. It was equal to about $1000 a week. So I went, of course, and Visconti handed me this thing and said, "This is a story by Enrico Boeto, and I see a movie in it. Here is a script that somebody else had done. It's not what I want. It shows you what kind of treatment it would be." He wanted a lot of battle scenes at the end, and so on, that weren't in the story. "This is how it could be done, but completely different. Here's one way of doing it, but you do it another way, but this might help you." It was all in Italian. So I had to read it, which was a job because my Italian is not so good. And then all I had to do, actually, in the end, was write the dialogue, which is what I did.

IC: Who was in that film?

PB: Alida Valli and Farley Granger. It's shown all around Europe, and it's always being shown at film festivals. It's never been shown at all in America. There's some reason for that, and I don't know what it is. It was turned down at first as something licentious because of the love scenes. They wouldn't cut it, and I don't know what happened, but it's never been allowed to go to America at all.

IC: Did Tennessee finally work on it too, even afterwards?

PB: Yes, he did indeed, because when I'd finished it and given it to Visconti, I said, "Well, it's all done." And he said, "Yes, I've read it, and it's fine, but the love scenes are not really tender." I said, "Well, I can't do it any other way." I see it as a natural concomitant of the rest of the film, and the natural result of the actions and the manner in which they're expressed. I don't see how I can suddenly change the style, just because it's a love scene. Well, it seems love is special, you know, either in films in general or to Italians in general, probably both. He wanted love scenes and not sex scenes. So Tennessee stepped in and said, "Alright, I will do two scenes particularly, the big love scenes," which were long and very important, obviously. He did it in a week.

IC: What would you say is the difference in the style?

PB: My feeling was that the characters in the film were not motivated by love ever. Anyway that's the whole point of the film, so why make them romantic and tender? That seems to me to be betraying the whole aesthetic of the film. If you believe you've done the right thing, it's almost impossible to do something else and do it well, because you don't know how to do the opposite. I couldn't write tender love scenes. I don't think I could at all, in any case, but certainly not in that film.

IC: When I first stopped in the Zocco Chico, I said I had dreamed all of this before, but then I finally realized that it was the stage set from the Tennessee Williams's play *Camino Real.*

PB: It used to be fantastic, that square.

IC: Did Tennessee spend a lot of time there? He certainly laid it down perfectly.

PB: Sure, he used to sit there, but he never saw it in the old days. He didn't see it until December 1948. It had already changed. It was better than it is now, but it wasn't the old milling about of several thousand people in native costume the way it used to be, selling animals.

IC: It was mostly Europeans, and you could have a drink then, I guess.

PB: Sure, you could drink. There were lots of Europeans sitting around. There were drunks around. It was full of Moroccans too, still in Moroccan costume.

IC: I think there's something about that world in *Camino Real* and the characters that he chose which had kind of an alcoholic fringe to it.

PB: Drunk types sitting around in bars. It wasn't a *kif* place.

IC: I've heard that the "Danse Macabre" was composed in the Zocco Chico.

PB: Yes, Camille Saint-Saens. He based it on a jubilee tune. He was here for quite a long time. I don't think he really came here to live, but he liked the place.

IC: The music of Morocco would be stimulating, I think, to a composer.

PB: I like generally to listen to folk music more than most composers. I don't know why. It doesn't show a very high degree of development.

IC: I know Bartok spent a lot of time recording Hungarian folk music, and Stravinsky was certainly interested in jazz and other folk music. I think it's probably not so uncommon as you feel.

PB: Well, I think the thing is that Bartok was a Hungarian musician interested in Hungarian music, Stravinsky was a Russian who was interested really only in Russian music. De Falla was a Spaniard, and he used nothing but Spanish music, and so on. Copland and Thomson use nothing but American folk music. But in my case, I like folk music all over, in every part of the world, completely dispersed, which is a different thing.

IC: You did some *fasoukh* experiments in 1933 in Hollywood. You came into contact with it somehow shortly after you first came in 1931.

PB: Yes. In Marrakech, in the Djemaa El Fna. I remember smelling something and it gave me a very strange feeling when I smelled it, and a promise, as it were, of something unknown. I didn't know what it was, but it was as though I'd smelled it before. In other words, it reminded me of a blank but something that I'd felt. And it was a strange sensation, and so I said I'll try and find it. I took someone named Abdul Kada ben Hammed ben Said there the next day, and found the same Negro, who must have been a Gnaoua, but I didn't know the existence of those, then. I recognized the odor and said, "That's what I want to buy." He said, "Oh, that's bad. You don't want to buy that. Nobody nice buys such things." You know, the old story. So of course, I insisted and got it. I got everything I could get and came back with a big collection. Among it was the *fasoukh.*

IC: Does it remind you of some previous experience you don't remember?

PB: Yes, but why should it? I'd never smelled any. It was a sort of smell that you'd stop and say, "My God! What is that?" It's such a crazy odor. You couldn't believe it. You couldn't believe your nose, as it were. The only word I could ever find for it was "black." It smelled like something black, and of course, it is black. But I wonder if I hadn't known it was black before I smelled it whether I would associate the word "black" with it anyway. That's what I feel. But I don't know why. It's dangerous because it's arbitrary. It's like Rimbaud's ascribing colors to the vowels. But I'll bet you that if you conducted a Gallup poll and got hundreds of people to smell it and say, "If this reminds you of any color, what color is it?" you'd get a preponderance of black.

IC: Could you tell me what *fasoukh* is and what you know about it?
PB: I don't. I can't.
IC: Well, it is used in certain kinds of magical rites, isn't it? As a kind of incense?

PB: It's used primarily, from what I can understand, as a purifier, a warder off of evil. At the same time, you can do evil with it if you work it backwards, against a person. And I'm not sure exactly how you do that, but I think one thing is to put a big piece of it under a stone at the entrance of a doorway, for instance, so that the man goes over it each time he goes in and out.

IC: But it is ordinarily something that would be burned.

PB: It's burned, yes, It's a black resin of some sort. Very sticky, like tar. I've always heard there was blood. I didn't hear necessarily that it was human blood, either. But it was made with dates and whatever resins from whatever trees. I don't know what they are. No one's ever explained the composition of it.

IC: What about those experiments you mentioned? What did they consist of? In burning the *fasoukh*?

PB: In a closed room. I think there were eight people. Without warning, I burned it. I gave bits of it to put on their cigarettes, and said, "Smell," and waved their hands.

IC: And what were the reactions? Do you remember anything in particular?

PB: Everyone felt very strange in about ten minutes and everyone began looking at everyone else and said, "Do you feel strange in your—" And then one would say, "Elbows," and the other would say, "Shoulders," and then they all agreed that they felt dislocated in the joints everywhere.

IC: Could it be compared to *kif* in terms of its effect?

PB: Well, it's obviously something like that. It's a chemical in a plant, but I don't think it's *kif*. There's no splitting of the self, where there is with *kif*, for instance, the awareness and non-awareness at the same time.

I got a wonderful oil that year, too. Oil of tea, pressed tea. It smelled fantastic.

IC: It was a perfume, right?

PB: You put one drop on a cigarette and the whole house smelled of fresh, hot tea. Very strong. Marvelous odor. Like mint tea. I never found any again. The next year I came back looking for it all through the perfume *soukhs* of Fez and Marrakech. Never found any more. I smelled hundreds of bottles, and they would say, "This is it," but no.

IC: You believe odors can have a powerful effect.

PB: Absolutely. Witness Mohammed Larbi, who would pass out whenever he smelled *Djaoui,* ordinary light *Djaoui.* I suspect that any odor can be used if you get a reflex started.

IC: Do you still remember how to shrink a head?

PB: Pretty well. I remember I saw some on sale for four dollars apiece. I could have bought a whole lot of them. I was a fool.

IC: Where was that?

PB: I think it was Colombia.

IC: Ever see a blond one in there?

PB: No.

IC: You mention that the scorpion season had arrived.

PB: It begins after the end of the hot weather. They go into their holes, and you can get them out. You try in March or May, they don't answer. I think they're asleep. But this time of year they're awake, and they grab hold of the little piece of palmetto. Stuff which is very good for salads, incidentally. You used to be able to buy it in the market. They're rather flat-shaped holes in the roots of the palmetto. Generally with an arched roof to the hole, and also the bottom's slightly arched. The shape of their bodies.

IC: And you stick in some of the palmetto and they come out for it?

PB: Well, they grab hold of it. You may have to stick it in a foot. They're big holes.

IC: Do you wet it or anything else?

PB: Wet it with saliva. The Moroccans chew the end of the palm frond and then stick it down the hole. I've never found it necessary to chew it up.

IC: And then what happens when you pull the scorpion out? Do they sting?

PB: Yes. They're ready to sting. They come out with their tails up over their heads. And then you quickly cut off the little thorn on the end of the tail.

IC: How do you hold it so that it won't sting you?

PB: You don't hold it. You get the scissors in there quickly. I do it very fast. He tries to sting the scissors' points, you see, and you get them over his tail.

IC: Then you just cut the stinger off. Then after that you can just hold it in your hand, I suppose.

PB: Sure. You can hold it in your hand, you can put it in your pocket, you can put it on your head and let it crawl all over you. It can't do anything to you, much as it would like to. I freed mine out here, outside the house. I didn't see any reason for keeping him.

IC: Are you interested in talking at all about Jane as a writer, or about anything that you feel that you share in point of view or attitude?

PB: The interesting thing is whatever parallels there might be between her writing and my writing, not the personality in my writing or vice versa. Of course, she's put me in her work, obviously. I can see that Mr. Copperfield is a kind of caricature of me, that's very clear, and her Mrs. Copperfield is another caricature.

IC: Well, you did make a trip to South America.

PB: Yes, and she actually used the names of the hotels we stayed at.

IC: But I know that there were some stories you wrote, and one in particular, about a couple taking a boat trip in South America . . .

PB: That's right, in South America. Something that we never did. An imaginary trip. If Jane and I had made this trip, that might have been the mainspring, but I wouldn't dare say because I don't remember. It's certainly not about Jane and me.

IC: I think it is unique in some way that both you and Jane are writers who are well known as writers, who have succeeded in certain kinds of ways similarly, writing novels or stories. Was there ever any interchange of information, help, or support on any of these things, or were they done very separately?

PB: All very separate.

IC: Naturally, you would work alone.

PB: When I was about sixteen, I published a poem in *transition,* and she read it a few years later, and that was her favorite poem. She had never met me or anything, and then we happened to meet, two or three years after that by sheer accident. She didn't know that I was the person who had written the poem she liked.

IC: What was the name of the poem. Do you remember the poem itself?

PB: Yes, but I don't remember the name of it, I'm afraid. It was in *transition.* ["Delicate Song," *transition* 19/20, June 1930, 303] It was about boats in the harbor and grapes. "It was a long trip back," that was the first line.

Then she wrote a novel in French when she was about 17 or 18. She was in school in Switzerland then, studying in French, speaking nothing but French year after year, until she wrote the novel in French. It was called "Le Phaeton Hypocrite," "The Hypocritic Phaeton." She knows what it means; I don't. Probably Phaedo, a character and also a kind of carriage, I believe. The book was never printed. I remember we took it to Paris in 1938 with the intention of getting it published. Then she lost it, and there was only the one copy. She was impossible. She's lost everything, except the few things that are in print.

IC: She has written a lot more that the material that has been printed?

PB: But it doesn't exist. Left it in a cab, it blew out the window. One time about 300 pages blew out the window, a novel she was writing in Mexico City.

IC: It must be quite a shock when those things happen.

PB: Well, she's kind of gotten used to it.

IC: Does she care about it, or does she take a kind of ironic attitude toward the whole thing?

PB: It's very hard to know what her attitude is. I think she cares very much and at the same time has to convince herself that it doesn't matter.

IC: Is she still working now? Does she write any more?

PB: She would like to. I don't think she is working now, no. I don't think she finds it possible to work any more. Anyway, she still hopes to.

IC: I'd like to see *In the Summer House* some time. I have the feeling that it's somewhat similar in a way to "You Are Not I." Isn't it played as a division of personality like that? A three-way split of character?

PB: All her things are like that, in a sense. They always have characters which are each other's negatives, shadows. A concave character and a convex character. Like *Two Serious Ladies*.

IC: Does that idea appeal to you? Do you feel that you sometimes work convex and concave?

PB: It's a perfectly good idea. A perfectly good pattern. It doesn't appeal to me particularly. It just seems like an eccentricity.

Paul Bowles

Mike Steen/1969

From *A Look at Tennessee Williams* (New York: Hawthorne Books, Inc., 1969), p. 141–156.

Santa Monica
31 October 1968

Mike: Paul, you first met Tennessee in Acapulco in 1940?

Bowles: That's right. He came to the house. We lived on the Avenida Hidalgo there. And one morning we were just about to go out to the beach, and the servant came and said there was a gentleman at the door and I went, and he said, "I'm Tennessee Williams. I'm sent here by Lawrence Langner. He told me you were here. The Theatre Guild is going to do my play *Battle of Angels*." I said, "Come in, but you must excuse us because we are about to go to the beach for the day and since we have been invited, we can't take you. But here is the house. Here is the patio. Here are hammocks. Here's a new bottle of rum and there's plenty of Coke. You just call the servants and they'll bring you whatever you need, books." And when we came back at five o'clock in the afternoon, he was lying in the hammock, and he'd drunk a good deal of the rum and lots of Coke, and was very happy and was reading books. And that's how we got to know him. Actually we hadn't spoken with him at all before we went out. It seemed like a rather seedy way to treat someone, but there was nothing else we could do. So we just turned the house over to him. Left him in it.

Mike: Did he stay as your house guest during the time he was in Acapulco?

Bowles: No. No. He was staying in a hotel there, not far. I think he was staying at the Miramar, up at the Quebrada, which was at the top of the same street we lived on. We lived down near the square. It has changed enormously since then but this was long ago and it was a small town. And he stayed on awhile. And then I had to go back to New York to do the music for *Twelfth Night* for the Theatre Guild with Maurice

Evans and Helen Hayes. So I went back and I didn't see him again at all. I stopped in and heard a rehearsal of the music to *Battle of Angels*. It was very fine. And then I heard it had closed at the Plymouth in Boston. Never got into New York at all. Just too bad. And I didn't see him again until December '43, when he suddenly appeared one night at my New York flat with Donald Windham and Margo Jones and the script which he called *The Glass Menagerie*. He left it with me and said, "We have a production lined up and you'll only have the weekend. If you can write the music for it over the weekend, it will be fine." And I had no contract. I had nothing. But I did, I wrote the music over the weekend. And Monday it was all done. That was quick! And then the show did come off and I flew out to Chicago, arrived in a terrible blizzard, I remember. It was horrible. A traumatic experience. And the auditorium was cold. Laurette Taylor was on the bottle, unfortunately. Back on it, really. She had got off it with the first part of the rehearsals but suddenly the dress rehearsal coming up was too much. The night of the dress rehearsal she was nowhere to be found. And finally she was found, unconscious, down behind the furnace in the basement, by the janitor. And there was gloom, I can tell you, all over the theatre because no one thought she would be able to go on the next night. She pulled herself together and gave, as you know, an historic performance the next night, and from then on. It was marvelous. And on opening night in New York, George Jean Nathan sent her a bottle of Scotch, a pinch bottle, and she sent him a little wire saying, "Thanks for the vote of confidence."

Mike: The Chicago reviews of *Glass Menagerie* were all good ones, weren't they?

Bowles: They were very good, yeah. But no one in New York knew it was going to be a hit from that, because it had critical success but not popular success in Chicago.

Mike: Then you also did the music to *Summer and Smoke?*

Bowles: Yeah, that was in '48, five years later. The autumn of '48. And, let's see, I came over to this country and went on the road with them. Yes. We went to Buffalo. Gypsy Rose Lee was along on that. I don't know why. She accompanied the show with her husband, Julio de Diego, the painter. That was a very enjoyable junket, the whole trip. We went to Cleveland and we went to Detroit and then came in to New York.

Mike: Margo Jones directed it, didn't she?

Bowles: That was Margo, yes.

Mike: Well, why would you need to travel with them? Were you writing additional music during the out-of-town trials?

Bowles: Sometimes, certain cues. But the composer always goes on the road with the show. I've been with all my shows. I don't know why. Because oftentimes it's unnecessary. But they seem to feel happier if you're there. In almost all shows there are changes required, up to and sometimes after opening night.

Mike: When you say you came to this country to do *Summer and Smoke,* you mean you came here from Tangier?

Bowles: Yes, that's right.

Mike: What year did you move to Tangier, Paul?

Bowles: I moved there definitively in '47. Then Tennessee came over to Tangier the winter of '48–'49, yeah, after the show went on. I remember he had a Buick Roadmaster with a convertible top which went back automatically. But it didn't! And we had some horrible experiences. We tried to get through the frontier, I remember, from Tangier into the Spanish zone. We got there late and it began to rain and the thing balked and wouldn't shut. We had to get all the luggage out into the customs shed, and there two small Spanish soldiers were looking at it and they took out Tennessee's suits, his underwear, his shirts, his typewriter, manuscript paper, razor, and they confiscated it all. And they were holding his suits up and saying, "This one will fit me." "I like these pants." "I'm going to take this." They were just taking everything. Stealing it. So we packed everything back into the car and went back to Tangier. And then Tennessee made an indignant call the next day to the American consulate and told them about it and they got busy and three days later we started out again. The consulate had called the frontier just before we left and when we arrived they threw the gates up and were screaming, "Diplomatico! Diplomatico!" We went straight through. Never stopped us at all. Didn't even have to show our passports. We got all through the Spanish zone to the border of the French zone, and then they asked us for our gasoline coupons, which we should have got at the Spanish frontier. So we didn't have any. So we had no gas, and we stayed there four hours trying to finagle some. And finally we got enough to go on to a horrible little town called Petitjean and we had a real mess as a result of not having enough gas to get on to Fez. And

Tennessee got very frightened because it began to pour rain, and the sides of the mountains were coming down with mud blocking the roads, the mountain passes. And he just went through hell until we got to Fez. He was worn out by the time we got there. He just stayed in the hotel for two weeks without budging.

Mike: Was it just you and Tennessee?

Bowles: No, Frank was along. The three of us. And Frank did most of the driving, unfortunately, because Tennessee had vibrations in those days and complained about them a lot and when he would take the wheel he would say, "I feel them coming on." And then he would have to move over and let Frank take the wheel.

Mike: What about your return trip from Fez back to Tangier?

Bowles: We never made it. I stayed in Fez and he and Frank drove on to Casablanca and took a ship from there to Italy. And I remained the whole winter down in Fez.

Mike: Where was Jane at this time? In Tangier?

Bowles: I'm trying to remember. No, no, she wasn't in Tangier. She was, I think, in Paris.

Mike: Did you ever do much other traveling with Tennessee? Didn't you travel with him in Italy some?

Bowles: Yes, yes—oh, Lord! In the—let's see—it was the summer of '53; I motored up to Barcelona and met him there. And I had with me Ahmed Yacoubi and Mohammed Temsamani, two Moroccans. Temsamani was the chauffeur. And Ahmed had trouble with his passport. He couldn't get a visa in order to go through France, so the only solution was for him to fly with Tennessee from Barcelona straight to Rome and I had to go by car. And so that was done. When I got to Rome, Ahmed and Tennessee had already been there several days. And Tennessee had arranged with Luchino Visconti for me to do the music for a film there, which I did. It was called *Senso*. Alida Valli and Farley Granger. I remember we were very lucky to get another flat on the same floor as Tennessee in the Via Firenze. And every night I would be working hard because I worked hard all summer. Day and night. And everyone else would be going out to the movies. The American movies. And I felt very put upon to have to stay at home alone every night. But I did, all summer.

Mike: Didn't Tennessee keep an apartment in Rome each year?

Bowles: He did. I don't think he was always on the Via Firenze, but

he did have that one for several years. He loved Rome. He was there all
the time in those days. You couldn't drag him away. I went on to Istanbul. That was the year I went to Istanbul to do a piece on it for *Holiday*
magazine. And when I came back to Rome Tennessee was still there.
And then we motored back up through Italy, France, and Spain, all the
way down to Tangier.

Mike: Did you get to know Anna Magnani in Rome with Tennessee?

Bowles: No, no. I've never seen Anna Magnani at all. And there
were a lot of people there, but not she. We also went down to Positano,
I remember, and stayed there awhile. And Maria Britneva was along.
I can tell you!

Mike: What about another female companion of Tennessee's, Marian
Vacarro? Didn't she often travel with him?

Bowles: Yes, she came to Tangier on two separate occasions with
him. Once in '61, I think, and again in '64. That's right, yeah. She was
very amusing.

Mike: I think she's always been one of his closest female friends,
along with Jane and, of course, Carson McCullers and Maria Britneva
and Lilla van Saher.

Bowles: We spent a weekend out at Carson's once, I remember, at
Nyack. Tennessee, Jane, and I with Carson, her sister, and her mother.
But Reeves was not around. Reeves McCullers. I saw Carson again in
Paris a few years later and I think that was the winter Reeves committed
suicide, very shortly afterwards. But Tennessee was not in Paris then.
I've seen Tennessee in so many places and under so many different
conditions that it's like a patchwork quilt. It's very hard to get any
chronology straight. He's suddenly here, and then he's suddenly there,
and I happen to be there and see him. But to remember exactly all the
various years and where I saw him is impossible.

Mike: With Tennessee liking to travel so much, did you ever feel he
was very good at languages when he'd be in the various countries?

Bowles: Not at all, naturally. No, no.

Mike: He speaks some Italian, doesn't he?

Bowles: Some. He is not a linguist. Oh, no. Not at all. He always
used the present-infinitive verbs instead of the proper forms. And I think
that people abetted him in that when he was speaking with Italians.
They would use it too, because I suppose that they thought it was easier.

Mike: He was always very popular in Italy, wasn't he?

Bowles: Oh, yes.

Mike: And didn't you feel that he was rather down-to-earth with people he'd meet and would accept people as friends rather readily? There was nothing snobbish about him.

Bowles: Oh, no, never. He is never snobbish.

Mike: He was always giving an immediate feeling of friendship.

Bowles: Too immediate. Yes. I think he was too friendly, really, with people too soon. He often regretted it later but he has a natural outgoing manner.

I have noticed that Tennessee always seemed to have friends in every city where we happened to be and I suppose the fact that he had these friends helped make the place bearable to him because I know he doesn't really like to travel. For someone who moves around so much, he's surprisingly unaware of his surroundings. And I've always suspected that he was more eager to get away from where he was than he was to get to another place, really.

Mike: Do you think that to get to another place would also be a desire to get to other people? That his eagerness to leave one place is also an eagerness to leave the people that he may be with at that particular time?

Bowles: Oh, I think very much it is an eagerness to leave the people. I am not sure that he's eager to get to the other place to see the other people. No. But I think he suddenly is fed up with a place and the people in it and feels that somehow any other place, or nearly any other place, will be more acceptable at that moment than the place he's in. So he leaves where he is and goes—it doesn't matter so much where, because he always changes his mind at the last minute anyway.

Mike: And never finds the place which he thinks will be the ultimate place. The place to really remain, or the situation to really remain in.

Bowles: I don't think he has ever found it, no. Not at all, because he is inherently extremely restless.

Mike: Of course, that could be beneficial to a writer: never to be content with any place or situation. Keeps them on the go and will influence their writing in a positive way.

Bowles: Surely. I don't see anything wrong with it at all. It is simply that he is never very interested in the place itself that he is in. I suppose that is a concomitant of being more interested in the people of the place he is in than in the place itself. That's natural.

Mike: But to feel a compulsion to move about that often could be within himself an unpleasant feeling. Don't you think?

Bowles: It probably is.

Mike: A lack of being able to be content.

Bowles: I don't think he is ever content for very long. And as far as compulsive behavior goes, it's always unpleasant because you're doing it before you have time to anticipate it. Half the pleasure of anything is anticipation.

Mike: But Tennessee also could be called a compulsive writer. And I think, even though I have heard him say that writing is a torture to him, it is his life. I really think it's a pleasure to him, that particular compulsion. He may deny it, but I think he really enjoys it.

Bowles: Of course he does. It gives him satisfaction. Whether or not he actually enjoys the moment of writing or not, I don't know. I suspect that he does enjoy that too. It certainly is satisfying to him.

Mike: The next play of Tennessee's you wrote the music for was *Sweet Bird of Youth.*

Bowles: Yes, it was ten years later, actually, I set *Sweet Bird of Youth.* I had the script in Tangier and I worked on it for about a month and then went to America. I continued working on it on the ship, I remember, the old *Vulcania,* going across. I went straight to Philadelphia, where Gadge was already rehearsing. The thing was in rehearsal, and it needed some more cues and bridges and tying up, so I finished the actual composition there in the theatre between rehearsals. The score was completed only two or three nights before opening night in Philadelphia. It worked very well, I thought. More successfully than the score for *Summer and Smoke.*

Mike: Did you think the play *Sweet Bird of Youth* was drawn very freely from Tennessee's own life and experiences?

Bowles: Yes, I do. Well, he said it was, so I'm not betraying a confidence by saying I think so too. How close the parallel was I wouldn't know. I should think very close, but certainly the ideas came from what he had been living during those years.

Mike: And the last play that you did the music for was *The Milk Train Doesn't Stop Here Anymore.*

Bowles: That's right, yeah. That was in the autumn of '62.

Mike: Did you do that work in Tangier?

Bowles: Let's see. No, I didn't at all. I had Virgil Thomson's apartment in New York in the Hotel Chelsea and I wrote it there. Almost all of it. And then I moved over to Oliver Smith's house in Brooklyn Heights and finished it over there. And we recorded it. That was done on tape. Also, *Sweet Bird of Youth* was recorded. I think that was the first time that I allowed them to actually use tape instead of live performances because in the old days the reproduction wasn't good enough. It costs exactly as much, as you know. You have got to pay your musicians every night for every performance anyway, whether you tape it or use them. Once tape got good enough, then you had a better performance really when you recorded it because you knew exactly what you had every night and everybody played perfectly because it was done in the studio. That play was well recorded. *Milk Train* was a much more difficult thing to fit music to, I thought. And I didn't like the script as much personally as the other three plays that I worked on. I still don't like it as much. I never believed in the character of Chris Flanders for a minute.

I remember in '46 Tennessee gave me some lyrics and asked me if I would like to use them to write songs. One was called "Gold Tooth Woman," I remember that. I didn't use that. But I did use four called *Blue Mountain Ballads* which I set to music: "Heavenly Grass," "Lonesome Man," "The Cabin," and "Sugar in the Cane." They made a suite which Schirmer published separately. They sell very well. They have gone on selling now for twenty years. They have gone into the repertory now. And then I did another one called "Three," which was published. And then he gave me one which I like very much called "Her Head on a Pillow," which I did set in '49 in Tangier and promptly mislaid. It was gone for about fifteen years and then I found it on the bottom of an old bag, a valise, and brought it out but I never did anything with it. Now I have lost it again. There is only that one copy. It is somewhere in Tangier. It is probably the best of all the songs of his that I have set. He writes excellent lyrics. The poetry I find harder to read, if you want to distinguish between his lyrics and his poems, his free-verse poems. I also did a series of six songs on commission from a singer, Alice Esty, who wanted to give a concert in Carnegie Hall five or six years ago. I chose a series of poems of Tennessee's which makes its own cycle. They are free verse. And they also set very well. But I chose them myself. I like to use as many Anglo-Saxon words as possible and as few foreign words, naturally, for the prosody. So I picked out the ones that

suited my purposes best and made a song cycle of them. And I have
never heard those, unfortunately. I would like to. I enjoyed setting them
very much.

Mike: Do you think that any of Tennessee's long works, his three-act
plays, could or should be set to music, or made into musicals?

Bowles: Certainly not musical comedies. No. Well, it's problematical
whether one could make opera out of them or not. They would lend
themselves much better to straight opera than they would to musical
comedy. I don't see that they're musical-comedy material at all. I can't
think of one that would make a good musical comedy. Not one. I can
conceive of an opera though, a lyrical opera of *The Glass Menagerie*.
It's not unthinkable. It would have to be very delicate. It could be done.
But I don't see the point, really, of adapting Tennessee Williams to
grand opera. They are wonderful plays. You don't need anything more.

Mike: Since you're a writer as well as a composer yourself, Paul, I
think any opinion you would have on Tennessee's writing would have
more value than most people's.

Bowles: When I first knew Tennessee, of course, I wasn't a writer.
I was only a composer. And I didn't start writing until the mid-forties.
But as soon as I did, Tennessee immediately took up cudgels for my
work and went out of his way to write reviews of my first two or three
books in *The New York Times* and *Saturday Review* and various other
publications. He couldn't have been a better friend. No one I know has
so consistently stood behind my writing as Tennessee all during these
years.

Mike: I believe he has the same attitude toward Jane's writing also,
doesn't he?

Bowles: Very much, very much. Perhaps even more, I don't know.
He loves Jane's writing.

Mike: Has he ever written reviews for any of her work?

Bowles: I don't think he has ever reviewed them. But he has written
blurbs for them, certainly. Several times.

Mike: I think he was quite a strong promoter of Jane's play, *In the
Summer House*.

Bowles: Oh, yes. He had great admiration for it from the beginning,
always. We were on the ship, Tennessee and I, going to Europe one
time, and I stayed in my cabin and wrote a story called "The Delicate
Prey." And so then I gave it to him to read on the ship. And I remember

the next day he brought it back and said, "It is a wonderful story but if you publish it, you're mad." And I said, "Why?" He said, "Because everyone is going to think you are some sort of horrible monster when they read it." And I said, "I don't care. I have written it and I'm going to publish it." And he said, "You're wrong, you're wrong to publish it. You will give people the wrong idea." But I disagreed with him on that. Perhaps now everyone does think I'm a monster. I still disagree with him. I think if you write something, you should publish it.

Mike: Well, I think that is certainly his belief now. I am surprised that he wouldn't have always had that same belief.

Bowles: Well, it shocked him, the story.

Mike: Well, certainly he has written stories that are shocking.

Bowles: Absolutely. Think of *Desire and the Black Masseur*. That's pretty shocking. Or even *The Mysteries of the Joy Rio*. No, my particular brand of shockingness shocked him more because it was mine and not his, I think. That's all. And it was just a friendly admonition on his part to try to dissuade me from publishing it.

An Interview with Paul Bowles

Oliver Evans/1971

From *Mediterranean Review* [Orient, New York] I:2 (Winter 1971): 3–14.

Paul Frederick Bowles was born in 1910 in New York City, the son of Claude Dietz and Rena Winnewisser Bowles. In 1938 he married the playwright Jane Auer. As much composer as writer, he studied with Aaron Copland in New York and Berlin and with Virgil Thomson in Paris. He has written operas, film scores, ballets, songs, and chamber music. He did the scores for *Glass Menagerie, Sweet Bird of Youth,* and for the ballets, *Pastorela, Yankee Clipper,* and *Sentimental Colloquy.* His books include *The Sheltering Sky* (New Directions, 1949); *The Delicate Prey* (Random House, 1950); *Let It Come Down* (Random House, 1952); *The Spider's House* (Random House, 1955); *The Hours After Noon* (Heinemann, 1959); *Yallah* (Obolenski, 1957); *A Hundred Camels in the Courtyard* (City Lights, 1962); *Their Heads are Green and Their Hands are Blue* (Random House, 1963); *A Life Full of Holes* (Grove Press). He has also translated Sartre's *No Exit* and written travel articles for *Holiday.* From 1942–45 he was music critic for the *New York Herald Tribune.*

The scene of the interview was the eastern end of a sixty-foot-long-room at the edge of a cliff on the Old Mountain in Tangier. The sea was audible, breaking against the rocks three hundred feet below. It was autumn and the wind roared in the trees. A Moroccan servant brought us tea. I sat with my machine at one end of the divan, and Mr. Bowles sat at the end near the fireplace, sometimes moving to the floor. There were several sessions of this sort, some beginning in mid-afternoon and some after dark. Mr. Bowles often got up and walked around the room as he tried to find the answers to the questions.

Interviewer: Mr. Bowles, you have a double identity, as writer and composer of music. Which came first?

Bowles: It's hard to say. I learned the piano as a child and studied theory and harmony as a child. Then as a child I also wrote blood-and-thunder stories. I used to stay after school and read them to the class. When school was over, the teacher used to say, "Those who wish to go may go; those who wish to stay and hear the new installment may do so." That was every day, you know. I was writing twenty pages a day.

Interviewer: Where was this?

Bowles: In New York, where I was born and grew up.

Interviewer: Were your parents from New York?

Bowles: No, they're New Englanders. My mother was a school teacher and my father was a dentist. And they met in New York. My mother was from Bellows Falls. And my father was a son of New Englanders from Rhode Island and Vermont.

Interviewer: Any relation to Chester Bowles?

Bowles: Yes, as a matter of fact. He's the grandson of my grandfather's cousin. I've never met him, I don't know him, but he's a blood relation.

Interviewer: You went to school in New York, then.

Bowles: Yes, to a so-called model school where each class was watched by about fifty student teachers who would sit around on camp-stools. The teachers were all model teachers showing the student teachers how to teach the children, who were supposedly all model pupils learning in a modern fashion.

Interviewer: Did you write poems also?

Bowles: Yes, but that was later. I got interested in poetry in my teens. Naturally you do, because you study it in school. Some of it was free verse, some were sonnets. I tried everything.

Interviewer: You still write poetry, as a matter of fact, don't you? I remember that when you were in California last year, teaching at the College*, you showed me a copy of a little book of verse that had just been published by Black Sparrow Press.

Bowles: Yes, *Scenes*. They are bringing out another collection this year.

Interviewer: I see. I take it that you finished high school in New York. Right?

Bowles: Yes, and then to a thing called The School of Design and

*Mr. Bowles served as Distinguished Visiting Professor at San Fernando Valley State College in the fall semester of 1968–69.

Liberal Arts, also in New York. I had life drawing and advertising layouts and lettering. I had a certain facility for it. Then my father said, "Enough nonsense." So I went to college. That was in 1928.

Interviewer: The University of Virginia?

Bowles: Yes. Because Poe did.

Interviewer: What did you major in?

Bowles: Nothing. I was just there because you're supposed to go to college. That's why I left.

Interviewer: When *did* you leave?

Bowles: At the end of the first semester. In March.

Interviewer: Where did you go?

Bowles: Paris. I ran away. Flipped a coin one night to decide whether I should take poison or go to Europe. It come out heads, which meant going to Europe. I was very happy. I don't know what would have happened if it had come out tails. I might have tossed again . . . Anyway, I arrived in Paris with twenty-four dollars—six hundred francs I believe it was in those days. And you couldn't live long on that. So I got a job on the *Herald* at the telephone switchboard. Elliot Paul was always coming in and out. The following winter I went back to New York, where I met Aaron Copland, and then I went back to the University of Virginia for the second semester, to take up where I had left off the year before. Copland came down to see me in the spring.

Interviewer: Had you been writing music in Paris?

Bowles: Yes, I was writing pieces. But I hadn't taken it up seriously with a master. I hadn't met Copland yet.

Interviewer: How long did you stay at the university this time?

Bowles: Another semester. Then I went to Yaddo, and back to Europe in the spring of 1931. First to Paris, where I met Gertrude Stein— I had been corresponding with her for a couple of years—and then to Berlin.

Interviewer: You knew Gertrude Stein well, I believe?

Bowles: Knew her well? We were very friendly, yes. She was a maternal figure, you know. She was like grandmother. Very warm and motherly—and lots of bosom.

Interviewer: She's not influenced your writing?

Bowles: No, not really, I shouldn't think. I remember I sent her a little story the following summer, when I was here in Tangier, and I have a letter from her in which she comments on it. She says, "I take

back some of the harsh things I said about your writing." That was nice.
Of course those things had been said about the poems. I wasn't writing
fiction at the time. And about the little story I sent her she said that it
makes a picture and that's always important. Something like that.

Interviewer: Did you stay long in Paris this time?

Bowles: No, I went to Berlin.

Interviewer: I believe Isherwood mentioned he knew you then.

Bowles: Yes. I met Spender that year too. But I didn't know Spender
as well as Isherwood. And I didn't really know Isherwood terribly well.
I was a bit too young and I didn't know what he was talking about.
Then in the summer I came here to Tangier and took a house on the
mountain right opposite. With Aaron Copland.

Interviewer: Your first visit to Tangier, then, dates back to . . .

Bowles: To 1931.

Interviewer: Did you like it immediately?

Bowles: Immediately. Oh, yes, I loved it more than any place I'd
ever seen in my life. In fact, I'd never liked any place strongly, I realized, until I came here. I'd always felt negatively about places before.
That is, I wanted to go here or there in order to get away from where I
was at present. But that's not liking a place, is it? On the contrary. Of
course, I liked France in those days, too. I loved France.

Interviewer: It was very different before the War, wasn't it?

Bowles: Well there *is* no more France. In fact, there's very little
Europe left.

Interviewer: When did you begin to write fiction seriously?

Bowles: After I met my wife. I had returned to the States. We met in
1937, in New York, and were married the following year.

Interviewer: Did she influence you to write?

Bowles: Well, yes. Not consciously. But her own novel—*Two Serious Ladies*—probably had some influence on me. It made me want to
write, too. For some reason the book stimulated me. I suppose the first
story was the one I wrote in, of all places, Brooklyn Heights in 1939:
"Tea on the Mountain." It's in the collection, *The Delicate Prey*. That's
the earliest one I've kept that's been published. For some reason I just
wrote it one day. But I didn't write anymore. Until 1945.

Interviewer: And in the meantime?

Bowles: Before the War? Not too many shows. For the Federal
Theater I did the score for *Horse Eats Hat,* an adaptation of Labiche's

Un Chapeau de Paille d'Italie, and Marlowe's *Doctor Faustus.* Then
one for Mercury Theater's version of William Gillette's old farce *Too
Much Johnson,* which was never produced, and two plays by Saroyan:
the Group Theater's *My Heart's in the Highlands* and the Theatre
Guild's *Love's Old Sweet Song.* The bulk of my theater work was done
during the War and directly afterward. That was when I did *Watch on
the Rhine,* the Helen Hayes *Twelfth Night, Liberty Jones, The Glass
Menagerie, Jacobowsky and the Colonel, Cyrano de Bergerac,* and a
good many unsuccessful ones. I did about thirty shows. The first was in
1936, for Orson Welles, and the last was for Tennessee Williams: *The
Milk Train Doesn't Stop Here Anymore.* Or rather, more recently still,
for Leonard Melfi's *Wet and Dry,* which was produced two years ago in
New York.

Interviewer: And still more recently—last year in fact—I heard
some theatrical music you wrote in California. It was a performance in
Schoenberg Hall, at U.C.L.A. You were good enough to give me a
ticket.

Bowles: Oh, yes. James Bridge's *Bachelor Furnished.* Yes, I wrote
that music in Santa Monica, in late 1968.

Interviewer: While you were teaching at Valley State?

Bowles: That's right.

Interviewer: As I remember, you said that although you wrote some
music that semester, you found it difficult to write fiction and teach at
the same time.

Bowles: Right. Whenever I had some time, I had to be preparing for
my next class, or reading over manuscripts from the creative writing
class. No, probably it was my fault, but I didn't manage to get any
writing done.

Interviewer: Coming back to your early music for the theater, written before the War, what were some of the other things you did?

Bowles: I also did a movie for Henry Wallace—that was in New
Mexico, in 1940. He was the Minister—they don't say Minister there,
do they?—the Secretary of Agriculture. First I was in the Theater
Project—as a composer, that is: I never wrote any plays. Then I transferred to the Music Project.

Interviewer: Your first book, I believe was *The Sheltering Sky*?

Bowles: Yes, and it was followed within a year by *The Delicate
Prey.* Of course I had been writing the stories ever since 1945.

Interviewer: I remember the dedication to *The Delicate Prey* reads, "To My Mother, Who First Read me the Stories of Edgar Allan Poe." I gather that Poe has influenced your work?

Bowles: Undoubtedly. Anything you read over and over as a child is an influence. And she did read me the stories of Poe. What she was always doing was trying to—unconsciously, I think, make me feel exactly as she'd felt when she was sixteen, and I was only seven or eight. And they had quite a different effect, naturally. I wasn't the sort of child who admired literature because of its style; I read because I liked the story. I still do, although I can't take a style that rubs me in the wrong way.

Interviewer: Yet I don't think in your own work the emphasis is on plot—at least not the kind of plot you find, say, in a detective story.

Bowles: No. Because that's not as interesting as the real material in life. I think one of the most difficult things is to see the drama that is really in front of one every minute—the drama that follows living. And one often doesn't. Actually see it. And if you can, then you're involved in the most momentous things every minute. They're around you all the time. In other people's lives, I mean. But one doesn't see them. I suppose one's protected from them. Jane, my wife, sees a great deal more than I do but then she can't work as a result. It has too much of an emotional effect on her, and she gets too involved in the actuality of it and can't transform it into material.

Interviewer: Coming back to the Forties, I take it you were living in New York, writing both music and fiction.

Bowles: Yes, mostly music. And I was Music Critic for the *Herald Tribune* from 1942 to 1946.

Interviewer: Many readers have commented on the rhythmical quality of your prose. Do you think your musical training has had anything to do with this—that there has been a carry-over from the rhythms of music to the rhythms of prose?

Bowles: Oh, absolutely.

Interviewer: And of course, as we were saying earlier, you have written poetry too.

Bowles: And songs! I've written a great many songs. Prosody, I think, has more to do with it than anything else—the value of the spaces between words.

Interviewer: And in a larger sense—I'm thinking now of the struc-

ture of a novel—do you think your knowledge of music has been helpful?

Bowles: Of course. One's attitude toward form and what constitutes
form is bound to be influenced by the fact of one's having been involved in musical form for years. That *is* form, as far as I'm concerned.
Yes, form as I see it has to do with the sense of speed, that is, the relationship between what's going on in the book and the duration of time
it takes to tell it. And to read it. If you want a slow movement, then
you find the right words to convey a sense of slowing down. Or for a
passage where one wants to suggest that the passing of time outside the
consciousness of the character is much greater or much smaller than it
seems to him, then you'd use musical devices for that too. I *do* think in
terms of music. I think in terms of syncopation, counterpoint, simultaneous motifs, solo and tutti passages. It helps to make things more
precise in my mind.

Interviewer: Speaking of precision, I remember that when I saw the
manuscript of *The Spider's House,* I was struck by its extraordinary
neatness almost as if it had been a musical score.

Bowles: Yes, composers have to be neat. Writers are generally
inclined to be sloppy. I didn't realize that—I've only discovered it
slowly, by meeting a few. I don't know many writers.

Interviewer: Could you tell me something about your writing habits?
I believe you once told me you wrote lying down.

Bowles: Yes, in bed.

Interviewer: That's a curious habit. Some writers think they must be
uncomfortable when they write . . . Hemingway used to write standing
up.

Bowles: I don't think it matters whether you're comfortable or uncomfortable. The important thing is to be able to leave where you are
and get into the book. The quickest way of getting there is the best way,
that's all. And for me the quickest way is to get there either just before
I go to sleep or just after I wake up. When life itself doesn't impinge at
all. I work late at night before sleeping, and again after waking up. I
may work three hours in bed before going to sleep. Composing music
was a much more nerve racking thing: it made me very, very nervous.
I never could sleep well during all those years. Not that I sleep too well
now, but certainly much better than when I was writing music. No, I get
the impression when I've finished a book that at least I've done some-

thing. When I finished a piece of music I never had the feeling that I'd *accomplished* anything, and that wasn't very satisfactory.

Interviewer: Do you need seclusion as much to compose music as to write?

Bowles: Not so much, no. Well, you do need to be alone, of course. I wrote most of my music in New York, for instance, but I never wrote any part of any book in New York. No. All the novels were written either in Asia or Africa, none of them in Europe or America—not a word of any of them.

Interviewer: How long does it usually take you to finish a novel?

Bowles: Depends. *The Sheltering Sky* took nine months. *Let It Come Down* took two and a half years. And *The Spider's House* took eight months.

Interviewer: Yet it's the longest.

Bowles: Yes. I wrote more pages a day, that's all. I don't know why. It's impossible to know.

Interviewer: When you're working on a book, do you make it a point to write a certain number of pages every day?

Bowles: As many as possible—that's all I can say. Generally one.

Interviewer: You don't actually count the words, I suppose, as Hemingway is said to have done?

Bowles: Oh no, that would drive me crazy. Really, count the words! It's beyond my comprehension. He must have been paid by the word.

Interviewer: I believe that with him it was a matter of conscience; he had simply committed himself to a certain quota.

Bowles: The novel's finished when you've told the story, as far as I can see.

Interviewer: All of your novels have foreign settings. Can you explain your interest in—

Bowles: In far away places and "backward" people? Well, I don't know that. Probably some fundamental defect in my character. You find it hard to answer when someone asks you why you can't get on with your own people—and it does come back to that, certainly, that one finds oneself ill at ease in the land where one was born and brought up, among one's equals. And one finds himself *not* ill at ease among others. And it puts one in a very strange position somehow, because one is quite aware that in these countries in many respects people are definitely inferior. On the other hand, one's also aware that in other respects they're superior. And then one realizes there really is no comparison possible. And one just says, "I find it more congenial." It may or may not be rationalizing some defect in one's character, as I say—or rather in one's development, not necessarily in character.

Interviewer: I think it's probably true that literary people, in particular, often find themselves ill at ease in civilized society, so-called.

Bowles: Of course. Because they reject, at this moment in history, the mass society. I think that's it. And I do too.

Interviewer: You never liked living in the States?

Bowles: No, I hated it. No, I don't want to live there. I'll have to eventually, I suppose. The world is closing in, you know.

Interviewer: Aren't there *any* places you liked in the States? Some cities you preferred over others?

Bowles: I don't like cities anywhere. I like the country. I don't want to be with a lot of people—even backward people! Much less Americans, who are forward people. I like the world as it is, you know—the trees, the wind, the globe and whatever's on it. To take a walk in the city is to me just a waste of time, whereas to take a walk in the country is always wonderful.

Interviewer: Yet the life in your Moroccan streets is very colorful. It's a constant spectacle, with something always going on.

Bowles: Going *on* rather than going *by*. There's no metropolis here yet, thank God. Yes, I know that, because when I leave this country to go anywhere else, I feel that everywhere else is slightly dead: a certain human element is missing. Taxis always rushing by, and none of the little groups that one sees everywhere in Morocco, with just a few people standing around talking or maybe haggling over something . . . Yes, it's wonderful that here there are those little—what shall I call them?—rocks in the brook that just stay there while everything else rushes by them in the water, people who just stand or sit all day while time goes by and people go by. That's the proof that life goes on, somehow, whereas in New York there isn't any proof. It's all going by, nothing going on.

Interviewer: Do you feel that artists, generally, have a hard time of it in America? I gather you do, because you have chosen to live elsewhere and I'm sure that being an artist has had something to do with that choice. What, exactly, is the danger as you see it?

Bowles: I don't know that there is any, to all artists. I certainly wouldn't recommend to a young writer that he leave the States just because he is a writer. Personally I felt antipathetic toward the whole set-up, but whether that was because I was a writer or not I haven't any idea. We'll say that thirty or forty years ago, when I was in my formative stage, there didn't seem to be any place for the artist there: he was considered to be an outsider. I resented that more than anything else, I suppose: the general attitude that any artist, particularly a creative artist—even more than an interpretative artist—was an outcast, a pariah. Naturally, if you were rejected, you rejected back. Whereas in France I remember very well that if I wanted to send a manuscript of music through the mail there was always a special rate for *papiers d'affairs.* There was a list of rules and regulations for writers, composers, lawyers . . . they were acknowledged to be important members of society. But not in the United States. There are no provisions made for their existence at all.

Interviewer: Nor in England either, do you think?

Bowles: I'm sure not. Well, give me a list of the great English composers. You won't find any.

Interviewer: What about Britten?

Bowles: He's not a great composer. His music is so eclectic, so unoriginal, so impersonal.

Interviewer: You said Poe was an influence on your work. What were some of your other influences?

Bowles: Gide and Proust, and then Camus and Sartre. I admire Sartre greatly, you know. Mine is the standard performing translation of *No Exit*—we have the rights to it for a certain number of years.

Interviewer: What about the Russians?

Bowles: Very little. I don't read Russian, and I hate to read anything in translation, so that's cut me off from the Russians and the Germans. I remember in Berlin, in 1931, Copland was reading Kafka's *The Trial* in German and he said, "This is an author you'd like." And I said, "Oh yes, he used to write for *transition,*" You see, some of his things were published in English, in *transition,* after his death. I loved him even then, in translation. And then I tried to read him in German, but I didn't really know enough to stay with it very long. Then I forgot what little German I had learned. I was never able to read anything in the original German. But I have read Kafka in English, again and again. He's marvelous, of course. My favorite was *Amerika*. It's curious about Kafka.

The criticism of works that one knows is always fascinating to follow from decade to decade, the way it changes. The attitude toward Kafka has been through so many evolutions, and now it's coming around to the attitude that I always had about it, which was that it was—just fiction. That it is not about God and it's not about all the things that Auden used to scream at me that it was about. All right, if you want, it is about that, but it's also just fiction. The fictional level really demands no explanation; you accept it as feeling.

Interviewer: I'm not sure I agree with you about that, but I will agree to this extent—that he would not be as widely read as he is if the fictional level hadn't been interesting in its own right. But I do think that what Kafka leaves out is ever so much more important than what he actually says. You do most of the work yourself.

Bowles: Yes, that's why it's great, of course. That's why it's not like anyone else's. Oh, I agree.

Interviewer: What other writers do you particularly admire?

Bowles: Living or dead?

Interviewer: Either, or both.

Bowles: I'm always more interested in living writers than in dead ones. Once they die I lose interest. For instance, when Camus was killed it seemed to me much less interesting to read his posthumous works precisely because he wasn't going to produce any more. And yet I admired him enormously, while he was alive—I still admire him, of course. I've been rereading him—last year I reread *L'Etranger*. I admire it tremendously. It's a work of genius. And then of course there's *Alice*.

Interviewer: *Alice*?

Bowles: *In Wonderland*. It's one of the books I've most enjoyed in my life. I'm always rereading it. And then there's D. H. Lawrence. I rejected him for many years, because of his style. Finally his message got through to me, in spite of that repellent style of his, but it took years. I would take up a book of Lawrence and throw it down in a rage every time, because I hated the language so much. Now I've read all his things, with excitement for years. He has an extraordinary talent for rendering places. In *The Plumed Serpent,* for example, the way he describes Lake Chapala, it really feels and smells like Lake Chapala. Camus does the same thing with Algiers—takes you out on a balcony and lets you listen to the sounds in the street. He does it with very deft strokes here and there, a very few words. Sometimes even a single word will bring the whole scene right before you.

Interviewer: What is it you look for in the fiction of other writers? Is it the story that interests you chiefly, or is it an idea or a moral message?

Bowles: A moral message is the *last* thing I look for. I reject moral messages, unless they're my own. I don't like other people's moral messages, no! I suppose what I look for is accurate expressions, for accurate accounts of states of mind, the way in which the consciousness of each individual is reported in the book. How the author makes us believe in the reality of his characters, in the reality of his settings.

Interviewer: And is this what you try to do yourself, as a writer— to create a character's state of mind so that it gives the impression of absolute reality? Or are you more interested in getting across an idea, a message? Some of your stories *are* parables.

Bowles: Yes. Well, both. It depends on the story, really.

Interviewer: And is it true, as has sometimes been charged—I believe it was Leslie Fiedler who called you a "pornographer of terror"— that you have occasionally written stories intended primarily to shock?

Bowles: Not primarily, no. That was not meant to shock. It's supposed to evoke a certain atmosphere, really. When I write a story I think more or less the same way as if I were writing a poem. It's quite different from writing a novel.

Interviewer: What about "A Distant Episode," which I think shocks at the same time it teaches?

Bowles: Precisely. If there's anything to teach in "A Distant Episode," it can only be taught through shock. Shock is a *sine qua non* to the story. You don't teach a thing like that unless you are able, in some way, to make the reader understand what the situation would be like to *him*. And that involves shock.

Interviewer: Would you agree that the writer who *merely* shocks doesn't give his reader a vision of life?

Bowles: I think so, yes.

Interviewer: That he's concentrating solely on effect, and that this may have nothing to do with the way he feels about life?

Bowles: Well, it does have *something* to do with it. But it's uninteresting because it has to do only with his personal neuroses, because if he's interested in shocking, it's a therapeutic thing to help himself, obviously. So he's not really free. Insofar as he wants only to shock, he's a victim. No, I can see that a lot of my stories were definitely therapeutic. Maybe they should never have been published, but they were. But they certainly had a therapeutic purpose behind them when I wrote them. For me personally. I needed to clarify an issue for myself, and the only way of doing it was to create a fake psychodrama in which I could be everybody.

Interviewer: Some critics have pointed out that the quietness of your style increases the sense of horror, so that the effect of shock is created through understatement. Is this deliberate on your part?

Bowles: Understatement is better than "enough" statement, and certainly better than too much. But I doubt that it *creates* the horror; it's just a concomitant effect.

Interviewer: How do you feel about the way readers react to your books? Does it seem to you that they get out of them what you intended?

Bowles: Some people, yes. I haven't lived in America for so long, except for the brief period in Santa Monica, when I was teaching. I don't know many literary people. And I've never discussed my books with writers I do know.

Interviewer: Do you think that's a disadvantage?

Bowles: It must be. Not having known the other, I can't say for certain. But I should think that never taking part in any literary life at all would be a disadvantage, yes.

Interviewer: But you do read a great deal?

Bowles: I read, yes. But that's not taking part. You understand, I don't want to take part in literary life, that's the whole point. On the other hand, I think you're right to ask if it is a disadvantage. It probably is. It's also a disadvantage to live out of your country.

Interviewer: I imagine there are compensations.

Bowles: Oh, yes! A great many. This house, for instance. It would be extremely difficult in the United States simply to go out in the month of May and choose an absolutely silent house and move in, occupy it for the summer, and then move out again. It would probably cost a thousand dollars a month. It would have to be miles from everything, which would mean being dependent on a car.

Interviewer: You are fortunate in being able to live where you like.

Many writers would envy you that. Have you never found it difficult
financially?

Bowles: Well, there's no guarantee of an annual income. I've always
just trusted to luck. Have to. There's no guarantee whatever. No one
has ever subsidized me or agreed to take over expenses. Fortunately I
was always able to live on what I earned in the theater. That gave me a
decent living, even during the Depression—enough to travel on, but I
never made a great deal.

Interviewer: You never took odd jobs, like so many writers in the
Thirties?

Bowles: No, I never did. Not out of snobbism, but it simply seemed a
waste of time. I was always busy working. During the years that I was
writing music, I was always writing music. Very busy. I had no time to
wait on tables and wash dishes! Actually, it was not too difficult to
make a living on Broadway in those days. If I did three or four shows in
a year, I had plenty to live on. For those days. I could make, oh, seven
to ten thousand a year. Always did, while on those shows. And I had
money saved up. Naturally, being a New Englander, I always built a
bank account. I still get royalties from the music I wrote for *Glass
Menagerie* and *Summer and Smoke,* and occasionally from my translation of *No Exit.* And small royalties from time to time from various
music publishers. The books are mostly out of print, though *The Sheltering Sky* was brought out in a paperback. So was the last novel, *Up
Above the World.* I've never worried very much about financial security. I'm going to die eventually, after all. The main thing is to get your
life behind you and be ready for the end. You do whatever you can
while you're alive, and then it's finished. I feel as though life were
going by very fast, that eventually it will be finished, the hour will
come. And then it's too late to do anything.

Interviewer: You live very much in the present, then?

Bowles: Completely, completely, completely. You can't do anything
else, really, if you're like me.

Interviewer: I've often wondered if you plan your books consciously, in advance, or whether you allow them to shape themselves as
you go along?

Bowles: Each one is different. I didn't plan *The Sheltering Sky* at all.
I knew it was going to take place in the desert, and that it was going to

be basically the story of the professor in "A Distant Episode." It was an autobiographical novel, a novel of memory, that is.

Interviewer: You mean you identify with the professor?

Bowles: No, not directly. I'm thinking in terms of one's career. One's first novel often writes itself: everything comes out in it and it's generally the best novel that one writes. In that sense it was autobiographical:—the one I'd been hatching for ten or fifteen years without knowing it. And it came out that way. But the next one, *Let It Come Down,* I did plan very much. It was completely surface-built, down to the details of the decor, choice of symbolic materials on the walls, and so on. The whole thing was planned. It had to be. It was an adventure story, after all, in which the details had to be realistic. There would have been no other way of lending it any semblance of reality. It's a completely unreal story, and the entire book is constructed in order to lead to this impossible situation at the end. But each book is different in every way from each of the others. It seems to impose its own rhythms, you know.

Interviewer: What about *Up Above the World*?

Bowles: You mean how it got written? Well, I started it about seven years ago, then laid it aside. Then a year or so later I looked at it again, got some more ideas and wrote some more, than laid it aside a second time. Finally, the third time I started working on it in earnest, and finished it. It was published in 1966.

Interviewer: In the meantime you published a couple of other books, I believe.

Bowles: Yes, a collection of travel sketches, *Their Heads Are Green and Their Hands Are Blue*; that was in 1963. And in 1964 a Moghrebi translation: *A Life Full of Holes.*

Interviewer: *Up Above the World* seems to me a very different kind of novel from the others—more of a "whodunit."

Bowles: I didn't consider it a serious book like the others. It was like what Graham Greene calls an "entertainment." Actually I wanted to do it under another name, but the publisher wouldn't agree.

Interviewer: Do you see any preparation for it in the early stories?

Bowles: The short stories, you mean?

Interviewer: Yes. Perhaps it's the Latin-American setting I'm thinking of.

Bowles: Well, of course there is that. But actually there is more preparation for it in *Sheltering Sky*: in both novels a husband and wife are traveling; the husband disappears and the wife is left to cope with the situation.

Interviewer: I believe you told me you had some help from William Burroughs on that book; I mean *Above the World.*

Bowles: Yes, I went to him for some of the technical information about drugs—the effects of various dosages, that sort of thing. But then I cut it out.

Interviewer: You mentioned a Moghrebi translation, *A Life Full of Holes*. That was the first of the "oral novels" you've been collaborating on wasn't it?

Bowles: Yes, but they're not exactly collaborations. I only get the authors to talk, you see. The stories are their own. My function is only to translate, edit, and to cut; now and then I have to ask a question to clarify a point.

Interviewer: The oral novel, as popularized by Oscar Lewis, has now become an accepted literary form. Unless I am mistaken, you were also a pioneer in this *genre,* were you not?

Bowles: I suppose you could say that. Yes, as early as 1954—before Oscar Lewis—I was taping stories by a young Moroccan, Ahmed Yacoubi, and translating them. Three of them were published. Then I did *A Life Full of Holes,* with Driss Ben Hamed Charhadi. And with Mohammed Mrabet I have done two novels, *Love With a Few Hairs* and *The Lemon,* and a collection of short stories, *M'Hashish.*

Interviewer: What about your work in progress? Are you willing to talk about it, or don't you find it advisable?

Bowles: I find it absolutely inadvisable.

Interviewer: Hemingway felt very strongly about that—that if you talk about it you lost it. Do you agree with that?

Bowles: Absolutely, and I remember my astonishment when I read that Huxley had no anxiety on that score. He must have been like Gertrude Stein in that respect. She was always willing to talk about everything. She *wanted* to talk about everything—her own work, just what she meant, what she was writing at the moment, and it wasn't always possible to follow her. But certainly she was willing to talk.

Interviewer: Let me ask you a question about *The Sheltering Sky,* then. In an article I wrote about your work—it came out in *Critique* and I believe I sent you a copy—I suggested that your use of the desert as a symbol resembled Eliot's use of it in *The Waste Land* and Dante's use of the *selva selvaggia* in *The Divine Comedy*. Were you aware of these two similarities, consciously, when you wrote the book?

Bowles: No, I didn't think of Dante. I didn't think of Eliot. I didn't think of anything. Of course I had read *The Waste Land*. I could see the implications, but I said to myself, "That will all be taken for granted; that will be in it anyway." I wasn't thinking about it at all. I was thinking about the story. No, what *The Sheltering Sky* was, really, was a working out of the professor's story, in "A Distant Episode." In my mind it was the same story retold; it described the same process in other terms.

Interviewer: Port, then, is the professor?

Bowles: They're all the professor. What I mean is what I wanted to tell was the story of what the desert can do to us. That was all. The desert is the protagonist.

Interviewer: I remember that I interpreted the sky in that novel as something that protects people from what might lie behind it, and that John Lehmann, who read the article, disagreed with me. Is the desert or the sky the chief symbol in the story, or are they related?

Bowles: It's all one: they're both the same, part of nature.

Interviewer: A nature which, like the sea in Stephen Crane's "Open Boat," is not inimical but merely indifferent.

Bowles: Precisely. Not caring. Unaware. And if you use the word God in place of nature, then *I* think you get even closer to it.

Interviewer: In that connection, I would like your comment on your third novel *The Spider's House*. *The Sky* gives the naturalistic view of man—a puny creature defeated by a nature, or by a God, that is indifferent, that doesn't care. *Let It Come Down* extends this view of man, I think, and gives it an existential context. Both these books seem to me to be not anti-religious, but non-religious. But *The Spider's House* seems very different—a religious book. A religious parable, actually. Aren't you saying in it that men need religion to be happy?—because that seems to me to be the big difference between it and the other two.

Bowles: Yes. *The Spider's House* is a novel which is partially at least about a given period in history. Right? While the other two are not, really. *The Spider's House* is definitely a time thing, isn't it? About the moment when the old is destroyed and the new breaks the shell and sticks its ugly head out. It is, yes, it's true that it's a sort of *apologia*.

Not for anything that one can ever do again. It's simply an evocation of that which has been lost. We'll never have it again. It's finished, it's smashed, it's broken. We've killed God and that's the end of it. There won't ever be that again.

Interviewer: The message of *The Spider's House,* then, is negative.

Bowles: How do you mean?

Interviewer: Well, it paints an idyllic picture of a place where people once had faith and were happy, but says that that kind of faith and happiness are things of the past. That we can never have them again.

Bowles: No, naturally, never again. That's finished and everybody knows it. But how is that negative?

Interviewer: I'm wondering if it isn't true that the reader comes from your work with a feeling of despair. *The Sheltering Sky* leaves one with that feeling, and *Let It Come Down* even more so. One might, perhaps, have been deceived into thinking that *The Spider's House* did not, but if the kind of security that it depicts is no longer possible, then that leaves the reader with despair, too.

Bowles: This hypothetical reader . . . Well, perhaps. Though I don't know why, unless the reader himself is in doubt about the existence of God.

Interviewer: What if the reader should happen to be religious?

Bowles: Religious meaning orthodox? He won't like the books anyway. He'll find them lacking in the qualities he demands. They're written from a point of view which precludes the existence of supernatural consciousness.

Interviewer: The opium of the people?

Bowles: Well, I don't see it that way, naturally.

Interviewer: I see. Now, Mr. Bowles, you have said that you are interested, as a reader, in fiction for its own sake, for the sake of the story, rather than for the sake of the ideas or the message that it might contain.

Bowles: Yes, I shy away from anything that propagandizes, generally. If I'm aware of the pitch, I resent it.

Interviewer: I am trying to reconcile this with your liking for existential fiction—Camus and Sartre, particularly.

Bowles: It seems to me that the books of Sartre I admire are precisely those without specific messages. The books have always interested me very much, but primarily for their technique, not as novels of ideas. I don't care whether Sartre is telling us that we have a choice, you know, to decide our destiny or not. That's his little song. That's what he personally gets out of it all. I'm not particularly excited by his personal conclusions, interesting though they almost always are. His fictional method can be considered independently of his philosophical messages. He has the most brilliant mind around in a long time. I can't help admiring him. But the method that Sartre uses does not necessarily have to be translated into strictly philosophical message. He has a different method, if you've noticed, of establishing reality. Philosophically, what interests me in Sartre and Camus is that they are both showing us how to live sensibly without the help of God.

Interviewer: I know you admire Lawrence, and I read a statement by Henry Miller recently, describing the way he—Miller, I mean—works. It reminded me very much of Lawrence, and I wonder if you would give me your comment on it. By the way, what is your opinion of Miller?

Bowles: I don't think of him as a novelist, exactly. Oh, I don't mean that he's not a good writer—I liked *The Colossus of Marousi*. But I didn't find the *Tropics* particularly good. I read them both, first in English and then in French. They're better in French. But at the time that I read them in the late Forties, my feeling was that a lot of the writing in both those books was shoddy.

Interviewer: Anyway, Miller said, "I think it's bad to think. A writer shouldn't think much. I'm not very good at thinking. I work in some deep-down place." And again: "I don't just know exactly what's going to happen. I know what I want to write about, but I'm not concerned too much with how to say it."

Bowles: That *does* sound like Lawrence. I think he's right.

Interviewer: But isn't this perhaps true only of himself, personally? Surely all writers who think are not bad writers? He has the idea, you see, that the imagination and the intellect are invariably at odds.

Bowles: Well, it's an admission of a certain weakness, certainly. But I sympathize, not being very good at "thinking," myself.

Interviewer: Doesn't this amount to a rejection of technique? Because technique implies calculation, and calculation is intellectual.

Bowles: That's the theory of a lot of contemporaries, of course. They're not interested in technique.

Interviewer: The theory of flow, yes. But isn't selection necessary in art?

Bowles: Well, it's much less likely that a good work will come out of a free association than out of planning. You're taking a much greater risk, that's all. It can happen, of course. But it's almost always flawed, like most emeralds. However, I think calculation should only come in at a certain point. It's not a substitute for imagination, and it can be very dangerous—in certain work, not all.

Interviewer: There is certainly a tendency among romantic writers— and I include the Beats and the surrealists in this category—to discourage conscious control: they feel that only by ignoring external form can they be faithful to a higher or rather deeper form.

Bowles: Organic form. Yes. But I doubt very much that with no conscious control at any point during the work it would be possible to construct that organic form. I don't think one could follow the surrealist method absolutely, with no conscious control in the choice of material, and be likely to arrive at organic form.

Interviewer: You are an artist, and you have had experience with different kinds of art in different cultures. Do you believe that there are art forms that can transcend the barriers of time and place, that are inevitable, so to speak, and can appeal to all people regardless of cultural differences; or do you think one needs to develop taste through exposure, and that the appeal of art forms is limited in time and space? Take music, for instance. I don't know how Western music sounds at first to Oriental ears, but certainly Oriental music sounds very strange to the Western ear the first time it's heard, and you have to be exposed to it before you can develop any kind of standard.

Bowles: Naturally. You have to listen. But I doubt very much that there is a music that appeals to everyone. I don't really see how it is possible to believe in inevitable form.

Interviewer: Well, according to the Jungian critics, there are certain patterns in art that are universal, and in the art of every society one can reduce the basic elements of composition to a very few possible combinations—archetypal patterns—and these patterns are inevitable.

Bowles: Well, obviously the basic experiences are universal—those having to do with birth, puberty, marriage, and death even though they are perceived and understood differently. A human being is a human being whether he lives in New Guinea or New York.

Interviewer: Yes, and I believe it would be possible to argue that your story, "The Fourth Day Out from Santa Cruz," which is a parable, is universal in that sense: wouldn't the truth of that story hold good for human beings everywhere? Wouldn't what happens to your sailor in that story be just as true of a sailor on an American ship as on a Spanish ship or on any ship that sails with human beings? Isn't it a condition of human behavior everywhere?

Bowles: Maybe not. Maybe not. Human behavior is contingent upon the particular culture that forms it. Maybe the behavior of the sailors in that story is only a condition of modern life. I don't think it would necessarily have been the same on an Indian ship, for instance. Not all cultures insist on the destruction of innocence.

Interviewer: Well, of course your sailor had not lost his innocence, and that's what I mean. The story shows us how he loses it. The theme is initiation, and that's a universal theme, isn't it?

Bowles: Maybe.

Conversations in Morocco: The *Rolling Stone* Interview

Michael Rogers/1974

From *Rolling Stone* 161 (23 May 1974): 48–50, 52, 54, 56, 58.
Reprinted by permission of Michael Rogers.

On the fourth floor of a small grey apartment house at the sunny outskirts of Tangier, Morocco, lives an American who may well rank as the premier expatriate of his generation; a rare blend of talents—composer, novelist, short-story writer—who has spent the last 40 years of his life on the move, through Europe, South and Central America, Africa and the Far East, and who settled at last in the odd and exotic blend of cultures that is Tangier.

"The Greeks used to call Greece the navel of the world," says Paul Bowles. "I always thought it was Tangier." It seems a fair call: The compact white city perches at the very tip of northern Africa, almost precisely between continents, a mix of influences European, African and Arabic.

Tangier is built on a hillside that slopes down to a long stretch of gleaming white beach, and on the heights of the city, one can sit in cool, tiled hotel patios, or at sidewalk cafes, sipping Pernod and gazing across the warm waters of the Strait of Gibraltar to the rocky outline of southern Spain. Further down, in the old town—the narrow twisting passageways of the medieval medina—one can pass through the separate odors of fresh mint, fresh shit and newly ground spices, all in less than a dozen steps. Above, French-language bookstores, plazas, fountains, galleries, immense hotel swimming pools; in the medina, trachoma-blinded beggars and bolts of bright fabric, fly-covered beef carcasses and dimly lit magic stalls. Tangier is for one who likes sharp contrasts and diverse territory, and for almost 25 years now, it has served Paul Bowles as home base.

Bowles, most likely, could hardly have settled for less. In the course of his 63 years, he has been involved in a series of artistic scenes from Gertrude Stein and company in Paris (it was Stein who first suggested that the then 21-year-old Bowles visit Tangier), to pre-war Berlin (where

Bowles provided a last name for Christopher Isherwood's cabaret girl
Sally), to the Beat scenes of the Fifties—Kerouac, Ginsberg, Burroughs
and Corso, in New York and Tangier. Even a quick glance through
Bowles's recently published autobiography, *Without Stopping,* makes it
clear that in the course of his travels, Bowles has made the acquaintance
of virtually every major artistic figure of the past four decades.

Bowles now considers Tangier his home, and it seems to fit him well.
"What to do if you get lost in the medina?" he told one visitor. "But
that's the point—you're supposed to get lost." Bowles has made good
use of his surroundings. In the late Fifties, he began to travel up into the
remote Moroccan hill country, recording the rural folk music and ultimately producing an album for the Library of Congress. In recent years,
Bowles has translated stories and novels from the unwritten Moroccan
language Moghrebi, with the results appearing in a variety of magazines, including *Rolling Stone.*

Bowles's tiny Tangier apartment is a constant flux of Moroccan
storytellers, visiting artists and curious tourists. Last summer, during a
trip to North Africa, I stopped in Tangier and recorded the following
conversations with Bowles over the course of several afternoons.
Bowles himself is as interesting an individual as his history indicates—
and more than that, a fine talker and teller of stories. And Tangier itself
is an endless source of stories to be told.

The city has a reputation for sex, drugs and general decadence, and in
fact, the sunny streets—and darker passageways—swarm with diverse
hustlers pushing everything from counterfeit Rolexes and stolen American passports (age, sex and height to approximate request, delivered
within six hours, 100 American dollars) to bad hashish, superb kif,
prescription opium, little boys, little girls, old ladies, spells, curses and
vicious poisons made to order.

The Western tide has placed Tangier in flux: Women, veiled and
hooded, brush past others made-up and miniskirted; Hondas and Ya-
mahas share even the narrowest medina passageway with mules and
donkeys. But the warm night air still vibrates with odd intrigues, unidentifiable sounds, the promise of forbidden and mysterious goings-on.
"In defense of the city," Bowles once wrote of Tangier, "I can say that
so far it has been touched by fewer of the negative aspects of contemporary civilization than most cities its size. More important than that,
I relish the idea that in the night, all around me in my sleep, sorcery

is burrowing its invincible tunnels in every direction, from thousands
of senders to thousands of innocent recipients. Spells are being cast,
poison is running its course; souls are being dispossessed of parasitic
pseudoconsciousnesses that lurk in the unguarded recesses of the mind.
There is drumming out there most nights. It never awakens me; I hear
the drums and incorporate them into my dreams."

On a bright Monday afternoon in Tangier, I walk a short distance into
the suburbs. Here the streets widen and grow quieter, lined with large
and well-kept houses, the summer homes of wealthy Europeans, or the
embassies and government offices. By the time one reaches the American consulate, there is considerable open ground and even occasional
goats picking at the scrubby grass covering the vacant areas.

Just across the street from the American consulate, Paul Bowles lives
in a several-storied structure of concrete that would not look altogether
out of place in Southern California. ("The Moroccans," Bowles notes,
"are always happy if something ancient can be made to look as if it were
built yesterday.") An elevator of recent European manufacture carries
one to Bowles's fourth-floor apartment.

The apartment is small, dimly lit, dominated by a wall of books and
a low, round wooden table surrounded by variously colored cushions.
More cushions lean against the walls, and a small, ornately carved table
contains a set of oddly assorted objects—half of unidentifiable function—that Bowles has picked up on his travels. An immense philodendron plant brushes the ceiling above some small windows, and past the
windows, a jungle of potted plants on an enclosed porch filters the
sunlight that reaches the room to a soft green glow.

The dim apartment is really the only setting during my visit where
Bowles will appear to be comfortable and in place. Bowles himself, at
first impression, seems fragile: of average height, but thin, with gray-
white hair that emphasizes the paleness and angularity of his face. He
moves carefully—pouring tea, fitting a cigarette into a short black
holder—but not so much with the caution of age as simply, it seems,
with some inner conviction that there is no point to hurry. His gaze is
evaluative, his voice generally quite low.

Bowles cannot quite figure out what his interviewer wants. ("I don't
have opinions," Bowles tells me later in the week, after a visit from
Tennessee Williams. "Why don't you talk to Tennessee? Tennessee has
opinions. I reserve judgment.") But Bowles is, clearly, a person of

unflagging curiosity, and he seems curious to discover exactly what his visitor with the tape-recorder is up to. Reclining on the cushions, over cups of strong tea, we begin to talk.

Before coming to see Bowles, I have been in the medina visiting a friend in one of the cheap hotels currently popular with longhairs and backpackers. In better days the hotel played host to F. Scott Fitzgerald for a summer; the French proprietor is still more than happy to display the signature in the register. Now, however, the fading lobby contains only the transient young people who, almost without exception, pass their few days in Tangier monumentally stoned.

For young American visitors, Morocco has one immense attraction: hashish.

But there isn't any. Yes, you can get sort of pressed leaves from the kif cuttings, but it's not hashish and it's no good.

What exactly is kif?

Kif has none of the impurities. It uses a small percentage of the plant, the small leaves around the clusters of flowers, cut very finely and usually mixed with black tobacco. You can get about 200 grams of kif from a kilo of plants. The tourists here buy the leftovers—the big leaves.

That's the hashish you see on the streets?

Yes. It's only the Americans and British who've come in the last 15 years who have shown them how to make it. There's no good Moroccan hashish. It's not a product they ever used. The first ones who made it were mostly American blacks who brought presses with them and showed the Moroccans how to do it. What the Moroccans sell as hashish is just the garbage left from kif-cutting. You wouldn't smoke it, normally. The hashish in Morocco is an American product and it's sold to Americans. The only thing they had here was kif and majoun.

Majoun?

Cannabis jam. Made with honey and nuts and kif and sometimes dates and figs.

Very strong?

Depends. It can be very strong.

What does it taste like?

You should try some.

GOOD OLE-FASHIONED MOROCCAN MAJOUN
2 lb. kif
1/2 lb. unsalted butter
1/2 lb. wheat grain
1/4 lb. dates
1/4 lb. figs (dried)
1/4 lb. walnuts
1 oz. caraway seed
1 oz. aniseed
1 lb. honey
part of whole nutmeg

Add kif (plus stalks) to 2/3-full cauldron of boiling water. Add butter, let simmer. Stir occasionally over low heat for eight hours.

Grind wheat grains. Chop walnuts, dates and figs very fine. Pound caraway and anise and nutmeg in mortar, then mix fruits, nuts and spices with the honey.

After eight hours, remove kif cauldron, let cool and scoop butter off top. Discard remaining water and kif. Put a small amount of wheat powder in frying pan and stir in some butter, heating until brown. Continue until all butter and wheat are used, then knead resultant paste into fruits/nuts/spices/honey mixture.

Will last indefinitely if stored in hermetic glass or metal containers. Serve two teaspoons, on biscuits, per day.

What is the official Moroccan government position on cannabis?

Well, they're trying to get rid of it, but it's very hard because everybody smokes. Once in a while, they have a campaign and go into the cafes and break the pipes over their heads.

But they don't arrest the smokers?

Not really. They arrest the dealers, certainly, and if you have a big wad of it they'll fine you according to the weight—a very high fine. But, like all the laws here, they're made in such a way that everyone has to break them; therefore, anybody can be grabbed at any moment. You can't keep within the law because the law is so arranged that you have to break it. But they don't generally arrest you unless they want something—usually money.

Did you smoke when you first came to Morocco?

The first four years I was here I didn't smoke at all. If they passed the pipe, I smoked it, but I didn't inhale because for four years I thought it was just very bad tobacco. It shows you how innocent you can remain living here year after year. Finally, I realized that it was a special plant.

And then?
Well, I smoked huge quantities regularly over a period of about 25 years. That's a very long time. I chain-smoked all day, in a way I couldn't have done with tobacco. An overdose, I'm sure, for anybody. So there must be a certain amount of habituation. It's certainly not an addicting drug, but you can make anything addicting if you want. Soda crackers.

Did you ever smoke when you were trying something creative?
Theater scores, yes, but serious music, no.

How about writing?
Oh, I wrote with it a great deal. In fact, I used it consciously in most of the books. In *The Sheltering Sky,* I got to the death scene and I didn't feel up to tackling it, so I ate a lot of majoun and just lay back that afternoon and the next day I had it resolved.

Have you tried the stronger psychedelics?
Mescaline, yes. LSD, never. LSD is too raw and too hard to get the proper dosage. I've seen it do things to people I've known—depersonalize them. After a few years and a lot of acid, they no longer have the same minds. They may be working fine internally, I don't know, but they're no longer good conversationalists.

Did you ever meet Timothy Leary?
Yes, he was here in '61, and he seemed . . . well, he was on the top of the wave, and riding. But when he was here three years ago, it seemed as if the wave had broken over and crashed, you know? Whether *up* was there, or there. He spoke with a constantly changing choice of symbolism, as if what was coming out of his mouth was a reflection of a kind of stroboscopic display going on in his head, where nothing seemed to last longer than one sentence. And, although he made sense on whatever he was saying for a moment, by the end of the evening it was very depressing, because he was exactly where he came in. It's his fighting spirit, though, that I admire.

On Tuesday, when I go to visit Bowles, I meet Mohammed Mrabet, a Moroccan storyteller. About 35, quite handsome with dark, wavy hair, and in superb physical condition, Mrabet lounges around Bowles's apartment and tells endless series of stories. Bowles has tape-recorded and translated some of these from the unwritten Moghrebi to English and by now Mrabet has two novels and two collections of short stories to his credit.

His literary success is a source of some amusement to Mrabet, who does not, himself, think too much of writers, intellectuals and kindred occupations. Mrabet wears two wrist watches, each consistently reading a different time. He tends to laugh loudly at random points in conversations and refuses, generally, to speak English, although one soon suspects that he understands it rather well. When he does use English, it is likely to be something like this: Grinning across a low table, white teeth gleaming, he will announce in a husky, smoke-roughened voice, "Hey. You, my friend." The grin widens and the eyes wander just a bit and then suddenly return. "Someday I come to your house and kill you." He leans back; big smile.

Another afternoon I wander into Bowles's apartment and find Mrabet there, sitting on the low cushions with his pipe.

"Mrabet—*como estás?*"

"Uhhhhh . . ." Mrabet groans softly, concentrating on his pipe. *"Muy, muy mal."*

"So bad? Why is this?"

"Ahhhh . . ." Mrabet shakes his head very slowly. Clearly he is greatly burdened. "Today," he says, "I have syphilis of the mouth . . . tuberculosis of the liver . . . cancer of the heart"—he gazes up mournfully—"and also, this morning, I was in a fight with three Spaniards and"—he pauses, looks down at his pipe—"they kicked all of my teeth out." And then, grinning toothily, he reaches for his cup of tea.

Mrabet is quite a storyteller.

It starts at night; he tells five or six stories in a row, one right after the other, and each one you wish you could put down. I always say, don't tell it now, I'd like to record it—but he tells it anyway and it gets lost. He can never remember them.

He makes them up on the spot?

I don't know whether he makes them up or synthesizes them. I don't think he knows. The Moroccans don't make much distinction between objective truth and what we'd call fantasy.

Power to the perceiver.

That's what they say, strangely enough. What do you want to believe? What do you want to think? There's a truth for everyone, and no one truth carries away all the others. Statistical truth means nothing to them. No Moroccan will ever tell you what he thinks, or does, or means. He'll tell you some of it and tell you other things that are completely false and then weave them together into a very believable core, which you swallow, and that's what's considered civilized. What's the purpose of telling the truth? It's not interesting, generally. It's more interesting to doctor it up a bit first of all, so it's more decorative and hence more civilized. And besides, how could anyone be so idiotic as to open himself to the dangers involved in telling the unadorned truth to people? You even have two pockets in your kif pouch—one for the kif you smoke yourself and one for the less good you give your friends.

But everyone knows that, right?

Oh sure, but they're not sure which part you keep the good in and which you keep the bad in. You change from day to day.

Lord.

Well, the Moroccans can read each other's lies pretty well, so it's a whole art of pulling the pieces together and trying to get the truth from the other's invention. Europeans have the reputation of swallowing everything, because they're too polite to say, "Well, I don't believe that." They say, "Oh, really?" and perhaps some of them really do believe what the Moroccans tell them. I don't know . . . they must think we're pretty foolish people. I think they look upon us with a certain amount of pity and some tolerance. There's a popular song which begins, "Our love was so nice at the beginning and then it turned Christian. . . ."

Which means?

Which means it became . . . ah—messed up, not straight. They'll say, "Now you're talking like a Christian," and that means, now you're saying what you don't believe.

On the other hand, they trust us. If you say, I'll take your wrist watch and give it back tomorrow, they would certainly rather give it to you than to a Moroccan. They'd rather work for you than for a Moroccan, because they believe you'll more likely pay them their wages. If you ask them why we exist, they will explain immediately that Allah made the Christians for us to live on. The Christians are for the Moslems to live off of, by milking. That's what life is all about.

They used to capture us, of course, and carry us off and make slaves of us, for centuries. The Barbary pirates—all Morocco was pirates, the whole coast of the Mediterranean, at least.

Is there still a slave trade in Morocco?

There are slaves in the south, but on paper they've been liberated. They just don't want to scatter because they couldn't live as well as they do being slaves. But nothing is said about it. There are still slaves, certainly. Occasionally there are slave raids. About 11 years ago, just two weeks before I arrived in the village of Taza down in the Sahara, they had come over the border and raided the whole village and carried off women and children. There's still a large slave market, but not in Morocco. Officially, naturally, no country would admit that it has one. It's probably either Mali or Mauritania. I'm not sure which.

The classiest of the Moroccan pirates Bowles mentions lived at the foot of the Rif mountains along the Mediterranean. The Riffians were apparently the original source of the old image of pirates swimming out to their hapless prey with long cutlasses clenched in their teeth. If it was a slow day and the pirates felt too lazy to pursue their victims, there was an alternate game plan: After dark, a line of 15 or 20 pirates would stand on a rise at the shoreline, each with a lighted lantern in hand. In what must have been a very precise—if perhaps kif-flavored—choreography, they would raise and lower the lanterns sequentially, up and down the line, and thereby create the effect of a row of lanterns hanging on the side of a gently bucking sailing vessel. The ship passing through would draw closer to investigate its apparent companion, wreck on the rocks, and the Riffians would then be able, at their leisure, to walk out on the shoals and conduct business.

These Riffian pirates seem to occupy something of the same romantic position in Moroccan folklore as do the cowboys in America. Even the 70-year-old kif-cutter beneath the steps of one's hotel beams more brightly when he announces *"Soy del Rif."* Mohammed Mrabet is from the Rif, as well, and he likes particularly to tell stories about his grandfather—a good old Riffian boy who displayed, among other things, the classical Moroccan attitude toward one's women. Once, for example, Mrabet's grandfather was up in the high country hunting with his rifle, and at the end of the day he started back down toward his village. Still high above the village, he looked down to view his own house. (The Riffians are noted for eagle-sharp eyesight, and at this point in the story Mrabet places one hand over his brow for shade and narrows his eyes to slits.) Ah ha! The returning hunter sees nothing other than one of his own wives, standing in the doorway of their house. Mrabet's grandfather decides to teach this wife a lesson for flaunting herself so publicly. He takes aim from the heights with his rifle, sights carefully, and—blam! Mrabet rocks back on the low pillows with the percussion of the blast and then grins, pointing with one index finger exactly between his eyes.

What? Mrabet's grandfather shot his wife dead for standing in the doorway of her own house?

Mrabet shakes his head vigorously, affirmatively. Of course, he explains—a woman who would come out of her house like that can only be a *puta*—a whore.

The listener thinks he will have to ponder this one a bit, and while he does, Mrabet decides that he will explain how his grandfather got the rifle in the first place.

It seems that word arrived in his village that a man in the neighboring village had rifles for trade, and, being without a firearm, Mrabet's ancestor decided he would obtain one. He put a tether on one of his best young bulls and led it over the hills to the next village and located the man with the rifles. They discussed the matter, bargaining back and forth, and at last arrived at what each thought an equitable arrangement: the young bull for one rifle. The man turned over the rifle, and Mrabet's grandfather surrendered the bull's tether. When Mrabet's grandfather had the rifle in his hands, however, he suddenly felt a powerful urge to use it. He looked all around, but could find nothing to shoot, except the man who traded him the rifle, so he shot the man, picked up the bull's tether, and walked home.

I was thinking about some of Mrabet's stories and wondering about the Moroccan sense of machismo, *which seems somewhat unqiue. According to Mrabet, what is a real man?*

For them? I suppose someone who has suffered as much as they have.

It's a question of suffering: How much can you take? The more suffering you can take, the more you've been mistreated, the more you've been in jail, the more of a man you are. They think we live a very namby-pamby, white-bread sort of life.

What about women in Morocco?

Well, if you hear noise in the street and send a Moroccan to the window and say, "What is it? A lot of people in the street?" they say, "No, only two." But you can hear a terrible noise so you say, "Only two?" and they'll answer, "But the rest are women." Women are not people. Women are decoration and they're sent by God to perpetuate the race. For instance, you can't get characteristics from the maternal side of the family—it's impossible. They can't explain how a baby can look like its mother since the mother is just a vessel.

Does Islam teach that?

Not exactly. Islam teaches that women are very dangerous creatures and one must stay away from them if possible. Have no truck with them, except, naturally, it's a necessity to marry and have children. That's the only reason you're supposed to go near a woman at all.

Better to marry than burn in hell. . . .

Right. But it's no good being married without having children— you'll go to hell anyway. Unless you happen to not be able to have children, and that is always sad. You're not a real man either.

I've heard that a certain amount of hostility has arisen toward European homosexuals who come to Tangier—a corrupting influence— something like that.

(quiet laugh) That would be the day, the Europeans come here and corrupt the Moroccans.

Ah. It's really a very bisexual culture, isn't it?

Well, yeah. More or less. Although they wouldn't define it as bisexual. Remember Mrabet, last night, saying that if a man went to jail for defending his rights, he's a good man, but if he goes to jail for ruining a girl or a boy—one always adds the "boy."

I think that's what gives Moroccan machismo *its odd character—in most* machismo *cultures, the homosexual is scorned and secretly feared.*

Well, that's something that may be changing here. There never was such a concept at all before, but as it's become more urbanized, there has come up a younger generation which could be called homosexual, I suppose. They're all bisexual, but there are also now those who are very obviously homosexual, more than bi. But that's conditioning—15 years ago, it was taken for granted all over Morocco that anybody slept with anybody. No holds barred. But nowadays—I've asked, I've gone into it with them, and they say it's old-fashioned to be bisexual, because you can see on television and in the films that there's no question of it; therefore it's out of style. Passe. Demode. People don't go in for that any more.

Fickle fashion.
Ce n'est la mode.

One afternoon the doorbell of Bowles's apartment rings, and Bowles is mildly upset—as upset as he ever seems to become—since a constant flow of visitors this afternoon has tended to make our taping rather sporadic. He says he will go to the door and look through the peephole and when he does, he stands for a moment, staring, and then opens the door. In strides Tennessee Williams, appearing tan and fit, with two pairs of glasses on chains around his neck, a medium-blue jacket over a nicely styled Italian sports shirt and, in one hand, a fifth of Johnny Walker Red.

"Tennessee!" says Bowles.

"Paul!" says Tennessee, and then introductions are made. Tennessee is accompanied by his secretary, a tall blond ex-BOAC steward faintly reminiscent of a well-tamed Malcolm McDowell. Tennessee has just fled the villa he had taken for the summer at *Positano,* abandoning it, patriotically enough, to some recent Vietnam veteran. ("A beautiful boy," Tennessee confides. "But he just didn't know when to stop.")

Tennessee sips his Johnny Walker and Bowles puffs his cigarette and they briefly reminisce. Their previous meeting, it is clear, was under somewhat less pleasant circumstances somewhere in the United States. ("Baby!" Tennessee tells him. "They were holding me *captive* there!") As the talk proceeds, Tennessee grows more effusive, a bit flushed beneath the Italian tan, and Bowles seems to shrink back in his cushions, nodding, evaluating, interjecting a name or a date here and there, but for the most part simply listening and fiddling with his cigarette holder.

After half an hour Tennessee has grown mellifluous behind the
Scotch and punctuates his conversation with long laughter that starts as
a cackle and winds up, long past when one might expect it to end, as
something closer to choking. He laughs, invariably, for a very long
time. At about this point, Tennessee decides to return to his hotel; his
secretary efficiently slips the sleek sports coat on his shoulders and caps
the Johnny Walker and then Tennessee departs, as quickly as he arrived.

"Oh," says another American, a young woman who has arrived in the
middle of Tennessee's visit. "Did you hear his laugh? The poor man has
suffered *so much*."

Bowles leans back, fits another cigarette into his holder, considers the
observation. "Yes," he says slowly, "that's true, but he's also achieved
a success in his lifetime that almost no artist ever manages."

The young woman is briefly silent, considering this.

"He looks much better than he did, though," Bowles says, nodding.
"Much, much better."

Tangier seems to attract a steady flow of American writers, doesn't it?
I guess so. Some like it and stay and some leave right away.

Truman Capote was among the latter, right?
Well, he couldn't have liked it all that much. He stayed about two
months, in '49. He's never come back. And while he was here, he
wouldn't even go to the medina. Said he wasn't interested.

Gore Vidal was here at the same time?
Just for a week. I think he came principally to annoy Truman Capote.
I know he did.

Both of them strike me as people to whom Morocco might not appeal.
No, I wouldn't expect them to be interested in it. I don't think they're
really interested in any kind of ethnology except American. And that's
all right. I think it's probably more important for a novelist to be interested in his own country.

*There was something of an American writing scene here in the sum-
mer of 1961, wasn't there?*
Sort of. Let's see . . . in '57, Allen Ginsberg and his sidekick, Peter
Orlovsky, and another man named Alan Ansen came here, and were
staying in a hotel where Bill Burroughs lived. They were trying to put

together all these yellow papers on the floor of Bill's room. The whole floor was covered with pages of manuscript, without numbers. He was just writing them and throwing them on the floor, all over the place, rat droppings among them—oh, it was a mess. And some of the pages were illegible but they managed to put it together for Olympia one way or another, and when they got the manuscript out they called it *Naked Lunch*. I didn't believe it would be possible.

This was 1957?

Yes. Four years later, they all came back in a more relaxed frame of mind, and also brought Gregory Corso along, and Tennessee was here; and Brion [Gysin] and Bill Burroughs, so there was a good nucleus . . . not that anything happened. I took Allen to Marrakech. He's a good person to travel with, easy to get along with, never complained about the food or anything.

Was everybody working that summer?

Oh, they were all working like mad, if you call it work. They were writing things together, and it was sort of fun to watch them work. The next year I went back to New York and they kept on working like that. Kerouac said, "I've got to write an opera. How do you do it?" No, it was a *ballet*. A ballet with spoken lines. And Kerouac would say, "Hey, Gregory, look, this guy comes in the bar and he begins bothering a girl there and someone stands up for the girl. What would he say?" And Gregory would say, "Don't bug the chick." And Kerouac would say, "Gee, that's great"—literally, in 1962, they hadn't thought of it. Only Gregory knew how to say it. And Kerouac immediately typed it down . . . Don't bug the chick. Then Peter Orlovsky would come in and say, "Why not put in"—I don't know—"somebody riding a bicycle." "Yeah, that's great," Kerouac would say. Everybody making suggestions. I'd never seen anyone write that way.

What did it turn into?

Well, he got paid for it, that's all that matters. He did an article for *Esquire,* too. I remember, the same time I was there. I read it later. It was pretty silly.

One night we are at a large party—a yearly event timed to coincide with the full moon—in the gardens of a villa at the beach. The gardens are

huge—a lush collection of everything from cacti to ferns—covering a
gentle hillside, and the winding rock paths have been lit with hundreds
of candles, placed every step or so. A large patio contains a number of
low tables and cushions, arranged around a bonfire of logs, each five
feet in length, bound together with wire and placed on end to stand as a
blazing column in the center of the gathering.

"She's not a snob," Bowles says of our titled hostess. "She invites
anybody she thinks would be amusing." Indeed, the guests range from
elaborately costumed young men with faces painted as checkerboards to
plump English novelists in suits and ties; exceedingly beautiful women
and equally beautiful boys and the older, well-maintained faces of the
Tangier summer regulars. A band of Moroccan musicians—12 or 13 in
number—has been hired to entertain, and they remain in constant motion around the fire for the entire evening. They are Jilala, and as they
circle the blaze they keep up a steady and hypnotic beat on large flat
hand drums, punctuated by a low-pitched, modulated wailing on long
cane transversal flutes.

The music is odd, dissonant, at first impression rather monotonous.
But it possesses a quality sufficiently compelling that soon a number
of the party-goers are dancing along with the band as they circle the
bonfire. The music goes on for hours and so do some of the dancers. At
one point, the band approaches the cushions where Mohammed Mrabet
reclines and they beckon for him to join. He shakes his head and smiles
in an unusually sheepish manner. One of the flute players is particularly
persistent and he begins to tug at Mrabet's arm while the rest of the
band draws closer. Mrabet throws the musician's hand away with some
violence; clearly, Mrabet doesn't want to dance, and the band moves
away to another group of Europeans.

Jilala is one of the dance cults in Morocco [says Bowles]—I
shouldn't think that more than half of the population of Morocco is
clearly affiliated with one or another of the dance brotherhoods. The
ceremony is a kind of purification ritual—the adept dances to the music
until he is inhabited by the saint, and then he can slash or burn himself
without harm.

And that's why Mrabet didn't want to dance last night.

Yeah. Because nobody there was in a trance and he very easily falls
into one, and didn't want to be an exhibitionist. He can go into the

trance much faster than most—three or four minutes and he's off—and
he only does it when there's no one around except the musicians. Partially because of the accidents he's had. We had a Jilala party three
weeks ago and he did dance, but in the first place he cut his hand badly,
and then he gave another man a black eye, he cut his face, cut someone's leg . . . there's always blood flowing because he gets much too
violent. He throws himself around and hurts himself and other people.

Sounds pretty spectacular.

Some of it is very spectacular. Once they have danced themselves
into the trance state, the Aissaoua, for example, eat scorpions and
cobras, bite off their heads and swallow them, or drink boiling water, or
they'll break bottles and chew the glass—I've watched them do it—or
throw themselves into piles of cactus. I've seen dancers with skin
simply bristling with thousands of cactus needles, and blood
everywhere. That's the Aissaoua.

The Jilala throw themselves into fires and burn themselves. You can
see a dancer jump into a fire and lie in the coals—and you think, my
God, he's dead—and then he comes out with an ecstatic expression on
his face and rubs handfuls of embers all over his body, in his mouth,
smearing himself, and half an hour later he's dancing again, and he's
washed off, and there's no sign of anything—no burn marks. Or, I've
seen people slash themselves with knives until they're bathed in blood
and lying on the floor rubbing it on their faces—and then they'll get up,
kiss everyone, kiss all the musicians, pay the musicians, walk out and
wash off, and there'll be no scars. It's not a trick. I don't understand it
at all.

Mind over matter?

It must be. Mrabet says the trance state is a way of going out of one's
house. If you are inside your house and you set it on fire, you will get
burned. But if you go outside your house, and your house burns, you
won't be harmed.

It's not a trick?

It's more a kind of hypnotism. A child in a given dance cult is exposed to the cult's music from infancy, until it operates as a hypnotic
device. They often can't even help it.

One of my drivers a few years ago was a Jilala; his whole family were Jilala. One night he took his family out to see a movie and they left the old grandmother at home. She went to bed, and to sleep, and then a Jilala party started in another house about a quarter-mile away. Still asleep, the old lady got up, started walking—somnambulistically—toward the sound of the music. The music stopped when she was half-way there, in the middle of a canebrake, and she fell down in a coma, among some cactus and lying on an anthill. When the family returned, they searched all night with lamps but didn't find her until morning. She was covered with ants and cut by the cactus but they couldn't awaken her from the state. At last they realized what had happened, and they had to go after the Jilala band, who had already left town, and bring them back to play for the old lady again, and it was only after a specific program had been gone through that she regained consciousness.

That sort of thing requires an incredible belief.
It isn't even belief, it's certainty—knowledge. And, of course, we can't have it. No matter how we train ourselves there would be an element of the impossible, of disbelief. As for them, there's no possibility of doubt. They know when they leave their bodies, nothing bad can happen.

But, for them, even death is not something to fear. One must never fear death because that ruins life. Death is a part of your life, and to push it away is a sin. It's almost a sin to weep if someone dies.

Almost opposite to Western religion, where it's at least a social sin not to weep.
Yet it's the Christians who promise immortality. Here, they always say, "The worms begin eating and eating and everyone has a wonderful time under the ground and finally there's nobody left," and that's part of life. Christianity, I never understood. Catholicism, perhaps, makes some sense in its formula. But all the various Protestant clans make no sense whatsoever. So pagan, the whole thing, but it's not even free pagan. Fake, kitsch, directed pagan.

Is Morocco pretty unstable politically?
Extremely unstable. Everyone feels that it's hanging by a silken thread, and wonders how it's managed to hang this long and not break.

King Hassan has quite a high lifestyle. . . .
Oh, certainly, fantastic marvelous palaces all over the place, and—

I don't know—175 different kinds of automobiles in his garages, racing cars, helicopters to fly between his palaces.

Is there a cohesive revolutionary movement in Morocco?

None whatever, my God. Revolution? There's no such word. The trials are still going on from the last coup attempt, against Hassan's plane. The executions are still going on—hundreds, so far.

Hundreds?

It's common enough. I remember in 1956, after the restoration of Mohammed V, when the Sultan returned from Madagascar, there was a great celebration at his palace. A German photographer went there, and there was such a crowd he could see nothing of what was going on, so he just raised his camera over his head and snapped away.

I saw the pictures and they gave me nightmares, and it takes a great deal to give me nightmares. Hundreds of people had been killed, their arms and legs sawed off, and their torsos tossed in an immense pile, dripping blood—with people in white costumes, smiling, dancing on top of the pile.

Lord.

The country people who move to the city will change the face of the nation. They settle outside in shacks, miles and miles of shacks, because they've sold all their land and animals—they were told that the city's paved with gold. When there is a new form of government, it will probably come from the disenfranchised people. There's more and more of them all the time.

Morocco is changing very quickly.

The country is in such a state of transition you can't even use the present tense, really. The impact of technology on the culture, for example. Television, automobiles, gas pumps—they know how to make them work, but they have no idea why they work. Several years ago there was a student at Meknes military school who was explaining something to Brion Gysin and he said, "It works by magic—just like an airplane." And everyone realized that, God, here he is just about ready to go to St. Cyr in Paris, a man of 18 or 19 who's studied geometry and all the rest, but says it works by magic like an airplane.

And that means, of course, at any moment it might not work—and they're delighted when the machine breaks. Since it's magic, it's ob-

vious that when you break it, then you've really won, you've proven
that it doesn't exist. They love to see machines fail, or medicines fail,
and then say, see—man can't do anyting, only Allah can do it. All
these things we think are so important are just toys and one day they'll
all break and then we'll have to live in front of Allah without toys. But,
of course, as long as the toys are here . . .

*I've noticed that in your fiction you like to set up situations with the
civilized man—the faintly decadent European—who deals with a less
civilized culture and loses disastrously.*
Yes, the degenerate European who feels able to cope with his own
culture and therefore imagines he can cope with any culture, imagines
wrongly.

*It's a common fantasy among travelers of my generation that it's pos-
sible to shed, say, one's Americanism, go barefoot and wear a* djellabah
and thus be part of a native system.
Well, that's a recurrent fantasy. Rousseauesque.

True.
But there is no such thing as going backwards, really. You can't
identify with a culture that is several centuries behind what you know. If
you were able to become part of a truly archaic culture, it would imply
something wrong with the psychic organism, I'm afraid. If a Westerner
encounters an archaic culture with the idea of *learning* from it, I think
he can succeed. He wants to absorb the alien for his own benefit. But to
lose oneself in it is not a normal desire. A romantic desire, yes, but
actually to try and do it is disastrous.

*What is the situation in Tangier with respect to hostility toward the
European and American residents?*
I don't find hostility. I find hostility on the part of groups of small
children, but then groups of small children are likely to act like mon-
keys anywhere in the world.

How about toward American longhairs?
Well, that attitude has changed considerably. When they first came,
they were welcome and everyone thought they were marvelous, but it
didn't last long because they were poachers, actually, on the Moroccan's territory. They tried to sell their chicks, as they called them, to the

Moroccans. They would buy up large quantities of kif and begin selling
it. But those were the prerogatives of the Moroccans and naturally they
got very indignant about it. If anybody was going to get pinched as
pushers, they were going to be and not the Americans. The Americans
were supposed to be their *clients.*

Finally, the police started coming to, say, a house where eight or ten
hippies were living and they'd take the whole house to the station. The
hippies would have a certain number of typewriters and tape recorders
and cameras, so the police would herd them all out, keep them overnight, and empty the house of all their belongings. The next morning
they'd take them in station wagons down to the port and put them on the
ferry to Spain. That got around pretty fast and Tangier was quickly
marked off the list of possible Shangri-las.

*Last night I was walking in the medina about midnight when I saw a
Moroccan, middle-aged, dressed in what appeared to be a pirate's
outfit—lots of jewelry, an odd kind of turban thing—and he was carrying a long sharp cutlass and chasing a bunch of kids down an alley. The
kids were laughing and he was yelling something and swinging this
sword around his head like a scythe, but nobody on the street seemed
very bothered.*

Perhaps he was a *mejdoub.*

Which is?

A *cherif.* Supposedly one of the direct descendants of Mohammed,
but a demented one. Everything they say, goes. Because they're a kind
of prophet. If they misbehave in public, break things, whatever, they
just calm them down. If he's not a *cherif,* then he's merely crazy.

What does it take to be considered crazy in this country?

Well, a bit more than by our standards. The place is full of what
we would call lunatics. As long as they don't hurt anybody, it's all
right. When they do hurt someone, they either put them away or they
don't.

I'd imagine there are some horrible kinds of mental conditions here.

Well, there's one very strange phenomenon here that I don't know of
anywhere else. Perhaps in someplace like Malaysia . . . it's a mass
psychosis around a character called Aicha Qandicha. You ever heard
of it?

Aicha Qandicha.

She's a woman—a spirit in the form of a woman. Practically every Moroccan has had contact with her in some way or another. She's a legion, she's manifold, like Santa Claus. I have a book that says, about 25 years ago, there were 35,000 men in Morocco married to her. A lot of the people in Ber Rechid—the psychiatric hospital—are married to her.

She appears to people?

She appears to men, yes, never to women. Women don't need to worry about her. Except that they're even more afraid of her. I don't know why—you say her name and they go to the corners of the room and whisper a prayer to clean the room of her name. Especially when they've just come from the country, the women are terrified of Aicha Qandicha.

If you're a man, it's always late at night that she calls you, when you're walking, and it has to be by running water. With a certain amount of vegetation. She will call you from behind. She often calls you in the voice of your mother. If you turn around, you're lost, because she's the most beautiful woman in the world and once you look at her you have no power against her at all. You must never see her, keep going, and if possible, have a piece of steel in your hand. Anything made of steel, plus the right prayers, and so on.

What exactly happens if you look at her?

Then you're married to her and that's that. You begin behaving very strangely. There are several well-known husbands of Aicha Qandicha around Tangier. They walk along brooks and river beds, hoping to hear her voice—you see them wandering. They'll come into cafes and sit down and be quite normal, but if anybody mentions Aicha Qandicha, they very quietly get up and leave. Most people know better than to mention it. But they all know when the man comes in.

A contagious psychosis . . .

Right. And when they find Aicha Qandicha again, they may make love to her right there, doesn't matter who's there. What you see if they're sort of screwing the ground, that's all. Children standing around, watching, laughing. Of course, then the police catch them and take them away. They don't beat them, just shut them up. Then they ship them to Ber Rechid.

Amazing . . .

Mental illness is very different in Morocco from in Europe or America. Based on different things. There was an American here who decided to set himself up as a psychiatrist in Casablanca, taking both Moslems and Christians, but his interest was in Moslems. And all he could discover in 13 years of practice was that everything was undifferentiated for the Moroccans. And Freudian therapy had nothing at all to do with it. You want a cup of tea?

One afternoon we go up into the hills above Tangier and sit on a grassy slope high over the deep water of the Strait of Gibraltar. In the distance, to the north, one can just make out the mountains of southern Spain. As is much of Tangier, the houses of the very rich are mingled with the more humble, and as we sit, surrounded by large walled estates—many inhabited by Tangier's European residents—a goatherd hurries his flock of 30 or 40 up the hill and the goats part noisily to flow around us.

The air is quite cold for Tangier in the summer—the weather in all of North Africa has been odd this year—and Bowles pulls his coat closer around his shoulders.

Did Tangier change much after Independence?

When Morocco was still colonial it was a place where any European could have anything. You could do anything, because you ran it. Americans used to go up to the police and take hold of them and slap them in the face. The police couldn't do anything about it—Americans could be tried only by a court of Americans at the consulate. They couldn't even be taken to a police station.

That's an incredible amount of freedom.

Yes, and they abused it. Certain Americans, the drunken types, with large racing cars—Aston Martins or something—they misbehaved.

That must have been quite a scene, those days. Was that when Barbara Hutton was giving her big Tangier parties? What was one of those like?

Big. Sort of a multiple party. She would have, say, in one part of the house, an Andaluz orchestra and then on the roof a Cuban orchestra. One party she had a whole village of blue men from the Sahara with

about 30 camels and their women and tents and fires and everything. In
the patio she had a whole group of Gypsies from Granada singing and
dancing and playing. That sort of thing. Hundreds of guests and lots
of secret police in every room, watching to make sure that no one took
the pearls, rubies and emeralds off the walls, since everything was en-
crusted. You could see where people had pulled gems out of the cushions as they sat. At that party a friend of mine knew the head of police
and how much each thing was insured for, and he went around telling
me, "This is insured for one million, this for . . ."

She still keeps her house here?

Oh yes. She may be in it right now, I don't know. With her seventh
husband. Who I knew before he married her, and who was a very
charming man, but since he's married her, everyone says he's gone
completely crazy and doesn't know any of the people he knew before.
Before he became a prince.

A prince?

She made him a prince. His name is now Prince Champassak. Before
that, he was a mining engineer in Marrakech; a Eurasian, half Vietnamese and half French. She bought the title for him. She said, "I've been
all sorts of things, but not a princess, and now I want to be a princess."

So she bought a title?

The story I heard is funny. She went to Rabat, to the Hilton, and
called up the Vietnamese embassy and said she wanted to buy a title
immediately. A Vietnamese title. And she would pay $50,000, but she
wanted it the next day. And they said, but Madame, this is scarcely
possible. And she said, well, you try. And then someone remembered
that there was an old Vietnamese working in the embassy as a typist or
something, who was a broken-down aristocrat who did own an estate
and was titled. One of the embassy people went to this old typist and
said, there's a crazy American woman who'll pay $10,000 for a title,
want to sell yours? And the typist said yes, so he got $10,000. She paid
$50,000.

So now she's a princess.

Yes. Princess Champassak. And the prince has a very nice house
of his own that she gave him out by the country club, with enormous
stables, and a tunnel built from the house to the stables, heated by a

furnace, so you can walk four or five hundred feet underground to get to the stables. The sort of thing nobody needs in Morocco. Still it was a good way to get rid of some money, and it gave people some jobs.

With such a small European population, there's a high proportion of extremely wealthy people here.

Yes, there are a lot of them. Thank heavens there aren't any more. Prices would go up.

Paul Bowles's wife, Jane, was an accomplished novelist and playwright (*The Collected Works of Jane Bowles,* Farrar, Straus & Giroux 1966) who suffered a serious stroke in March of 1957. Following six years of hospitalization in Spain, Jane Bowles died in May of 1973.

I've heard that Mrs. Bowles's stroke was caused by some sort of Moroccan medicine. . . .

Oh, well, because of the stroke, no one will ever really know. The doctor here couldn't tell what it was. Other doctors were inclined to think it hadn't been a stroke because the lesion was microscopic. She had taken something the day she had the stroke, but no one knows for certain what caused it. She was doing Ramadan, for one thing, which is very strenuous.

Ramadan?

A month of fasting. She was fasting, but she wasn't doing the real Ramadan, because she was drinking. You're not supposed to drink when you fast. She was drinking brandy and doing Ramadan. I should think that in itself would do it. And then this rather evil maid we had here gave her something, and afterward, when she came out of her initial coma, the first thing she wanted to know was what she'd taken. What this woman had given her. When she was back in her right mind, she denied that she'd taken anything, to protect the woman. But she admitted to me she had taken some majoun. Whether it was majoun or something else, there's no way of telling.

The maid may have poisoned her?

This maid was a horror. We used to find packets of magic around the house. In fact, in my big plant, in the roots, she hid a magic packet. She wanted to control the household through the plant. The plant was her

proxy, or stooge, and she could give it orders before she left and see
that they were carried out during the night. She really believed these
things.

What was this packet of magic?
Well, it was a mess. It was a cloth bound up very tight and inside
there were all kinds of things . . . pubic hairs, dried blood, fingernails,
antimony and I don't know what all. I didn't analyze it, no Moroccan
would touch it, and I had to pick it up. Everyone around saying, don't
touch it, don't touch it. I threw it down the toilet.

Why did you keep this maid around?
Mrs. Bowles wouldn't let me fire her. She said, I hired her and when
I see fit, I'll fire her, but you can't. And unfortunately the maid knew
that. She was very hostile. She always carried a switchblade and when
she saw me alone she'd bring it out—swish—a real quick draw.
[Bowles gestures as with knife toward throat.] That's what you'll get,
she'd say to me. She tried to put my eyes out one night. A monster, a
real monster. I could show you pictures of her that would freeze you.

How long did you have her around?
About 15 years, I guess. We finally gave her a little house in the
medina.

You ever see her these days?
No, I don't want to see her. She's never come back. She writes
threatening letters to me, though, which I keep.

Very strange.
Very strange.

Magic and poison.
Well, that's part of everyday life. I'm not afraid of magic, but I'm
afraid of poison.

The Moroccans make nasty poisons?
Oh, horrible. Because they don't work right away. Little by little.
There was a man here, an Englishman, two years ago, who was poisoned. When he woke up in the mornings, he would find incisions,
designs cut into his feet. During the night someone came in and carved
these cabalistic designs with a penknife on his feet. He couldn't even

walk, they were so cut up. Obviously, he must have been very drugged, and every morning he would find these new tic-tac-toe sorts of things on his soles. He finally died.

How did he get himself in such a situation?
I have no idea.

On my last afternoon in Tangier, we go up into the hills again, to a small cafe that is one of Bowles's favorites. On a terraced hillside leading down to the Strait, this cafe boasts a whole set of outdoor cubbyholes with woven mats, gently shaded and overlooking the water, where one may pass the afternoon with glasses of sweet mint tea and a pipe. The only other Westerner visiting the cafe is a very spaced American girl, accompanied by four Moroccans. We take seats, leaning back against a low wall, the tea is brought, and I begin to shoot some pictures of Bowles.

Soon it becomes clear that a group of young Moroccans, seated not far from us with pipes, tea and a Japanese cassette machine playing Dylan, are upset about the photography. "No pictures," one of them says, not at all friendly. "No pictures."

"They're afraid you're taking pictures of them smoking," Bowles says quietly. At first I try to be more careful, then I leave off the photography entirely, but the Moroccans do not take their eyes off us. Dylan sings "Blowin' in the Wind," the breeze comes up off the Strait, and the Moroccans glower. After several minutes we go inside to sit.

What's the future for the expatriate population here in Tangier?
Oh, the population itself is diminishing. The tens of thousands of little European artisans and shopkeepers and so on, are leaving—and have already left, most of them. This year there was a big Moroccanization program, and now all companies have to be controlled at least 51% by Moroccans. If you have a bakery, a cobbler's shop, you have to turn half of it over to Moroccans. Of course, you don't—what you do is sell out cheap. About 60,000 French have left Morocco in the last four months.

That's a big change.
Certainly. Who will want to live here, after a few years, when there's no way of eating properly, or having anything done? No—it would be

impossible. What will come of it, I don't know. Eventually maybe Europeans and Americans won't be able to visit countries like this. Practically no Arab country receives tourists any more.

The Tangier way of life is disappearing fast.
Very fast. But then it is all over the world, too.

If you had to leave Morocco, where would you go?
Where would you go?—that's the point. I don't know whether one would have a choice. If one had to leave here, I'm sure one would be taken willy-nilly to the United States. If someone, say, should happen to make Hassan dead, things could change very quickly. As the American consul says, one small bag down at the dock at dawn and we'll have boats to get you out. But you won't be able to take anything with you. You'd have to start out again from the United States, and decide where to go, but with nothing . . . you'd have to buy everything all over again. It'd be a job.

And there's no place like Tangier, or the Tangier of ten years ago?
I don't know of any place in the world like it. There were, but now. . . .

Interview with Paul Bowles

Daniel Halpern/1975

From *TriQuarterly* [Evanston, IL] 33 (Spring 1975): 159–177.
Reprinted by permission of Daniel Halpern.

Daniel Halpern: Why did you first come to Morocco?

Paul Bowles: Gertrude Stein suggested it. She had been here three separate summers, staying at the old Villa de France, and she thought I'd like it. She was right. I loved it. And I still love it. Less, naturally. One loves everything less at my age; also it's a little less lovable than it was forty years ago.

Halpern: What is it that keeps you in Tangier?

Bowles: It's changed less than the rest of the world, and continues to seem less a part of this particular era than most cities. It's a pocket outside the mainstream. You feel that, very definitely, when you come in. After you've been over to Europe, for instance, for a few days or a few weeks, and you come back here, you immediately feel you've left the stream, that nothing is going to happen here.

Halpern: You were eighteen when you first left America. What lured you to Europe?

Bowles: Everyone wanted to come to Europe in those days. It was the intellectual and artistic center. Paris specifically seemed to be the center, not just Europe. After all, it was the end of the twenties and just about everybody *was* in Paris.

Halpern: Did you know many writers and composers in Paris?

Bowles: Practically no writers. I met a lot but I didn't know them. Composers? Naturally, Virgil Thomson, and Henri Sauguet and Francis Poulenc. . . . Not very many, no.

Halpern: Did you see much of Gertrude Stein while you were there?

Bowles: I did see a lot of her in 1931. She had read some of the poems I had published, and she didn't like them. I went around in 1931, and I remember she mentioned Bravig Imbs, a poet at that time who wrote for various magazines, and she said, "Yes, Bravig Imbs is a very bad poet, but you're not a poet *at all*." She also had things to say about my music. I played her my music in 1931 and she said, "It's interesting." And then I went back in 1932 to her country house in Bilignin and played some newer music for her, and she said, "Ah, last year your music wasn't attenuated enough, and this year it's too attenuated." That's all she had to say. Except that she told me come to Tangier. She was liking me at the time, which meant that I could trust her recommendation. The next year, when she was not liking me at all, she suggested I go to Mexico, adding after a pause, "You'd last about two days."

Halpern: Was she in favor of your giving up music and devoting more time to your writing?

Bowles: I suspect she thought I had no ability to write. I remember we were sitting in the garden at Bilignin and she said, "I told you last week what was the matter with your poetry. What have you done with it since then, with those particular poems? Have you rewritten them?" And I said, "No, of course not; they've already been published that way. How could I rewrite them?" And she said, "You see! I told you you were not a poet. A real poet would have gone up and worked on them and then brought them down and showed them to me a week later, and you've done nothing whatever."

Halpern: What was it about writing that made you put composing aside?

Bowles: I'm not sure. I think it had a lot to do with the fact that I couldn't make a living as a composer without remaining all the time in New York. I was very much fed up with being in New York.

Halpern: When did you begin to write?

Bowles: At four. I have a whole collection of stories about animals that I wrote then.

Halpern: But it was as a poet that you first published, in *transition*?

Bowles: I had written a lot of poetry (I was in high school) and had been buying *transition* regularly since it started publishing. It seemed to me that I could write for them as well as anyone else, so I sent them things and they accepted them. I was sixteen when I wrote the poem they first accepted, seventeen when they published it. I went on for several years as a so-called poet.

Halpern: What ended your short career as a poet?

Bowles: I think Gertrude Stein had a lot to do with it. She convinced me that I ought not to be writing poetry, since I wasn't a poet at all, as I just said. And I believed her thoroughly, and I still believe her. She was quite right. I would have stopped anyway, probably.

Halpern: Were there any important early literary influences?

Bowles: Well, I suppose everything influences you. I remember my mother used to read me Edgar Allan Poe's short stories before I went to sleep at night. After I got into bed she would read me *Tales of Mystery and Imagination*. It wasn't very good for sleeping—they gave me nightmares. Maybe that's what she wanted, who knows? Certainly what you read during your teens influences you enormously. During my early teens I was very fond of Arthur Machen and Walter de la Mare. The school of mystical whimsy. And then I found Thomas Mann, and fell into the *Magic Mountain* when I was sixteen, and that was certainly a big influence. Probably that was the book that influenced me more than any other before I went to Europe.

Halpern: Before you actually begin writing a novel or story, what takes place in your mind? Do you outline the plot, say, in visual terms?

Bowles: Every work suggests its own method. Each novel's been done differently, under different circumstances and using different methods. I got the idea for *The Sheltering Sky* riding on a Fifth Avenue bus one day going uptown from Tenth Street. I decided just which point of view I would take. It would be a work in which the narrator was omniscient. I would write it consciously up to a certain point, and after that let it take its own course. You remember there's a little Kafka quote at the beginning of the third section: "From a certain point onward there is no longer any turning back; that is the point that must be reached." This seemed important to me, and when I got to that point, beyond which there was no turning back, I decided to use a surrealist technique—simply writing without any thought of what I had already written, or awareness of what I was writing, or intention as to what I was going to write next, or how it was going to finish. And I did that.

Halpern: What about your second novel, *Let It Come Down?*

Bowles: That was altogether different. I began to write that on a freighter as I went past Tangier one night. I was on my way from Antwerp to Colombo, in Ceylon, and we went past Tangier and I felt very nostalgic—I could see faint lights in the fog and I knew that was Tangier. I wanted very much to stop in and see it, but not being able to, since the boat went right on past, I created my own Tangier. I started by imagining that I was standing on the cliff looking out at the place where I was on the ship. I transported myself from the ship straight over to the

cliffs and began there. That was the first part I wrote. I worked backward and forward, as it were, from that original scene.

Halpern: Where Dyar and Hadija stand on the top of a cliff and see
freighters going by.

Bowles: That's right. Then on the ship, before I got to Colombo,
I worked it out—the sequence of events, the patterns of motivations,
the juxtapositions. Again I decided to use exactly the same writing
technique I had used with *The Sheltering Sky*. To get it up to a place
from which it could roll of its own momentum to a stationary point, and
then let go and use the automatic process. It's quite clear where it
happens. It's on the boat trip.

Halpern: When you wrote the scene in which Dyar was high on
majoun, the evening he had dinner with Daisy, were you yourself
under the influence of kif?

Bowles: No. The whole book was written in cold blood, up to that
point. But for the last section of the book I went up to Xauen and stayed
in the hotel there for about six weeks, writing only at night after dinner.
After I had worked for half or three quarters of an hour, and it was
going along, I would smoke. That made it possible for me to write four
or five hours rather than only two, which is all I can usually do. The kif
gave me a much longer breath.

Halpern: Are you in the habit of using kif in order to write?

Bowles: No, I don't think that would be possible. When I was writing
Up Above the World I smoked when I felt like it, and worked all day
wandering around in the forest with a pen and notebook in my hand.

Halpern: To what extent does the ingestion of kif play a role in your
writing?

Bowles: I shouldn't think it has an effect on anyone's writing. Kif
can provide flashes of insight, but it acts as an obstacle to thinking. On
the other hand, it enables one to write concentratedly for hours at a
stretch without fatigue. You can see how it could be useful if you were
writing something which relied for its strength on the free elaboration of
fantasy. I used it only once that way, as I say—for the fourth section of
Let It Come Down. But I think most writers would agree that kif is for
relaxation, not for work.

Halpern: Do you revise a great deal after you've finished the rough
draft?

Bowles: No, the first draft is the final draft. I can't revise. Maybe
I should qualify that by saying I first write in longhand, and then the
same day, or the next day, I type the longhand. There are always many
changes between the longhand and the typed version, but that first typed
sheet is part of the final sheet. There's no revision.

Halpern: Many critics like to attribute a central theme to your writing: that of the alienation of civilized man when he comes in contact
with a primitive society and its natural man.

Bowles: Yes, I've heard about that. It's a theory that makes the body
of writing seem more coherent, perhaps, when you put it all together.
And possibly they're right, but I'm not conscious of having such a
theme, no. I'm not aware of writing about alienation. If my mind
worked that way, I couldn't write. I don't have any explicit message;
certainly I'm not suggesting changes. I'm merely trying to call people's
attention to something they don't seem to be sufficiently aware of.

Halpern: Do you feel trapped or at a disadvantage by being a member of Western civilization?

Bowles: Trapped? No. That's like being trapped by having blond hair
or blue eyes, light or dark skin. . . . No, I don't feel trapped. It would
be a very different life to be part of another social group, perhaps, but I
don't see any difference between the natural man and the civilized man,
and I'm not juxtaposing the two. The natural man always tries to be a
civilized man, as you can see all over the world. I've never yearned to
be a member of another ethnic group. That's carrying one's romanticism
a little too far. God knows I carry mine far enough as it is.

Halpern: Why is it that you have traveled so much? And to such
remote places?

Bowles: I suppose the first reason is that I've always wanted to get as
far as possible from the place where I was born. Far both geographically
and spiritually. To leave it behind. I'm always happy leaving the United
States, and the farther away I go the happier I am, generally. Then
there's another thing: I feel that life is very short and the world is there
to see and one should know as much about it as possible. One belongs
to the whole world, not to just one part of it.

Halpern: What is the motivation that prompts your characters to
leave the safety of a predictable environment, a Western environment,
for an unknown world that first places them in a state of aloneness and

often ends by destroying them, as in the case of Port and Kit in *The Sheltering Sky* and Dyar in *Let It Come Down*?

Bowles: I've never thought about it. For one thing there is no "predictable environment." Security is a false concept. As for the motivation? In the case of Port and Kit they *wanted* to travel, a simple, innocent motivation. In the case of Nelson Dyar, he was fed up with his work in America. Fed up with standing in a teller's cage. Desire for freedom, I suppose; desire for adventure. Why *do* people leave their native habitat and go wandering off over the face of the earth?

Halpern: Many of your characters seem to pursue a course of action that often leads them into rather precarious positions, pushed forward by an almost self-destructive curiosity, and a kind of fatalism—for example, the night walks of Port, or the professor in *A Distant Episode*. Could you say something about this?

Bowles: I'm very aware of my own capacity for compulsive behavior. Besides, it's generally more rewarding to imagine the results of compulsive than of reflective action. It has always seemed to me that my characters act naturally, given the circumstances; their behavior is foreseeable. Characters set in motion a mechanism of which they become a victim. But generally the mechanism turns out to have been operative at the very beginning. One realizes that Kit's and Port's having left America at all was a compulsive act. Their urge to travel was compulsive.

Halpern: Do you think that these characters have an "unconscious drive for self-destruction"?

Bowles: An unconscious drive for self-destruction? . . . Death and destruction are stock ingredients of life. But it seems to me that the motivation of characters in fiction like mine should be a secondary consideration. I think of characters as if they were props in the general scene of any given work. The characters, the landscape, the climatic conditions, the human situation, the formal structure of the story or the novel, all these elements are one—the characters are made of the same material as the rest of the work. Since they are activated by the other elements of the synthetic cosmos, their own motivations are relatively unimportant.

Halpern: Why do you constantly write about such neurotic characters?

Bowles: Most of the Occidentals I know *are* neurotic. But that's to be expected; that's what we're producing now. They're the norm. I don't think I could write about a character who struck me as eccentric, whose behavior was too far from standard.

Halpern: Many people would consider the behavior of your characters far from standard.

Bowles: I realize that if you consider them objectively, they're neurotic and compulsive; but they're generally presented as integral parts of situations, along with the landscape, and so it's not very fruitful to try to consider them in another light. My feeling is that what is called a truly normal person (if I understand your meaning) is not likely to be written about, save as a symbol. The typical man of my fiction reacts to inner pressures the way the normal man *ought* to be reacting to the age we live in. Whatever is intolerable must produce violence.

Halpern: And these characters are your way of protesting.

Bowles: If you call it protest. If even a handful of people can believe in the cosmos a writer describes, accept the workings of its natural laws (and this includes finding that the characters behave in a credible manner), the cosmos is a valid one.

Halpern: Critics often label you an existential writer. Do you consider yourself an existentialist?

Bowles: No! Existentialism was never a literary doctrine in any case, even though it did trigger three good novels—one by Sartre (*La Nausée*) and two by Camus (*L'Etranger* and *La Peste*). But if one's going to subscribe to the tenets of a formulated belief, I suppose atheistic existentialism is the most logical one to adopt. That is, it's likely to provide more insight than another into what attitudes to take vis-à-vis today's world.

Halpern: But you do share some of the basic tenets of existentialism, as defined by Sartre.

Bowles: He's interested in the welfare of humanity. As Port said, "What is humanity? Humanity is everybody but yourself."

Halpern: That sounds rather solipistic.

Bowles: What else can you possibly know? *Of course* I'm interested in myself, basically. In getting through my life. You've got to get through it all. You never know how many years you've got left. You keep going until it's over. And I'm the one who's got to suffer the consequences of having lived my life.

Halpern: Is this why so many of your characters seem to be asocial?

Bowles: Are they? Or are they merely outside and perhaps wishing they were inside?

Halpern: Do you think of yourself as being asocial?

Bowles: I don't know. Probably very, yes. I'm sorry to be so stubborn and impossible with all this, but the point is I just don't know any of the answers, and I have no way of finding them out. I'm not equipped to dig them up, nor do I want to. The day I find out what I'm all about I'll stop writing—I'll stop doing everything. Once you know what makes you tick, you don't tick any more. The whole thing stops.

Halpern: You are against Sartre's taking life so seriously. Yet when you say about your life that you are just trying to get through it the best you can, it sounds to me as if *you* took living very seriously.

Bowles: Oh, everyone takes his own existence seriously, but that's as far as he should go. If you claim that life itself is serious, you're talking out of turn. You're encroaching on other people's lives. Each man's life has the quality he gives it, but you can't say that life itself has any qualities. If we suffer, it's because we haven't learned how not to. I have to remind myself of that.

Halpern: Then life is a painful experience for you?

Bowles: You have to keep going, and try at least to keep a pleasant face.

Halpern: Life seems to be inaccessible to many of your characters. By their going beyond a certain point, past which they are pulled by an unconscious force, they place themselves in a position where return to the world of man is impossible. Why are they pushed beyond that point?

Bowles: It's a subject that interests me very much; but you've got to remember that these are all rationalizations devised after the fact, and therefore purely suppositious. I don't know the answers to the questions; all I can do is say, "Maybe," "It could be," or "It could be something else." Offhand I'd suggest that the answer has to do with the romantic fantasy of reaching a region of self-negation and thereby regaining a state of innocence.

Halpern: Is it a kind of testing to find out what it's like beyond that point?

Bowles: It could be. One writes to find out certain things for oneself. Much of my writing is therapeutic. Otherwise I never would have started, because I knew from the beginning that I had no specific desire to reform. Many of my short stories are simple emotional outbursts.

They came out all at once, like eggs, and I felt better afterward. In that sense much of my writing is an exhortation to destroy. "Why don't you all burn the world, smash it, get rid of everything in it that plagues you?" It is a desire above all to bring about destruction, that's certain.

Halpern: So you don't want to change the world. You simply want to end it.

Bowles: Destroy and end are not the same word. You don't end a process by destroying its products. What I wanted was to see everyone aware of being in the same kind of metaphysical impasse I was in. I wanted to know whether they suffered in the same way.

Halpern: And you don't think they do?

Bowles: I don't think many do. Perhaps the number is increasing. I hope so, if only for selfish reasons! Nobody likes to feel alone. I know because I always think of myself as completely alone, and I imagine other people as a part of something else.

Halpern: And you want to join the crowd?

Bowles: It's a universal urge. I've always wanted to. From earliest childhood. Or to be more exact, from the first time I was presented to another child, which was when I was five.

Halpern: And you were rejected?

Bowles: It was already too late. I wanted to join on my own terms. And now it doesn't matter.

Halpern: And so now you alienate your characters, the way you were alienated?

Bowles: I don't think the judge would allow that question. Life is much harder if one is alone. Shared suffering is easier to bear.

Halpern: Sartre says somewhere that a man's essential freedom is the capacity to say "No." This is something your characters are often incapable of. Do they achieve any kind of freedom?

Bowles: My characters don't attain any kind of freedom, as far as I'm aware.

Halpern: Is death any kind of freedom?

Bowles: Death? Another nonexistent, something to use as a threat to those who are afraid of it. There's nothing to say about death. The cage door's always open. Nobody *has* to stay in here. But people want freedom *inside* the cage. So what is freedom? You're bound by physical laws, bound by your body, bound by your mind.

Halpern: What does freedom mean to you?

Bowles: I'd say it was not having to experience what you don't like.

Halpern: By the alienation that your characters go through in their various exotic settings, are they forced into considering the meaning of *their* lives, if there is meaning to life?

Bowles: I shouldn't think so. In any case, there's not *one* meaning to life. There should be as many meanings as there are individuals—you assign meaning to life. If you don't asign it, then clearly it has none whatever.

Halpern: In *L'Etranger,* Meursault is put in jail, which is a way of being alienated, and at that point he considers "the meaning of life."

Bowles: Camus was a great moralist, which means, nowadays, to be preoccupied with social considerations. I'm not preoccupied in that way. I'm not a moralist. After all, he was a serious communist; I was a very unserious one, a completely negative one.

Halpern: What was it about communism that appealed to you?

Bowles: Oh, I imagined it could destroy the establishment. When I realized it couldn't, I got out fast and decided to work on my own hook.

Halpern: Back to destroying the world. . . .

Bowles: Well, who doesn't want to? I mean, look at it!

Halpern: It's one thing to dislike something you see and another to want to destroy it.

Bowles: Is it? I think the natural urge of every human being is to destroy what he dislikes. That doesn't mean he does it. You don't by any means get to do what you want to do, but you've got to recognize the desire when you feel it.

Halpern: So you use your writing as a weapon.

Bowles: Right. Absolutely.

Halpern: And your music?

Bowles: Music is abstract. Besides, I was writing theater music. It was fun but it's a static occupation. I always have to feel I'm going somewhere.

Halpern: Has your desire to destroy the world always been a conscious one?

Bowles: Yes. I was aware that I had a grudge, and that the only way I could satisfy my grudge was by writing words, attacking in words. The way to attack, of course, is to seem not to be attacking. Get people's confidence and then, surprise! Yank the rug out from under their feet. If they come back for more, then I've succeeded.

Halpern: If they enjoy your work you have succeeded—in the sense that their minds have been infected.

Bowles: Infected is a loaded word, but all right. They have been infected by the germ of doubt. Their basic assumptions may have been slightly shaken for a second, and that's important.

Halpern: And you don't think of your goals as being negative?

Bowles: To destroy often means to purify. I don't think of destruction as necessarily undesirable. You said "infecting." All right. Perhaps those infected will have more technique than I for doing some definite destroying. In that sense I'm just a propagandist, but then all writers are propagandists for one thing or another. It's a perfectly honorable function to serve as a corrosive agent. And there certainly is nothing unusual about it; it's been a part of the romantic tradition for the past century and a half. If a writer can incite anyone to question and ulti-mately to reject the present structure of any facet of society, he's per-formed a funciton.

Halpern: And after that?

Bowles: It's not for him to say. *Après lui le déluge.* That's all he can do. If he's a propagandist for nihilism, that's his function too.

Halpern: To start the ball rolling?

Bowles: I want to *help* society go to pieces, make it easy.

Halpern: And writing about horror is your method.

Bowles: I don't write "about horror." But there's a sort of meta-physical malaise in the world today, as if people sense that things are going to be bad. They could be expected to respond to any fictional situation which evoked the same amalgam of repulsion and terror that they already vaguely feel.

Halpern: Are you, as Leslie Fiedler suggests, a secret lover of the horror you create?

Bowles: Is there such a character as a secret or even an avowed lover of horror? I can't believe. If you're talking about the *evocation* of horror on the printed page, then that's something else. In certain sensitive people the awakening of the sensation of horror through reading can result in a temporary smearing of the lens of consciousness, as one might put it. Then all perception is distorted by it. It's a dislocation, and if it's of short duration it provides the reader with a partially pleasurable shiver. In that respect I confess to being jaded, and I regret it. A good jolt of vicarious horror can cause a certain amount of questioning of values afterward.

Halpern: Is that what you hope to accomplish through the horror you evoke?

Bowles: I don't use horror. If reading a passage of mine triggers the suspension of belief in so-called objective reality for a moment, then I suppose it has the same effect on the reader as if I had consciously used horror as a device.

Halpern: I'd like to talk a little about your translating. Many critics are convinced that the stories from the Moghrebi are really yours.

Bowles: I know, but they're not. That's critical blindness. If they were mine, they'd be very different. They're translations. Each Moroccan writer has a different style in English because the cadence of each one's speech is different in Moghrebi. I keep the tapes. Anyone who listens to them and understands the language can hear the differences.

Halpern: Has your writing been affected by the translations you've done?

Bowles: A little. I noticed that it had been when I wrote *A Hundred Camels in the Courtyard*. I was trying to get to another way of thinking, noncausal. . . . Those were experiments. Arbitrary use of disparate elements.

Halpern: You did some translating of Borges' work, didn't you?

Bowles: I did one short story, which I particularly liked, called "Las Ruinas Circulares"—back in 1944, I think it was. He was completely unknown in the United States. His cousin, Victoria Ocampo, was in New York. She was the editor of *Sur,* in Buenos Aires, and was the woman who eventually bought *La Prensa* and went to jail under Perón. She was a very spectacular woman. One afternoon she tossed me a book, which she said was a new work by her cousin (it was one that she herself had published). It was called *El Jardin de los Senderos Que se Bifurcan.* A marvelous book. Since then it has been translated as *Ficciones.* I had read some Borges four years before that, and already admired him. I think that was the first translation into English of a short story by Borges. I don't know whether *View,* the magazine it was published in, bothered to get permission from Buenos Aires or not, but I doubt it. They seldom did.

Halpern: Did you have much difficulty in translating that story?

Bowles: Well, Borges writes in classical Castellano, and the ideas are simply put; he's an easy man to translate. I should think the important thing would be to retain the particular poetic flavor of the prose in each story.

Halpern: Do you feel there is any importance to the Moroccan translations you've done?

Bowles: I think they provide a certain amount of insight into the Moroccan mentality and Moroccan customs, things that haven't been gone into very deeply in fiction. I haven't noticed many good novels about Morocco, so in that sense they're of use to anyone interested in the country. Literary importance? I have no idea.

Halpern: Why do you spend so much time on these translations instead of on your own writing?

Bowles: Because Jane, my wife, was ill, and to write a novel I need solitude and great long stretches of empty time; I haven't really had that since 1957. The summer of 1964, of course, I did go up on the mountain, Monte Viejo, you know, and write *Up Above the World.*

Halpern: Are you a great fan of Jane Bowles' work?

Bowles: I am indeed. I've read *Two Serious Ladies* ten times—I think I can quote most of it. Also, it was going over the manuscript of *Two Serious Ladies* that gave me the original impetus to consider the possibility of writing a novel.

Halpern: You met Jane before she started writing *Two Serious Ladies,* didn't you?

Bowles: Oh, yes. She began writing *Two Serious Ladies* in 1938, in Paris, the year we were married. She wrote a few scenes that were later much modified, but still they were the nucleus. And then she went on writing it in New York and finally in Mexico.

Halpern: Was it difficult living with another writer?

Bowles: That's hard to say, since I've lived only with Janie. She was the only writer I've ever lived with, and also the only woman I've ever lived with, so I don't know which difficulties come from her being a woman and which come from her being a writer. Naturally, you always have some difficulties with your wife, but whether these had anything to do with the fact that she was a writer, I can't tell you.

Halpern: Was there ever any question of competition?

Bowles: Competition between us? Competition's a game. It takes more than one to play. We never played it.

Halpern: Among your own books do you have a favorite?

Bowles: Of published volumes I like *The Delicate Prey* the most. Naturally that doesn't mean I'd write the stories the same way now.

Halpern: Do you have much contact with other writers?

Bowles: When other writers come through Tangier and look me up, I see them, yes. And I knew a few before I settled here. One of the first was Bill Saroyan, who came to New York with the script of a play for which he wanted me to write music. It was *My Heart's in the Highlands,* and the old Group Theatre produced it. About that time I met Auden. I always held him in great respect: he was erudite, and he had an unparalleled ability to use the English language. An infallible, like Stravinsky. And of course I knew Isherwood and Spender. There was one spring when I used to have lunch with them every day at the Café des Westens in Berlin. Although I never felt that I knew them, because they were English, and enough older than I to be intimidating. It was only much later, long after he had gone to America, that I knew Isherwood better. And Tennessee Williams. Certainly I've seen a lot of him and in many different places: Acapulco, New York, Rome, Tangier, Paris, Hollywood. . . . It used to be I who was the traveler, but nowadays Tennessee moves around a good deal more than I do. This is probably because he doesn't refuse to take planes. Truman Capote was here for a whole summer, staying at the Farhar, and we ate our meals together every day during those months. Gore Vidal came, and Allen Ginsberg, and Angus Wilson, and Cyril Connolly. And of course Bill Burroughs lived here for years. Even Susan Sontag came, although she didn't stay very long.

Halpern: What about Djuna Barnes?

Bowles: Yes, Djuna came here to Tangier and took my house on the Marshan one year. She was writing a book she called *Bow Down.* Later she called it *Nightwood.* I used to see a lot of Carson McCullers when we lived in Middagh Street, and then we used to go and visit her in Nyack—spend weekends up there. And of course Sartre, who came to America for a while. We'd have lunch together and then wander around the poorer sections of New York, which he wanted very much to see. That was the year I got the rights to translate *No Exit.* Later he was annoyed with me in Paris, so I don't know him any more.

Halpern: Annoyed about what, if I may ask?

Bowles: He was annoyed because I was unable to keep the director of

No Exit from changing the script. He considered that my province, which it should have been, but the point was that I didn't have a percentage in the show and he didn't know how Broadway works. I was simply the translator, so I had no rights whatever. He sent telegrams of protest from Paris before we opened, and I was obliged to send back replies that were dictated by John Huston. His anger should have been directed against John, not me.

Halpern: What about contemporary writers? Are there any you enjoy reading?

Bowles: Let's see, who's alive? Sartre is alive, but he did only one good novel. Graham Greene is alive. Who's alive in America? Whom do I follow with interest? Christopher Isherwood's a good novelist. They're mostly dead. I used to read everything of Gide's and Camus'.

Halpern: Let me have some opinions on the kind of writing that's being done in America today.

Bowles: There are various kinds of writing being done, of course. But I suspect you mean the "popular school," as exemplified by Joseph Heller, Kurt Vonnegut, John Barth, Thomas Pynchon—that sort of thing? I don't enjoy it.

Halpern: Why not?

Bowles: It's simply that I find it very difficult to get into. The means it uses to awaken interest is of a sort that would be valid only for the length of a short piece. It's too much to have to swim around in that purely literary magma for the time it takes to read a whole book. It fails to hold my attention, that's all. It creates practically no momentum. My mind wanders, I become impatient, and therefore intolerant.

Halpern: Is it the content that bothers you or the style of the writing? Or both?

Bowles: Both. But it's the point of view more than anything. The cynicism and wisecracks ultimately function as endorsements of the present civilization. The content is hard to make out because it's generally symbolic or allegorical, and the style is generally hermetic. It's not a novelistic style at all; it's really a style that would be more useful in writing essays, I should think.

Halpern: Let me go back to the critics for a moment. Do you think they have missed the point of your writing?

Bowles: They have, certainly, on many occasions. I've often had the impression they were more interested in my motive for writing a given

work than they were in the work itself. In general, the British critics
have been more perceptive; language is more important to them than it
is to us. But I don't think that matters.

Halpern: One thing that particularly interests many who meet you is
the great discrepancy between what you are like as a person and the
kind of books you write.

Bowles: Why is it that Americans expect an artist's work to be a clear
reflection of his life? They never seem to want to believe that the two
can be independent of each other and go their separate ways. Even when
there's a definite connection between the work and the life, the pattern
they form may be in either parallel or contrary motion. If you want to
call my state schizophrenic, that's all right with me. Say my personality
has two facets. One is always turned in one direction, toward my own
Mecca; that's my work. The other looks in a different direction and sees
a different landscape. I think that's a common state of affairs.

Halpern: In retrospect, would you say there has been something that
has remained important to you over the years? Something which you
have maintained in your writing?

Bowles: Continuing consciousness, infinite adaptability of human
consciousness to outside circumstances, the absurdity of it all, the
hopelessness of this whole business of living. I've written very little the
past few years. Probably because emotionally everything grows less
intense as one grows older. The motivation is at a much lower degree,
that's all.

Halpern: When you were first starting to write you were,
emotionally, full of things to say. Now that that has faded somewhat,
what springboard do you have?

Bowles: I can only find out after I've written, since I empty my mind
each time before I start. I only know what I intended to do once it's
finished. Do you remember, in *A Life Full of Holes*, the farmer comes
and scolds the boy for falling asleep, and the boy says: "I didn't know
I was going to sleep until I woke up."

Interview: Paul Bowles

Stephen Davis/1979

From *Stone Age* [New York] 2 (Spring 1979): 38–40, 59. Copyright © 1979 by Stephen Davis. Reprinted by permission of Stephen Davis.

Paul Bowles lives in the lovely hillside port town of Tangier, Morocco. He is the dean of American expatriate writers, perhaps the last of a breed that embodies the tradition that stretches from Henry James to James Baldwin. But at 69, Paul Bowles is also the great forgotten man of contemporary American letters. His four novels (*The Sheltering Sky, Let It Come Down, The Spider's House* and *Up Above the World*), each blazing with mysterious travel lore, cannabis wisdom and black magic, are no longer in print. As a writer Bowles is known mostly for his collections of short stories (*A Hundred Camels in the Courtyard, M'Hashish, The Delicate Prey*) and occasional finely-wrought stories and articles in magazines like *Antaeus, Rolling Stone* and *High Times*.

Commenting a few years ago on the unnerving force of Bowles's fiction. Gore Vidal wrote: "He coolly creates nightmare visions in which his specimens drown in fantasy, in madness, in death. His short stories with their plain lines of monochromatic prose exploit extreme situations with a chilling resourcefulness; he says, in short, 'Let us sink, let us drown' . . . His stories are among the best ever written by an American." But in spite of these and other accolades, Bowles is the kind of writer who, like Poe, will only be considered "great" after his death.

Paul Bowles didn't intend to be a writer. Born in New York in 1910, he began his career as a world traveler by running away to Paris at 16 to write poetry and music. There Gertrude Stein told the young man to forget poetry and concentrate on composing. Bowles studied with Aaron Copland, joined the Communist Party, wrote the music for scores of Broadway productions (including some of Tennessee Williams's early triumphs) and traveled through Central America in the '30s, where he gathered the material for his first ficciones. There he met a young American girl named Jane Auer, who later as Jane Bowles would herself become an elusive literary legend for her novel *Two Serious Ladies* and the play, *In the Summer House*. She died in 1973, in Spain.

In 1931 Paul Bowles saw North Africa for the first time. He described the sensation in his 1972 autobiography, *Without Stopping*: "It was as if some interior mechanism had been set in motion by the sight of the approaching land. I based my sense of being in the world on an unreasoned conviction that certain areas of the earth's surface contained more magic than others, a secret connection between the world of nature and the consciousness of man, a hidden but direct passage which bypassed the mind. Like any Romantic, I had always been vaguely certain that during my life I should come into a magic place which, in disclosing its secrets, would give me wisdom and ecstasy—perhaps even death."

Moving permanently to the wide-open International Zone of Tangier after the war, it was in Morocco that Bowles came of age as a writer of fiction. And it was in the flamboyant, mystical cult of kif smoking that Bowles found his métier. "At night, after Jane and the maids had gone to bed, I enjoyed myself writing stories about Moroccans. Let's say that I'd start with disparate fragments—anecdotes, quotations or simple clauses deprived of context. The task was to invent a connecting narrative tissue which would make all of the original elements supportive of the resulting construction. It seemed to me that the subject of kif smoking provided an effective cement. By using kif-inspired motivations, the arbitrary could be made to seem natural, the diverse elements could be fused, and several people would become one."

Kif is Moroccan marijuana (actually only the potent leafy bract that envelops the seed) chopped ritually in a 60/40 ratio with native black tobacco. The strength of the cannabis (the best is grown in the nearby Rif and Djebala ranges) serves to pull the user firmly into the ganja zone, while the strong tobacco in the mixture provides a counterpoint rush of alertness. The result is a feeling of exaltation that easily lends itself to fantasy and baroque, ornamented storytelling. It is on the mingling of kif and good stories that Paul Bowles has built his career as the prime explicator of the heart of one particular darkness—that of Morocco and its fathomless mysteries.

Recently I tried to find Paul Bowles in Tangier. In Morocco it had been a hard winter. King Hassan's government had been trying to defend its phosphate-rich Western Sahara annexation against the Algerian-backed guerrillas of the Frente Polisario, and the rumors were filtering back from the desert that the Moroccan army was being whipped. Draft calls were going out, and many of the country boys who normally hang around Tangier's stagelike Zoco Chico had fled back into the hills. It had rained all winter, and all over northern Morocco houses were collapsing and people were dying in colorful fashion. A news report claimed that two woodcutters were trimming the roadside eucalyptus trees near Fez when the last tree they cut started to bleed red blood; one of the men died on the spot, the other in the doorway of the hospital. An old woman was also said to have emerged from her fresh grave in the holy city of Meknes in order to place a spell on her faithless husband. Good kif was scarce due to the rains and the price had risen accordingly. The populace was itchy and no one knew what to believe.

Finding Bowles was tough. His mailing address turned out to be a post-office box and he was unlisted in the phone directory. The genial Englishman who runs the Hotel Muniria said that Bowles didn't mix much. But in a cafe on Tangier's Boulevard Pasteur, we met a man named Omar who drives for a retired British World War II naval hero. Omar knew Bowles, so we jumped into a mini-cab and headed for an apartment building close to the American consulate. As we drew up Omar pointed out Bowles's immaculate rust-gold Ford Mustang with Moroccan plates. On the fourth floor Bowles cracked open his door to reveal his slender frame and plumes of kif smoke drifting from within. Since he wasn't expecting us, we made an appointment for a few days later.

When we returned we found a cozy, fire-lit flat, a small party, and good kif going round the room, which was stuffed with books and tapes. Bowles was dressed in a jacket and tie and introduced us to Mohammed Mrabet, a young Moroccan novelist with whom Bowles frequently collaborates. While Bowles made tea, his own driver, Hamid, told of an encounter with Aicha Qandicha, the fierce blue-breasted goddess who hangs around springs and wells and steals mens' souls (she's a stone-age goddess, this Moroccan version of Astarte; if you see her you put your knife between your teeth since only metal frightens her). When Bowles served tea he put a cassette of *Jilala* trance music on my spare cassette. Though he claimed he was "too kifed" to do it, we turned on the other recorder and talked a bit. During the interview Bowles smoked a mild kif mix in cigarette papers, and the canaries in his little balcony greenhouse warbled a melodious counterpoint to the mad Jilala ranting on the cassette:

Stone Age: Is it easier for the kif smoker to write short stories than novels?

Bowles: Probably, yes. I never really thought of that, but it might be so. But my book *Up Above the World* is a novel, and I didn't have any trouble writing that, and I certainly imbibed enough cannabis at the time I was working on it. In fact that was the first book where I really *used* kif for the purpose of writing. The real difficulty for me with novels isn't kif, but finding a novelistic theme worth doing.

Stone Age: How were you introduced to kif?

Bowles: Well, when I first came to Morocco I would occasionally accept a pipe of kif when it was passed to me, but since I didn't really inhale I didn't get any effects. But my Moroccan friends were always talking about *majoun,* which is sort of like a cannabis jam or candy. So while I was working on *The Sheltering Sky* I ran into a writing block and decided to try it out.

I got the address of a house in the Calle Ibn Khaldoun and bought a big jar of *majoun.* It was the cheapest kind and tasted like dusty old fudge, but it still turned out to be extremely powerful and really worked for me. The block on my writing involved the difficulty of writing my protagonist's death. I just couldn't find the proper style or method of description. But under the effects of this marvelous *majoun* I just handed the job over to my subconscious mind, and I'm sure that the cannabis provided a solution totally unlike anything else I might have written without it. So for the writer, for any artist, depending on the individual, cannabis can be an extremely useful tool.

Stone Age: One of the major themes in your writing is the power of superstition. When your driver told of seeing Aicha Qandicha a few minutes ago, did you believe him?

Bowles: Yes. I mean, I believe that he believes it.

Stone Age: Do you believe it?

Bowles: Well . . . no. But what does it mean to see something? If you're asking if I believe there's such a physical presence as Aicha Qandicha, the answer is no. Naturally not. How could I believe it? But when a Moroccan says he saw something, then I believe him. To me there's no difference between belief in a legend and belief in the thing itself. Once people believe in something, it becomes part of the truth for them. You can say it's a mass psychosis if you like, but that doesn't make it any less a part of their life.

Stone Age: What about the rituals of the trance brotherhoods like the Jilala, the Hamadcha, the Aissoua. During their ceremonies they drink boiling oil and mutilate their faces and bodies with razors and axes. The next day there are often no wounds. What is this level of reality at work here? Do you believe in it?

Bowles: Indeed! Of course I do! They just have a very different kind of consciousness than ours, I think. There are those who are able to, as they say, leave themselves behind, go out of the house, and leave the door open so their saint can get in and take over. The drumming merely provides the key to get in that door. We can only formulate it. I don't think we can possibly experience it. It's not really possible to derive any spiritual or healing benefits from contacts with the brotherhoods without having been brought up a devout Muslim.

Stone Age: In traveling through Morocco, you've encountered much that's alien or unknown to the Western mind. Has anything ever really frightened you?

Bowles: Frightened? No. Delighted, mostly. I expected to see what I saw, self-mutilations and the like, because I had heard it was there. Just a little hard to find. But I never felt frightened because I never felt that the violence was directed toward me. Usually I simply felt a complete outsider and often I didn't even believe in the reality of my being there. But that didn't frighten me, that's another thing. I never felt any hostility directed toward me at these religious ceremonies because I felt almost invisible, not physically invisible but spiritually invisible, non-existent, because according to these orthodox brotherhoods I have no soul. To them I'm not really there, so I don't present any danger to them. But nowadays it's another story. Hostility isn't religious but political. Whatever animosity you or I might encounter isn't directed toward you as a Christian or a non-Muslim but as a European.

Stone Age: What about the stories of Christians or Jews who have gotten too close to the street rituals of the brotherhoods and have been summarily sacrificed and torn apart on the spot?

Bowles: Well, I've heard these stories of course, but none has ever really been substantiated. The Moroccans love to tell them because it makes them seem more dangerous. The brotherhoods do tear apart live bulls and sheep from time to time when they get carried away, and we heard on good authority that they slaughtered a French woman at Sidi Kassem one year. I somehow disbelieve it, but I'm just not sure. Maybe my imagination isn't lively enough. Certainly the Moroccans have done some astounding things to Europeans, but usually for other reasons.

There was a Doctor Mauchon in Marrakech who was hacked into many tiny pieces outside his front door, because the Moroccans didn't like the idea that he established a hospital for them. They felt that it was a place that existed only to kill Moroccans and cut them up. I vividly remember in Marrakech in '31, people still wouldn't walk on the street the hospital was on. It was always empty because the people were really terrified.

And then there was the incident in Ouezzane where they killed every European in town—87 souls—inside of an hour without any weapons. Just ripped 'em apart. So I know that sort of thing exists, but I never felt it was about to be directed at me during a brotherhood ceremony. Even in Morocco it's not recommended to kill a lot of people at a religious ceremony. But politically it's very much recommended, of course.

Stone Age: Your most recent story, "Allal," was published in *Rolling Stone*. It's about a boy who eats *majoun* and turns into a snake. Is that an adaptation of a Moroccan source or your own invention?

Bowles: It was a fantasy, completely. I don't believe there's a local story about a man who becomes a serpent. If so I never heard it. Usually I don't use Moroccan source material purposefully, because the pieces would be too similar to the translations I do of Mohammed Mrabet's stories. I'm forced to invent most of my own material generally.

Stone Age: How do you formulate your own stories?

Bowles: Well, there's kif. With a story like "Allal," I thought about it for a long time before I started to write it, then I wrote it out very quickly. It has to be fast for me or it doesn't come out right. I always think of it as laying an egg: you lay it quickly and painlessly and that's that. A short story, anyway. That's why I like them better than novels. You can't write a novel as though you were laying an egg. Impossible.

Stone Age: Do you ever get homesick?

Bowles: Well, maybe one could get homesick for New York City. I don't know, it doesn't seem very likely. When I travel I get homesick for Tangier. Why, I really don't know. The really heavy fact for me is that I'm *here* and 68 years old and don't feel like pulling up stakes and going somewhere else. Can't think of anywhere else I'd rather live, so why not stay where you are if you have a pleasant life?

In the beginning everybody came here because you could live for nothing and get whatever you wanted. Right after the war Tangier was extremely cheap; you never asked the price of anything, you just took what you saw. It was amazing. You got a terrific rate on the dollar, higher than anywhere. People were living in Paris and all over Europe, but they kept their bank in Tangier and changed their money here. And also it was a very beautiful place to live.

Stone Age: What's the difference between that Tangier and today?

Bowles: They have very little in common really. The Tangier of those days was very small, a quarter of its size today. It was run by Europeans, the embassies, so it was spic and span, beautiful trees, flowers everywhere. Now it seems just a huge slum to me, the whole city. Makes me sad.

Stone Age: Do you follow Moroccan politics?

Bowles: No. Not in Morocco, it's not a good idea. I don't want to know anything about it because as a foreigner the less you know the better, if you're living here. And Moroccan politics aren't that interesting anyway, because in a monarchy like this one you can tell what's going to happen beforehand. I'm much more fascinated with Moroccan behavior, personal behavior.

Stone Age: What about the mechanics of living as an artist outside the United States but using the U.S. as your marketplace?

Bowles: They get much more complicated as the years go by, but that's mostly at this end. And then there's the general breakdown of the postal system all over the world. I used to be able to mail manuscripts from county post offices in Ceylon and they'd be in New York in two weeks. Those days are over. Also, with war on here we have a lot of censorship, on outgoing and incoming mail both, and that makes it harder. Particularly on outgoing.

Stone Age: What other writers do you admire?

Bowles: That's a hard question, because I'm very eclectic. I don't have an answer. Conrad, you know, and Kafka.

Stone Age: What about your contemporaries?

Bowles: I can't keep up with what comes out because it's unavailable. I'm very cut off here, and I don't know what's being published.

Stone Age: What are you reading right now?

Bowles: At this moment? A book of stories about the Sudan by a Sudanese writer. It's in English and not a bad translation either.

Stone Age: Was *The Sheltering Sky* [a harrowing tale of desperation and captivity in the Sahara] in any way autobiographical?

Bowles: No, not at all. None of it ever happened, to my knowledge. But I'd been to all the places I described, and other locations I visited while I was actually writing the book in 1948. Wrote most of the story while traveling around the Sahara, so it was a combination of memory writing and minute descriptions of whatever place I was in at the moment, all thrown together into the magma of the memory when I finished it.

Stone Age: Do you ever go back and reread your books?

Bowles: I have. And I've read them in every language except the ones I don't know.

Stone Age: Which translations are the most sympathetic?

Bowles: Recently I read *Up Above the World* in Portuguese and thought it was very good. I read *Let It Come Down* in Italian and thought it was better than in English. It was like a new book to me. But I don't like the French translations. They send proofs, I correct them, and the publishers ignore them. For instance, their translator misunderstood a list of Islamic holidays I was writing about, and they came out as suburbs of Tangier. When I mentioned the sacrifice of two sheep, the French translator turned them into two hogs. What an insult! It's because the translators at Editions Gallimard in Paris are on the phone most of the time. They're all receptionists! One minute it's, "*Allo, Allo, oui, il se trouva au deuxieme etage, oui monsieur,*" then they pull out their little desks and do their translations.

Stone Age: Do you have problems with your royalties?

Bowles: No, because nobody pays anything. It's simple. First, I haven't got any books in print by large publishers, and that's where you make money writing. I remember a summer in 1949 when Truman Capote came through and he said—and this is one of the few things I remember he did say—"Never trust a publisher. They're *all* dishonest! As soon as you begin publishing books, you begin robbing writers. And that's part of publishing." I've come to agree with him.

Stone Age: Do you think the natural enemy of the writer is the publisher and editor?

Bowles: I do, at least the way it's set up now. Very definitely. Publishing is what Marc Blitzstein referred to as the other side of the barricades. My feeling is that television has killed literature and love of books, perhaps forever. I hope I'm wrong.

Stone Age: Which of your books is your favorite?

Bowles: Oh . . . I suppose *The Delicate Prey,* if I've got to make a choice. I don't really think of it as a book but as a collection of stories, but in general I like that grouping.

Stone Age: Having been a composer, do you find parallels in writing?

Bowles: Well, if you're a composer, that's going to determine something about the form in which you construct your prose. Especially novelistic construction. There's definitely a connection in that it can affect your style. If you have an "inner ear," then you hear everything you write; you hear it out loud, every sentence, every phrase. When I write I hear it as I'm working. I hear it as it should sound before I ever type it.

Stone Age: Do you still write music?

Bowles: Occasionally. A little piece for my own pleasure on a little Phillips electric organ I keep around.

Stone Age: Are you still exploring Morocco, or do you feel you've seen what you've wanted to see?

Bowles: Not much these days. In the last two years I've only been down to Marrakech twice, which isn't getting around very much when you think about it. The main reason is that the hotels have gotten very expensive and I think very bad. You can't get a decent meal in any hotel I know of in Morocco, including the best, the Mamounia in Marrakech or the Minzah here in Tangier. Maybe at the Palais in Fez, but I doubt it.

Stone Age: When was the last time you were in the States?

Bowles: I think it was '69.

Stone Age: Do you think you'll go back again?

Bowles: I've thought about it . . . I doubt it.

The Art of Fiction LXVII: Paul Bowles

Jeffrey Bailey/1981

From *The Paris Review* XXIII:81 (Fall 1981): 62–89. Copyright ©
1981 *The Paris Review*. Reprinted by permission of *The Paris
Review*.

Like any Romantic, I had always been vaguely certain that sometime during my life I
should come into a magic place which, in revealing its secrets, would give me wisdom
and ecstasy—perhaps even death.

Paul Bowles in Without Stopping, on his first approach to North Africa.

Tangier has been Paul Bowles' home for the past thirty years, though he
first visited it fifty years ago, in 1931, on the advice of Gertrude Stein
and in the company of his friend and tutor, Aaron Copland. The city
which greeted him in those days with a promise of "wisdom and
ecstasy" bears little resemblance to the Tangier of the 1980s. The
frentic *medina,* with its *souks,* its endless array of tourist boutiques,
its perennial hawkers and hustlers is still there, of course, though fifty
years ago it had already been dwarfed by the European city and its
monuments to colonialism: the imperious French Consulate, the Café de
Paris, luxury hotels in the *grand style* (the Minzah, the Velasquez, the
Villa de France), the now forlornly abandoned Teatro Cervantes, and
the English church with its cemetery filled with the remains of knight
commanders, baronets, and the prodigal sons of former empires. But the
days of Tangier as the wide open international city of intrigue are gone
forever. Today it is simply one city of a third-world country in flux,
slowly but steadily coming to grips with the Twentieth century.

For those of a romantic bent, however, the power of Tangier to evoke
images of the inscrutable East remains potent, despite the ravages of
modernity. It still seems an appropriate place to find Paul Bowles,
whose name and fiction have been associated with the remotest corners
of the globe: North Africa, South America, Ceylon, the Far East. Any
American who comes to Tangier bearing more than a casual curiosity
about Morocco and a vague concern for music and literature considers
a visit with Bowles an absolute must; for some, it even assumes the
reverential character of pilgrimage. In no way, however, does Bowles

see himself as an object of special interest. Indeed, such an attitude strikes him as being amusingly naive, if not downright silly; to him it in no way relates to what he regards as the routine circumstances of his present life.

Since 1957, he has been living in a three-room apartment in a quiet residential section of Tangier. His flat, located in a Fifties-Futuristic building in sight of the American Consulate, is comfortably unimposing, though it does testify to his days as a world traveler: souvenirs from Asia, Mexico, Black Africa, as well as Morocco; a bookcase lined with personally inscribed volumes by Burroughs, Kerouac, Ginsberg, Vidal; an entry way in which vintage trunks and suitcases are stacked shoulder high, as if a voyage of indefinite length were perpetually in its offing.

Our first meeting took place in the summer of 1976, within a month of my coming to live and work in Morocco. Having set a tentative date to see him, I arrived at his door in the early afternoon of an August weekend carrying my tape-recorder, a notepad filled with questions and, for autograph purposes, a copy of his first novel, *The Sheltering Sky*. I found him newly awakened, his thick white hair tousled and pale blue eyes slightly bleary; he was obviously surprised that anyone would come to call at that hour of the day. As he finished his breakfast and lighted up his first cigarette (at that time he was a chain-smoker), his thin, somewhat wiry frame relaxed noticeably and he became increasingly jovial. He asked about my impressions of Morocco and easily slipped into colorful reminiscences of his early days in Tangier and, at my prodding, of personalities who had particularly intrigued me: Gertrude Stein, Alice B. Toklas, André Gide, Djuna Barnes.

Evidently, however, my timing hadn't been particularly good. The tape-recorder had just begun to roll when a series of visitors announced themselves with persistent rings of the doorbell: his chauffeur, his maid, a woman-friend from New York, an American boy who'd taken the apartment downstairs and, eventually, Mohammed Mrabet, the Moroccan story-teller whose works Bowles has been translating for over ten years. Each visit presented a break in the rhythm of our conversation, involving lengthy asides conducted in three languages: English, Spanish, and Arabic. Mrabet, handsome in a rugged and obscurely brooding way, was in a sardonically loquacious mood. Before leaving he asked me to bring him, on my return to Tangier, a pistol with nine chambers as there were apparently nine people upon whose elimination he was intent at that time. As it turned out, I had reason to be grateful for these interruptions. They enabled me to return and talk at length with Bowles that evening, the next day, and two more times over the following year and a half. This extra time also gave me the opportunity to reflect more intelligibly upon the details and effects of his long career as a writer, composer, and compulsive traveler.

An only child, born in New York City in 1910 and raised in the respectable conventionalism of middle-class professionals with a Unitarian background, Paul Bowles' youth was marked by a willful determination to realize himself as an artist. Between stints at the University of Virginia he managed, at age 18, to make his first trip to Europe where, besides writing and composing, he worked for the *Herald Tribune* in Paris and met a number of established artists, including Tristan Tzara. He returned to the States within a year and went to live in Greenwich Village; while writing music and surrealist poetry he supported himself by working at Dutton's Bookshop on Fifth Avenue. One of his friends of that period, Henry Cowell, introduced him to Aaron Copland with whom Bowles began to study. Parental influence forced him to resume his coursework at the University, though he was shortly to leave it again, never to return. In 1931, at age 20, he accompanied Copland to Berlin for the purpose of studying music in earnest. This he did, both with Copland in Berlin and, in Paris, with Nadia Boulanger. His experience in Europe brought him into contact with some of the greatest literary names of the time: Gertrude Stein, André Gide, Jean Cocteau, Ezra Pound. His love of independence and his self-acknowledged lack of discipline must have been a prominent element of his personality in those days. Gertrude Stein once remarked to him: "If you were typical it would be the end of our civilization. You're a manufactured savage."

By the mid-1930s he had returned to New York where his circle of friends and acquaintances came to include John Hammond, Joseph Losey, George Antheil, E. E. Cummings, and Georgia O'Keeffe. He focused his energies on developing a musical career, writing scores for Project 891 of the Federal Theater Project where he worked with Orson Welles. By the mid-1940s he had written scores for Saroyan's *Love's Old Sweet Song*, Philip Barry's *Liberty Jones*, Lillian Hellman's *Watch on the Rhine*, Tennessee Williams' *The Glass Menagerie*, and for the Theatre Guild's production of *Twelfth Night* (starring Helen Hayes and Maurice Evans), as well as three original ballets, *Yankee Clipper* and

Pastorela for the American Ballet Caravan and *Colloque Sentimentale* for the Ballet International, a one-act opera entitled *The Wind Remains*, and numerous sonatas and cantatas. He was also the recipient of a Guggenheim Fellowship. His project was a musical interpretation of Garcia Lorca's *Así Que Pasen Cinco Años.*

The Thirties and early Forties formed a period of leftist political involvement which Bowles now terms, "a bit of softheadedness." He joined the Communist Party at the end of 1938 and left it at about the time that Germany invaded Russia. "At the time I left the Party," he explains, "I was not totally disillusioned; I was merely less passionate, and at the same time much busier in my own life."

He'd met Jane Auer in New York City in 1937 and married her a year later. For several months, while he was working on his ballets, he and Jane Bowles lived in a communal house (dubbed "February House" by Anaïs Nin) run by W. H. Auden and George Davis for the support of serious artists of every description. They took rooms which had been occupied by Gypsy Rose Lee. Their co-communalists included Benjamin Britten, Peter Pears, Oliver Smith, and Thomas Mann's younger Son, Golo.

It was observing the birth of his wife's novel, *Two Serious Ladies,* that reawakened Bowles' interest in fiction-writing. When Bowles went to live permanently in Tangier in 1947, to be joined by Jane Bowles the following year (the permanence of his move was determined more by chance than by actual planning), he had decided to "cut the composing cord." Although he returned to New York on several occasions to work on Broadway projects, including Tennessee Williams' *Summer and Smoke, The Milk Train Doesn't Stop Here Anymore,* and *Sweet Bird of Youth,* Garcia Lorca's *Yerma,* and Jane Bowles' *In the Summer House,* writing has been his primary concern for the past thirty years. During that time he has produced four novels: *The Sheltering Sky, Let It Come Down, The Spider's House,* and *Up Above the World;* four volumes of short stories: *The Delicate Prey, The Time of Friendship, Things Gone and Things Still Here,* and *Midnight Mass* (published this year); and two travel books: *Yallah!* and *Their Heads Are Green and Their Hands Are Blue.* His autobiography, *Without Stopping,* appeared in 1972. In 1976, City Lights published his translation of the stories of Isabelle Eberhardt under the title *The Oblivion Seekers.* He has been the consulting editor of *Antaeus* magazine since he founded it in 1970. Since living in Morocco, he has done a considerable amount of translating from the Moghrebi dialect, most notably the stories of Mohammed Mrabet.

The following conversation was tape-recorded during the course of four visits to Mr. Bowles' home in Tangier.

Interviewer: For many people, the mention of your name evokes romantic images of the artist's life in exotic, far-away places. Do you see yourself as a kind of consummate expatriate?

Bowles: I'm afraid not. I don't see myself as a consummate anything. I don't see myself, really, I have no ego. I didn't find the United States particularly interesting and once I found places that were more interesting I chose to live in them, which I think makes sense.

Interviewer: Was this decision to leave the United States an early one?

Bowles: I made it at seventeen, so I guess you'd say it was an early decision. Some people absorb things more quickly than others and I think I had a fairly good idea of what life would be like for me in the States, and I didn't want it.

Interviewer: What would it have been like?

Bowles: Boring. There was nothing I wanted there, and once I moved away I saw that all I needed from the States was money. I went back there for that. I've never yet gone there without the definite guarantee of making money. Just going for the pleasure of it, I've never done.

Interviewer: Since your contact with foreign places has so obviously nurtured your writing, perhaps you would never have been a writer if you had stayed in the States.

Bowles: Quite possibly not. I might have gone on as a composer. I cut the composing cord in 1947, when I moved here, although, as I say, I went back several times to write scores for Broadway.

Interviewer: Did you cut the composing cord because writing and music were getting in each other's way?

Bowles: No, not at all. You do them with separate parts of the brain, I think. And you derive different kinds of pleasure from them. It's like saying, "Is it more fun to drink a glass of water when you're thirsty or eat a good meal when you're hungry?" I gave up composing professionally simply because I wanted to leave New York. I wanted to get out of the States.

Interviewer: Did giving up an entire career because you disliked life in America leave you feeling hostile toward the place?

Bowles: No, no. But when you say "America" to me, all I think of is New York City where I was born and brought up. I know that New York isn't America; still, my image of America *is* New York. But there's no hostility. I just think it's a great shame, what has happened there. I don't think it will ever be put right; but then again, I never expect anything to be put right. Nothing ever is. Things go on and become other things. The entire character of the country has changed beyond recognition since my childhood. One always thinks everything's got worse—and in most respects it has—but that's meaningless. What does one mean when one says that things are getting worse? It's becoming more like the future, that's all. It's just moving ahead. The future will be infinitely "worse" than the present; and in *that* future, the future will be immeasurably "worse" than the future that we can see. Naturally.

Interviewer: You're a pessimist.

Bowles: Well, look for yourself. You don't have to be a pessimist to see it. There's always the chance of a universal holocaust in which a few billion people will be burned. I don't hope for that, but it's what I see as a probability.

Interviewer: Can't one also hope for things like a cure for cancer, an effective ban on nuclear arms, an upsurge of concern for the environment, and a deeper consciousness of being?

Bowles: You can hope for anything, of course. I expect enormous things to happen in the future, but I don't think they'll be things which people born in my generation will think are great and wonderful. Perhaps people born in 1975 will think otherwise. I mean, people born in 1950 think television is great.

Interviewer: Because American technology has already contributed so much to making what you regard as an inevitably undesirable future, I guess it's understandable that living outside your indigenous culture became almost a compulsion with you.

Bowles: Not almost; it was a *real* compulsion. Even as a small child, I was always eager to get away. I remember when I was six years old, I was sent off to spend two weeks with someone—I don't know who it was or why I was sent—and I begged to stay longer. I didn't want to go home. Again, when I was nine and my father had pneumonia, I was sent off for a month or two and I kept writing letters asking, "Please, let me stay longer." I didn't want to see my parents again. I didn't want to go back into all that.

Interviewer: In *Without Stopping,* you were quite frank about your feelings toward your parents in describing the fondness you had for your mother and your estrangement from your father.

Bowles: I think most boys are fond of their mothers. The hostility involved with my father was very real. It started on his side and became reciprocated, naturally, at an early age. I don't know what the matter was. Maybe he didn't want any children. I never knew the real story of why he was so angry with me, although my maternal grandmother told me it was simply because he was jealous. She said he couldn't bear to have my mother pay attention to this third person. It's probably true.

Interviewer: Did this negative relationship with your father affect your becoming a traveler and an artist?

Bowles: Probably, I don't know. I've never really gone over it in my mind to see what caused what. I probably couldn't. It's obvious that a shut-in childhood is likely to make an introverted child and that an introverted child is more likely to be "artistic."

Interviewer: Your parents weren't enthusiastic about your going off to Europe when you were only eighteen?

Bowles: It wasn't a matter of their being enthusiastic or not, inasmuch as they knew nothing about my going. I had the money for my passage to France, plus about twenty-five dollars.

Interviewer: Were you running away from something?

Bowles: No, I was running toward something, although I didn't know what at the time.

Interviewer: Did you ever find it?

Bowles: Yes, I found it over the years. What I was ultimately running toward was my grave, of course: "The paths of glory lead but to the grave."

Interviewer: You began studying with Aaron Copland not long after you returned from that first trip abroad. How would you describe your experience with Copland?

Bowles: It couldn't have been better. He was a wonderful teacher.

Interviewer: Apparently Copland was able to compose professionally outside of New York, yet you say that you weren't.

Bowles: No, because I had to make a living at writing music. If I'd had a private income I could have composed anywhere, as long as I'd had a keyboard. A few composers don't even need that but I do. Aaron and I had a very hard time the first summer here in Tangier, in 1931. Gertrude Stein had told us that it would be easy to get a piano, but it wasn't. Nowadays it's impossible, but in those days you still could if you really looked. We finally found one. It wasn't very good, and the problem of getting it up the mountain to the house we'd rented was horrendous. The road wasn't paved so it had to come up on a donkey. Just as it was going through the gate the piano fell off with a WHAM!!! and I thought, "That's the end of our summer." It worked out all right, eventually. Aaron was writing a short symphony and although he couldn't finish it, he was able to do some work on it. Of course, he worked constantly.

Interviewer: Weren't you as diligent a worker as Copland?

Bowles: I wouldn't say so, no. When we were in Berlin, it seemed that I was always going somewhere else. Aaron was rather annoyed by that. I was supposed to be studying, but instead I would set out for Austria or Bavaria.

Interviewer: What was your impression of Berlin back then?

Bowles: Well, I wasn't there for very long, only four months; one whole spring. But it was crazy. Really crazy. It was like a film of Fritz Lang's. You had the feeling that all of life was being directed by Lang. It was sinister because of the discrepancy between those who had and those who didn't, and you felt it all very intensely. The 'haves' were going hog-wild while the 'have-nots' seethed with hatred. There was a black cloud of hatred over the whole east end of the city. It was that summer that the *Disconto-Gesellschaft* failed. You felt the catastrophe coming, which gave an uncomfortable tinge to everything that happened. Christopher Isherwood was living it rather than writing about it then.

Interviewer: How did you react when Isherwood gave your name to his best-known character creation?

Bowles: Sally Bowles? I thought it was quite natural, really. We'd all been here together through the whole season, and we used to eat lunch together every day. He didn't want to use her real name, Jean Ross, so he used mine. Where he got "Sally," I don't know.

Interviewer: From your recollection, did the real Jean Ross much resemble the character she had inspired?

Bowles: I'd say so. Yes. She was very attractive, and also very amusing. Christopher was always with her. They lived in the same rooming house on the Nollendorfstrasse. I lived on Guntzelstrasse, in a room with a balcony, I remember. Aaron took a flat that belonged to an American poet named Alfred Kreymborg on the Steinplatz, so I would go there for my lessons every day. We'd have lunch with Stephen Spender, Christopher, and Jean. We always had that nucleus. We generally ate at the Café des Westens opposite the Kaisergedachtniskirche.

Interviewer: Did you know that you were observing the genesis of "Goodbye to Berlin?"

Bowles: How would I? I had no idea that he was going to write a book. One was just concerned with living each day as it came. I met some of the people in *The Berlin Stories,* but I never suspected they were going to be "immortalized."

Interviewer: Have you ever felt any professional antagonism toward other artists?

Bowles: No, I've never been like that at all. I refuse to play. I told you I don't have much of an ego. I meant it. To take part in such games, you have to believe in the existence of your personality in a way that I don't. And I couldn't do it. I could pretend, but it wouldn't get me very far.

Interviewer: When you were a young man making the acquaintance not only of other young writers such as Isherwood and Auden but also getting to know more established writers, like Stein and Cocteau, were you consciously attempting to become a part of an artistic community? Were you looking to be nurtured by contact with other artists?

Bowles: I was never aware of wanting to become part of a community, no. I wanted to meet them. I suppose I simply felt that I was taking pot shots at clay pipes. Pop! Down goes Gertrude, down goes Jean Cocteau, down goes André Gide. I made a point of those things— meeting Manuel de Falla, for example—for no reason at all. I went to Granada, found his door, knocked, went in, and spent the afternoon. He had no idea who I was. Why I did that, I don't know. Apparently I thought such encounters were important or I wouldn't have bothered, because it involved a lot of work and sometimes a sacrifice of something I cared about. But exactly how I felt I can't remember, because it wasn't an intellectual thing. It was "unthought," and it's hard for me to recall the reason for it. Of course, I've never been a thinking person. A lot seems to happen without my conscious knowledge.

Interviewer: Has it always been that way, or has it developed over the years?

Bowles: It was always like that. All through my late teens, from sixteen on, I was writing surrealist poetry. I read André (Breton) who explained how to do it, and so I learned how to write without being conscious of what I was doing. I learned how to make it grammatically correct and even to have a certain style without the slightest idea of what I was writing. One part of my mind was doing the writing, and God knows what the other part was doing. I suppose it was bulldozing the subconscious, dredging up ooze. I don't know how those things work, and I don't want to know.

Interviewer: It sounds as though Breton served to inspire your earth writing. Did you have many "inspiration" writers?

Bowles: Not really. During my early years in Europe, I was very much taken with Lautréamont. I carried him with me wherever I went, but I got over that and didn't supplant him with anyone else. You may have such enthusiasms when you're very young, but you don't usually have them when you get older, even a few years older. There were many writers whom I admired, and if they were living I tended to seek them out: Stein, Gide, Cocteau, many others.

Interviewer: Your autobiography, *Without Stopping,* seemed to overflow with the names of artists, writers, famous people in general, whom you'd met.

Bowles: And yet I cut many of them out. I saw when I was finished that it was nothing but names, so I cut out fifty or sixty. The reason for all that was that Putnam wanted the book to be a roster of names; they stressed that at the beginning, before I signed the contract. If they'd just left me alone without all the stipulations, I think I could have done something more personal. Actually, I think the first half was personal enough, but the last half was hurried. Time was coming to an end and I had to meet the deadline. They'd already allowed an extra year in the contract, so I just rushed it off. I'd never do another book like that, under contract. A full year after I'd signed the contract I still hadn't begun to write. It took me that length of time to recall events and sequences. I had no diaries or letters to consult, so I had to go back over my entire life, month by month, charting every meaningless meander of its course. And as I say, that took more than a year.

Interviewer: You've never been a diarist?

Bowles: No. I had no letters or documents to go on at all.

Interviewer: Was that intentional? Would a diary have hindered your spontaneity?

Bowles: I don't know about that. It was just the facts of life. I never bothered. I felt that life was important, each day. I didn't see any reason to keep a diary. Then again, I never thought I'd be writing an autobiography.

Interviewer: How do you write?

Bowles: I don't use a typewriter. It's too heavy, too much trouble. I use a notebook, and I write in bed. Ninety-five percent of everything I've written has been done in bed.

Interviewer: And the typing?

Bowles: The typing of a manuscript to send out is another thing. That's just drudgery, not work. By work I mean the invention of something, the putting down, the creation of a page with words on it.

Interviewer: Did you write any of your novels under a deadline?

Bowles: No. When I finished them, I sent them in and they were published. I could't write fiction under pressure. The books wouldn't have been any good; they'd have been even less good than they were.

Interviewer: You don't seem to have a particularly high regard for your talent as a writer.

Bowles: No, no. I haven't.

Interviewer: Why not?

Bowles: I don't know. It doesn't seem very relevant.

Interviewer: Haven't people encouraged you along the way, telling you that you were good?

Bowles: Oh, yes. Of course.

Interviewer: You just didn't believe them?

Bowles: I believed that they believed it, and I wanted to hear them say they liked this or disliked that, and why. But I was never sure of their viewpoint, so it was hard to know whether they understood what they were liking or disliking.

Interviewer: Would you say that it was easier for a serious young writer to get published twenty or thirty years ago?

Bowles: I doubt that getting "serious" writing published was ever easy. But judging from the quantity of non-writing that gets into print today, I'd deduce that today there are fewer young authors writing with the intention of producing serious work. To quote Susan Sontag: "Seriousness has less prestige now."

Interviewer: In reading your work, one doesn't expect to be led to some conclusion through a simple progression of events. One has the sense of participating in a spontaneous growth of events, one on top of another.

Bowles: Yes? Well, they grow that way. That's the point, you see. I don't feel that I wrote these books. I feel as though they had been written by my arm, by my brain, my organism, but that they're not necessarily mine. The difficulty is that I've never thought anything belonged to me. At one time, I bought an island off Ceylon and I thought that when I had my two feet planted on it I'd be able to say: "This island is mine." I couldn't; it was meaningless. I felt nothing at all, so I sold it.

Interviewer: How big an island was it?

Bowles: About two acres. A beautiful tropical forest of an island. Originally it had been owned by a French landscape gardener. Sixty or seventy years ago he'd brought back trees, shrubs, vines and flowers from all over Southeast Asia and the East Indies. It was a wonderful botanical display. But as I say, I never felt I owned it.

Interviewer: Was writing, for you, a means of alleviating a sense of aloneness by communicating intimately with other people?

Bowles: No. I look on it simply as a natural function. As far as I'm concerned it's fun, and it just happens. If I don't feel like doing it, I don't do it.

Interviewer: One is struck by the violence in your work. Almost all the characters in *The Delicate Prey*, for example, were victimized by either physical or psychological violence.

Bowles: Yes, I suppose. The violence served a therapeutic purpose. It's unsettling to think that at any moment life can flare up into senseless violence. But it can and does, and people need to be ready for it. What you make for others is first of all what you make for yourself. If I'm persuaded that our life is predicated upon violence, that the entire structure of what we call civilization, the scaffolding that we've built up over the millenia, can collapse at any moment, then whatever I write is going to be affected by that assumption. The process of life presupposes violence, in the plant world the same as the animal world. But among the animals only man can conceptualize violence. Only man can *enjoy* the *idea* of destruction.

Interviewer: In many of your characterizations, there's a strange combination of fatalism and naiveté. I'm thinking in particular of Kit and Port Moresby in *The Sheltering Sky*. It seemed to me that their frenetic movement was prompted by an obsessive fear of self-confrontation.

Bowles: Moving around a lot is a good way of postponing the day of reckoning. I'm happiest when I'm moving. When you've cut yourself off from the life you've been living and you haven't yet established another life, you're free. That's a very pleasant sensation, I've always thought. If you don't know where you're going, you're even freer.

Interviewer: Your characters seem to be psychologically alienated from each other and from themselves, and though their isolation may be accentuated by the fact that you've set them as foreigners in exotic places, one feels that they'd be no different at home; that their problems are deeper than the matter of locale.

Bowles: Of course. Everyone is isolated from everyone else. The concept of society is like a cushion to protect us from the knowledge of that isolation. A fiction that serves as an anesthetic.

Interviewer: And the exotic settings are secondary?

Bowles: The transportation of characters to such settings often acts as a catalyst or a detonator, without which there'd be no action, so I shouldn't call the settings secondary. Probably if I hadn't had some contact with what you call "exotic" places, it wouldn't have occurred to me to write at all.

Interviewer: To what degree did the character of Kit resemble your wife, Jane Bowles?

Bowles: The book was conceived in New York in 1947, and eighty percent of it was written before Jane ever set foot in North Africa in 1948, so there's no question of its being related to experience. The tale is entirely imaginary. Kit is not Jane, although I used some of Jane's characteristics in determining Kit's reaction to such a voyage. Obviously I thought of Port as a fictional extension of myself. But Port is certainly not Paul Bowles, any more than Kit is Jane.

Interviewer: Have you ever written a character who was supposed to be Jane Bowles, or a character who was *directly* modeled after her?

Bowles: No, never.

Interviewer: Yet couldn't one say that you both exerted a definite influence on each other's work?

Bowles: Of course! We showed each other every page we wrote. I never thought of sending a story off without discussing it with her first. Neither of us had ever had a literary confidant before. I went over *Two*

Serious Ladies with her again and again, until each detail was as we both thought it should be. Not that I put anything into it that she hadn't written. We simply analyzed sentences and rhetoric. It was this being present at the making of a novel that excited me and made me want to write my own fiction. Remember, this was in 1942.

Interviewer: You hadn't had that strong an interest before?

Bowles: Oh, I'd written before, of course, although of the fiction I saved only one short story. All during my childhood I was writing, and that means from the age of four on. Even at four it gave me a very special kind of pleasure to make up my own stories and print them on paper. They were always about animals and barnyard fowl. My memory doesn't go back to a time when I couldn't read. I remember being ridiculed by my grandfather because I couldn't pronounce the word "clock." I said, "Tlot," but I indignantly spelled it out for him to prove that I knew the word. I must have spelled it "c-l-o-c-tay."

Interviewer: You learned to read at an unusually early age?

Bowles: Three, I guess. I learned from wooden blocks that had letters of the alphabet carved on them. Toys weren't encouraged. They gave me "constructive things," drawing paper, pencils, notebooks, maps and books. Besides, I was always alone then, never with other children.

Interviewer: Tell me, would you please, about Jane Bowles.

Bowles: That's an all-inclusive command! What can I possibly tell you about her that isn't implicit in her writing?

Interviewer: She obviously had an extraordinary imagination. She was always coherent, but one had the feeling that she could go off the edge at any time. Almost every page of *Two Serious Ladies,* for example, evoked a sense of madness although it all flowed together very naturally.

Bowles: I feel that it flows naturally, yes. But I don't find any sense of madness. Unlikely turns of thought, lack of predictability in the characters' behavior, but no suggestion of "madness." I love *Two Serious Ladies*. The action is often like the unfolding in a dream, and the background, with its realistic details, somhow emphasizes the sensation of dreaming.

Interviewer: Does this dreamlike quality reflect her personality?

Bowles: I don't think anyone ever thought of Jane as a "dreamy" person; she was far too lively and articulate for that. She did have a way of making herself absent suddenly, when one could see that she was a thousand miles away. If you addressed her sharply, she returned with a start. And if you asked her about it, she would simply say: "I don't know. I was somewhere else."

Interviewer: Can you read her books and see Jane Bowles in them?

Bowles: Not at all; not the Jane Bowles that I knew. Her work contained no reports on her outside life. *Two Serious Ladies* was wholly non-autobiographical. The same goes for her stories.

Interviewer: She wasn't by any means a prolific writer, was she?

Bowles: No, very unprolific. She wrote very slowly. It cost her blood to write. Everything had to be transmuted into fiction before she could accept it. Sometimes it took her a week to write a page. This exaggerated slowness seemed to me a terrible waste of time, but any mention of it to her was likely to make her stop writing entirely for several days or even weeks. She would say: "All right. It's easy for you, but it's hell for me, and you know it. I'm not you. I know you wish I were, but I'm not. So stop it."

Interviewer: The relationships between her women characters are fascinating. They read like psychological portraits, reminiscent of Djuna Barnes.

Bowles: In fact, though, she refused to read Djuna Barnes. She never read *Nightwood*. She felt great hostility toward American women writers. Usually she refused even to look at their books.

Interviewer: Why was that?

Bowles: When *Two Serious Ladies* was first reviewed in 1943, Jane was depressed by the lack of understanding shown in the unfavorable reviews. She paid no attention to the enthusiastic notices. But from then on, she became very much aware of the existence of other women writers whom she'd met and who were receiving laudatory reviews for works which she thought didn't deserve such high praise: Jean Stafford, Mary McCarthy, Carson McCullers, Anaïs Nin. There were others I can't remember now. She didn't want to see them personally, or see their books.

Interviewer: In the introduction that Truman Capote wrote for the collected works, he emphasized how young she'd been when she wrote *Two Serious Ladies*.

Bowles: That's true. She began it when she was twenty-one. We were married the day before her twenty-first birthday.

Interviewer: Was there something symbolic about the date?

Bowles: No, nothing "symbolic." Her mother wanted to remarry and she had got it into her head that Jane should marry first, so we chose the day before Jane's birthday.

Interviewer: Did your careers ever conflict, yours and your wife's?

Bowles: No, there was no conflict of any kind. We never thought of ourselves as having careers. The only career I ever had was as a composer, and I destroyed that when I left the States. It's hard to build up a career again. Work is something else, but a career is a living thing and when you break it, that's it.

Interviewer: Did you and Jane Bowles ever collaborate?

Bowles: On a few songs. Words and music. Any other sort of collaboration would have been unthinkable. Collaborative works of fiction are rare, and they're generally parlor tricks, like *Karezza* of George Sand and who was it: Alfred de Musset?

Interviewer: How did she feel about herself as an artist—about her work?

Bowles: She liked it. She enjoyed it. She used to read it and laugh shamefacedly. But she'd never change a word in order to make it more easily understood. She was very, very stubborn about phrasing things the way she wanted them phrased. Sometimes understanding would really be difficult and I'd suggest a change to make it simpler. She'd say, "No. It can't be done that way." She wouldn't budge an inch from saying something the way she felt the character would say it.

Interviewer: What was her objective in writing?

Bowles: Well, she was always trying to get at people's hidden motivations. She was interested in people, not in the writing. I don't think she was at all conscious of trying to create any particular style. She was only interested in the things she was writing about: the complicated juxtapositions of motivations in neurotic people's heads. That was what fascinated her.

Interviewer: Was she "neurotic"?

Bowles: Oh, probably. If one's interested in neuroses, generally one has some sympathetic vibration.

Interviewer: Was she self-destructive?

Bowles: I don't think she meant to be, no. I think she overestimated her physical strength. She was always saying, "I'm as strong as an ox," or "I'm made of iron." That sort of thing.

Interviewer: Considering how independently the two of you lived your lives, your marriage couldn't really be described as being "conventional." Was this lack of "conventionalism" the result of planning, or did it just work out that way?

Bowles: We never thought in those terms. We played everything by ear. Each one did what he pleased—went out, came back—although I must say that I tried to get her in early. She liked going out much more than I did, and I never stopped her. She had a perfect right to go to any party she wanted. Sometimes we had recriminations when she drank too much, but the idea of sitting down and discussing what constitutes a conventional or an unconventional marriage would have been unthinkable.

Interviewer: She has been quoted as saying, "From the first day, Morocco seemed more dreamlike than real. I felt cut off from what I knew. In the twenty years I've lived here, I've written two short stories and nothing else. It's good for Paul, but not for me." All things considered, do you think that's an accurate representation of her feelings?

Bowles: But you speak of feelings as though they were monolithic, as though they never shifted and altered through the years. I know Jane expressed the idea frequently toward the end of her life, when she was bedridden and regretted not being within reach of her friends. Most of them lived in New York, of course. But for the first decade she loved Morocco as much as I did.

Interviewer: Did you live with her here in this apartment?

Bowles: No. Her initial stroke was in 1957, while I was in Kenya. When I got back to Morocco about two months later, I heard about it in Casablanca. I came here and found her quite well. We took two apartments in this building. From then on, she was very ill, and we spent our time rushing from one hospital to another, in London and New York. During the early Sixties she was somewhat better. She spent most of the last seven years of her life in hospitals. But she was an invalid for sixteen years.

Interviewer: That's a long time to be an invalid.

Bowles: Yes. It was terrible.

Interviewer: Before that, though, your life together had been as you wanted it?

Bowles: Oh, yes. We enjoyed it. We were always busy helping each other. And we had lots of friends. Many, many friends.

Interviewer: What is life like for you in Tangier these days?

Bowles: Well, it's my home. I'm settled here and I'm reasonably content with things as they are. I see enough people. I suppose if I had been living in the States all this time I'd probably have many more intimate friends whom I'd see regularly. But I haven't lived there in many years, and most of the people I knew are no longer there. I can't go back and make new acquaintances at this late date.

Interviewer: All those trunks you've got stacked in your entryway bear testament to your globe-trotting days. Don't you miss traveling?

Bowles: Not really, surprisingly enough. And Tangier is as good a place for me to be as any other, I think. If travel still consisted of taking ships, I'd continue moving around. Flying to me isn't travel. It's just getting from one place to another as fast as possible. I like to have plenty of luggage with me when I start out on a voyage. You never know how many months or years you'll be gone or where you'll go eventually. But flying is like television: you have to take what they give you because there's nothing else. It's impossible.

Interviewer: Tangier is nothing like the booming international city it once was, is it?

Bowles: No, of course not. It's a very dull city now.

Interviewer: Things were still happening here in the Sixties when Ginsberg, Burroughs, and that group were here. To what degree were you involved with them?

Bowles: I knew them well, but I wasn't involved with their work. I think Bill Burroughs came to live in the *medina* in 1952. I didn't meet him until 1954. Allen Ginsberg came in '57 and began to supervise the retrieving of the endangered manuscript of *Naked Lunch*, which was scattered all over the floor of Bill's room at the Muniria. These pages had been lying there for many months, covered with grime, heelmarks, mouse-droppings. It was Alan Ansen who financed the expedition, and between them they salvaged the book.

Interviewer: Was Gregory Corso here then?

Bowles: No. He came when Ginsberg returned in 1961.

Interviewer: What was Tangier like back then?

Bowles: By the Sixties, it had calmed down considerably, although it was still a good deal livelier than it is these days. Everyone had much more money, for one thing. Now only members of the European jet-set have enough to lead amusing lives, and everyone else is poor. In general, Moroccans have a slightly higher standard of living than they did, by European criteria. That is, they have television, cars and a certain amount of plumbing in their houses, although they all claim they don't eat as well as they did thirty years ago. But nobody does, anywhere.

Interviewer: Moroccan life seems to be so incongruously divided between Eastern and Western influences—the *medinas* and *nouvelles villes, djellabas* and blue jeans, donkey-carts and Mercedes—that it sometimes seems downright schizophrenic. I wonder where the Moroccan psyche really is.

Bowles: For there to be a Moroccan psyche there'd have to be a national consciousness, which I don't think has yet come into being. The people are much more likely to think of themselves as members of a subdivision: I'm a Soussi, I'm a Riffi, I'm a Filali. Then there are those lost souls who privately think of themselves as Europeans because they've studied in Europe. But the vast majority of Moroccans have their minds on getting together enough money for tomorrow's meal.

Interviewer: Through the years that you've been here, have you ever had feelings of cultural estrangement, or even superiority?

Bowles: That wouldn't be very productive, would it? Of course I feel apart, at one remove from the people here. But since they expect that in any case, there's no difficulty. The difficulties are in the United States, where there's no convention for maintaining apartness. The foreigners who try to "be Moroccan" never succeed, and manage to look ridiculous while they're trying. It seems likely that it's this very quality of impenetrability in the Moroccans that makes the country fascinating to outsiders.

Interviewer: But isn't there a special psychological dimension to the situation of a foreigner living in Morocco? It seems to me that a foreigner here is often looked upon automatically as a kind of victim.

Bowles: Well, he *is* a victim. The Moroccans wouldn't use the word. They'd say "a useful object." They believe that they, as Moslems, are the master group in the world, and that God allows other religious groups to exist principally for them to manipulate. That seems to be the average man's attitude. Since it's not expressed as a personal opinion but is tacitly accepted by all, I don't find it objectionable. Once a thing like that is formulated you don't have to worry about the character of the person who professes it. It's no longer a question of whether or not he agrees with it as part of his personal credo.

Interviewer: Doesn't this rather limit the nature of a relationship between a Moroccan and a non-Moslem?

Bowles: It completely determines the nature of a relationship, of course, but I wouldn't say that it limits it, necessarily.

Interviewer: You've never met a Moroccan with whom you felt you could have a Western-style relationship in terms of depth and reciprocity?

Bowles: No, no. That's an absurd concept. Like expecting a boulder to spread its wings and fly away.

Interviewer: Coming to this realization must have been a frustrating experience.

Bowles: No, because right away when I got here I said to myself "Ah, this is the way people used to be, the way my own ancestors were thousands of years ago. The Natural Man. Basic Humanity. Let's see how they are." It all seemed quite natural to me. They haven't evolved the same way, so far, as we have and I wasn't surprised to find that there were whole sections missing in their "psyche," if you like.

Interviewer: Can Morocco be described as a homosexual culture?

Bowles: Certainly not. I think that's one thing that doesn't exist here. It may be putting in an appearance now in the larger cities, what with the frustrations of today's urban life. I would expect it to, since that's the world pattern. They're undifferentiated, if you like, but they don't have a preference for the same sex. On the contrary.

Interviewer: I suppose there are advantages to living in a sexually "undifferentiated" society.

Bowles: There must be, or they wouldn't have made it that way. The French *colons* found it an unfailing source of amusement, of course.

Interviewer: Isn't it paradoxical, though, because of the restrictions of Islam?

Bowles: But religion always does its utmost to restrain human behavior. The discrepancy between religious dogma and individual behavior is no greater here than anywhere else.

Interviewer: What do you know about Moroccan witchcraft?

Bowles: Witchcraft is a loaded word. To use it evokes something sinister, a regression to archaic behavior. Here it's an accepted facet of daily life, as much as the existence of bacteria is in ours. And their attitude toward it is very much the same as ours is toward infection. The possibility is always there, and one must take precautions. But in

Morocco only what you'd call offensive magic is considered "witch-craft." Defensive magic, which plays the same game from the other side of the net, is holy, and can only be efficacious if it's practiced under the aegis of the Koran. If the *fqih* uses the magician's tricks to annul the spell cast by the magician, it doesn't necessarily follow that the *fqih* believes implicitly in the existence of the spell. He's there to cure the people who visit him. He acts as confessor, psychiatrist, and father image. Obviously some of the *fouqqiyane* must be charlatans, out to get hold of all the money they can. But the people get on to the quacks fairly fast.

Interviewer: One hears a lot about the legend of Aicha Qandicha. Who is she?

Bowles: You mean who do I think she really is? I'd say she's a vestigial Tanit. You know when a new faith takes over, the gods of the previous faith are made the personification of evil. Since she was still here in some force when Islam arrived, she had to be reckoned with. So she became this beautiful but dreaded spirit who still frequented running water and hunted men in order to ruin them. It's strange; she has a Mexican counterpart. La Llorona, who also lives along the banks of streams where there's vegetation, and who wanders at night calling to men. She's also of great beauty, and also has long tresses. The differ-ence is that in Mexico she weeps. That's an Indian addition. In Morocco she calls out your name, often in your mother's voice, and the danger is that you'll turn and see her face, in which case you're lost. Unless, unless. There are lots of unlesses. A series of formulas from the Koran, a knife with a steel blade, or even a magnet can save you if you're quick. Not all Moroccans consider Aicha Qandicha a purely destructive spirit. Sacrifices are still made to her, just as they are to the saints. The Hamadcha leave chickens at her sacred grotto. But in general she in-spires terror.

Interviewer: The Moroccans have had an extremely violent history, and even now it seems that there's an innate belligerence in their char-acter; a constant undercurrent of violence. Do you think that's true?

Bowles: As far as I can see, people from all corners of the earth have an unlimited potential for violence. The Moroccans are highly emotional individuals. So naturally in concerted action they're formidable. There's always been inner-tribal violence here, as well as the age-old rustic resentment of the city-dwellers. Until 1956 the country was divided officially into two sectors: *bled el maghzen* and *bled es siba,* or, in other words, territory under governmental control and territories where such control couldn't be implanted. That is, where anarchy reigned. Obviously violence is the daily bread of people living under such conditions. The French called *bled es siba "La Zone d'Insécurité."* As an American you were just as safe there as anywhere else in Morocco, but it wasn't the security of Americans that the French were thinking of.

Interviewer: One also feels, don't you think, that the concept of time is completely different here?

Bowles: Well, yes, but it's partially because one lives a very different life. In America or Europe the day is divided into hours and one has appointments. Here the day isn't measured; it simply goes by. If you see people, it's generally by accident. Time is merely more or less, and everything is perhaps. It's upsetting if you take it seriously. Otherwise it's relaxing, because there's no need to hurry. Plenty of time for everything.

Interviewer: How did your association with Mohammed Mrabet come about?

Bowles: I began to translate from Moghrebi Arabic twenty-five years ago, when I'd notate stories Ahmed Yacoubi told me. Shortly afterward, tape recorders arrived in Morocco and I went on translating, but from tapes. I did the novel *A Life Full of Holes,* by Charhadi, and some things by Boulaich. When I met Mrabet I knew that there was an enormous amount of material there, and fortunately he wasn't averse to exploiting it. On the contrary, he's been telling tales into a microphone now for thirteen years, all from Arabic. The only difficulty with Mrabet is getting everything onto tape. I've lost some wonderful tales merely because at the moment he told them there was no way of recording them.

Interviewer: Isn't Mrabet continuing an oral tradition which is well-established here?

Bowles: He's very much aware of it. From his early childhood he preferred to sit with elderly men, because of the stories they told. He's impregnated with the oral tradition of his region. In a story of his it's hard to find the borderline between unconscious memory and sheer invention.

Interviewer: Why isn't he more popular within Morocco?

Bowles: It's not a question of being popular or not being popular.

He's practically unknown in Morocco. His books are all in English, though there are a few things in French, Italian and Portuguese. What little notice he's received here has been adverse. There have been a few unpleasant articles about him in the newspapers, but probably only because it was I who translated him. But since, at the moment, I'm the sole possible bridge between him and the publishers, I go on doing these books, even though the local critics may take a dim view of them. They feel that a foreigner can present a Moroccan only as a performing seal. They scent neocolonialism in a book translated directly from *darija*. At first they wrote that he didn't exist, that I'd invented him. Then they accused me of literary ventriloquy. I'd found some fisherman and photographed him so I could present my own ideas under the cover of his name, thinking that would give them authenticity. What they seem to resent most of all is not that the texts were taped, but that they were taped in the language of the country which, by common consent, no one ever uses for literary purposes. One must use either Classical Arabic or French. Moghrebi is only for conversational purposes. Then they object to the subject matter. For them contemporary prose must be political in one way or another. They don't conceive of literature as such, only as ammunition to implement their theories about economics and government. Most Moroccan intellectuals are confirmed Marxists, naturally. The same pattern as in other third world countries. I can see clearly why they'd execrate the very concept of such a phenomenon as Mrabet. His books could as easily have been written under the colonial regime as during independence, and this strikes the local critics as tantamount to intellectual treason.

Interviewer: Are you still taping storytellers whom you meet in cafés?

Bowles: There aren't any more. All that's completely changed. There's a big difference just between the Sixties and Seventies. For instance, in the Sixties people still sat in cafés with a *sebsi* (pipe) and told stories and occasionally plucked an *oud* or a *guinbri*. Now practically every café has television. The seats are arranged differently and no one tells any stories. They can't because the television is going. No one thinks of stories. If the eye is going to be occupied by a flickering image, the brain doesn't feel a lack. It's a great cultural loss. It's done away with the oral tradition of storytelling and whatever café music there was.

Interviewer: The music here is supposed to have a mesmirizing effect on its listeners. Is this true?

Bowles: That's one of its functions, but not the only one. If you're an initiate of certain religious groups, it can induce trance-like conditions. In less evolved cultures music is always used for that. But something similar exists in many parts of the world, perhaps even in our own. Strobe lights, acid rock and so on, I think all that's meant to alter consciousness.

Interviewer: Has your involvement with Moroccan music been a means of maintaining your contact with the music world at large?

Bowles: How could it be? It's just a natural interest which I've had since I first came.

Interviewer: What are your future plans, as regards writing?

Bowles: I don't think much about the future. I've got no plans for future books. The book of stories I'm writing at present takes up all my attention. More tales about Morocco. If an idea were to come to me which required the novel form, I'd write a novel. If it happens it happens. I'm not ambitious, as you know. If I had been, I'd have stayed in New York.

Paul Bowles Interviewed

John Spilker/1982

From *oboe* 5 (1982): 74–86. Copyright © Night Horn Books, 1982.
Reprinted by permission of Night Horn Books.

For some of our readers, the review of Paul Bowles' *Collected Stories* in *oboe* No. 4 may have been an introduction to this expatriate American novelist, short story writer, poet and composer. The publication of the collection itself has had the impact of a major retrospective of works by an extraordinary artist who has not always received the attention he deserves. In fact, Bowles has written four novels, the music for many of Tennessee Williams' early plays, an autobiography, and translations of several works by Moroccan writers, in addition to the stories in the collection. Black Sparrow Press has recently published a collection of his poetry, with a reprinting of the novels underway. American society, however, seems to make little place for a writer who fails to engage the media on a weekly basis, less still for one who has taken up permanent residence abroad. Perhaps it is an affront to our journalistic egocentricity. Perhaps we have too much at stake in resisting the ennui of American surfaces.

In any event, at a time when the din of a "postmodernist" search for substance echoes through geometric desolation, the clarity and strength with which Bowles writes deserves a closer look. In his review of Bowles' *Collected Stories,* John Spilker termed him the historian of events "for which our spirit maintains no certain names." There is something in Bowles' matter-of-fact narration, in its cool approach to hallucinatory event, which manages "to encompass the world and light its angular facade with transparency, showing us the bones of which our surroundings are inevitably made."

As we were laying plans for this issue, the idea of interviewing Bowles seemed a natural, though belated, companion piece to our review. However, he has lived in Morocco since shortly after the war, and last visited the U.S. in 1969. Travel funds being somewhat restricted, we opted for postage. An epistolary interview was conceived, an eager correspondent volunteered, and the beast of communication was en-

gaged. John Spilker, whose own fiction has appeared in earlier issues of
oboe, and who has lived and worked in Africa reports:

"I first contacted Paul Bowles in May of this year to suggest the somewhat unusual project of an interview conducted by mail. His response
was both prompt and accommodating. Our correspondence, begun in
earnest in June and concluded in August, resulted in the 'interview'
which follows. While its epistolary nature tends to inhibit the spontaneity
and informality associated with interviews, I suspect that a great deal is
gained in allowing a writer to respond in his chosen medium, the written
word. Too often interviews, by their very immediacy, are reduced to
snapshots of the everyday.

In reviewing the entire exchange, I find one comment by Bowles
which, since it was an aside, has gone unrecorded and, therefore, un-
answered. He claimed not to be 'a very good player of Questions and
Answers.' I feel that the precision he applies to the 'verbal elaboration of
ideas,' here as well as in his stories, makes him an excellent player. At
times, it may have seemed a bit like juggling in a dark room, but I
thoroughly enjoyed the game."

John Spilker: As recently as 1979, with the publication of your *Collected Stories,* Gore Vidal felt the need to "try to place Paul Bowles" for
readers of the collection. As part of this placement, he claimed that your
writing derives from such sources as Poe, Valéry, Roussel, Gide and
Stein. While I realize the claim is Vidal's, would you care to comment
on this ancestry? I am especially curious about Miss Stein's inclusion.

Paul Bowles: The names in Vidal's list should not be placed together
and labelled "sources." If they're to be mentioned in the same breath, it
should be with the observation that they're present in distinct capacities
and in varying degree. Poe was a childhood favorite, yes. Gide I read
between my mid 'teens and my late twenties. Valéry and Roussel came
still later. Stein I liked personally. A similar list could consist of completely different names, I think, and with equal relevance. (e.g.: Sartre,
Shiel, Kafka, Machen, Eliot). I assume we're talking about strictly literary antecedents; if we are, then I see no reason for including Stein at all.

JS: Many of our readers (myself included) may be unfamiliar with
Shiel and Machen. Could you place them for us?

PB: Matthew P. Shiel (I believe he was Irish) wrote a few novels I
thought highly worth reading. At the moment I can call to mind only
two titles which I've read: *Children of the Wind* and *How the Old
Woman Got Home.* Arthur Machen was perhaps better known than

Shiel. Among the books of his that I enjoyed in the 'twenties were *The Great God Pan, The Hill of Dreams* and *The Three Impostors.* (I'm not sure whether he was Welsh or English.)

JS: In a similar vein, Vidal mentions that when you went to Paris in 1928, you were influenced by the surrealists. What writers, or writing, did you encounter during that visit?

PB: I first went to Paris in 1929, and met no writers at all, as far as I can remember.

JS: What significance do you think surrealism has for us today?

PB: By 1931 surrealism had ceased to be a potent factor in French intellectual life, and thus no longer existed as a movement save through belated echoes in other European capitals. In the United States Madison Avenue quickly tamed it. Significance today? As a movement of considerable historical interest, surrealism is not practised today; there is no organization, there is no spokesman or leader. Surrealist creation was principally collaborative; the surrealists were a political party.*

JS: I'll step very gingerly here, because the term "surrealism" has suffered abundantly from careless misuse, Madison Avenue's included (though it was probably more calculated than careless), and you have just done an admirable job of trimming it to manageable proportions. Critics, however, have applied the term descriptively (not historically or politically) to your own writing. Do you feel that this application is totally inaccurate?

PB: If the critics who apply the term *surrealist* to my writing are referring to the novels or stories, then I consider the use of the word inaccurate, of course. If however they're considering the verse, they're entirely correct in applying the term. My prose has nothing to do with surrealism; I should think that would be clear.

JS: Many of your stories involve a passage from the ordinary to a world apparently gone quite mad, in which the rational order no longer holds. Why have you so often chosen, as a writer or as a man, to enter this territory?

PB: Here I must disagree. Take the *Collected Stories.* Out of thirty-nine, there are six which could be said to involve "a passage from the ordinary world to a world etc." The six: "The Scorpion," "By the

*The editor [of *oboe*] would like to note that there is an American surrealist group which was founded in 1966 in Chicago. Through their journal *Arsenal,* and other publications, they claim direct descent from the group of Breton et al, as well as contacts with Surrealist groups in other countries.

Water," "The Circular Valley," "You Are Not I," "If I Should Open My Mouth," and "Allal." The other thirty-three definitely do not fit your description. So I balk at the word "many." "A few" would be more exact. "If I Should Open My Mouth" and "You Are Not I" are tales of mental alienation, and "Allal" is a folk fantasy told in realistic terms.

JS: A problem in terminology, perhaps. I was thinking of such stories as "Tapiama," "A Distant Episode," or "He of the Assembly" from the *Collected Stories;* beyond that, the drugged confusion suffered by the Slades in *Up Above the World,* or Port's fever-inspired sense of the world in *The Sheltering Sky.* In each of these, the protagonist experiences a radical disruption of perceived reality, whether through intoxication, sickness, "mental alienation" or extreme suffering. If the rational order holds externally, if there are rational explanations for each experience, it no longer seems so for the character with whom we, as readers, have become involved. My question has to do with the recurrent passage into a territory of *perceived* dislocation. Why have you chosen in these works (leaving aside the question of many or few) to confront your characters with realities beyond their reason?

PB: You might as well ask me: Why do you like peas better than carrots? Or: What is your purpose in preferring beef to lamb? It gives me pleasure to explore states of dislocation; there is no point in asking why an individual is the way he is, unless the aim is to psychoanalyze him. I don't find your "why" a literary one.

JS: My "why" neither aims to psychoanalyze nor questions your preference—it's intended as a question of literary purpose. Don't you feel that the presence of such "states of dislocation" in your stories allows you to accomplish certain things, or to engage the reader in ways that stories centered on a more conventional (perhaps falsely stable) orientation cannot?

PB: I can only say: What *is* my writing but a constant exploration of possible modes of consciousness? You could almost qualify the entire body of work as a series of variations on the theme of human perception. (That is, if you didn't mind sounding like a critic.)

JS: On the same subject, reviewers have found in your work a "hypnotic combination of beauty, dread and strangeness," "an atmosphere of something vaguely amiss" (both from Tom Clark), a "sense of strangeness and terror" (Vidal again)—a splendid nightmare. Their reaction is more primal than critical, an involuntary shudder. What is it, in your opinion, that makes these stories so disturbing?

PB: If there are "shudders," they are not mine, so I can't know their cause. But no serious person writes in order to produce such a reaction; he hopes to convert readers to his way of experiencing the phenomenon of existence. It may be that what you call the "shudder" is the first step in the conversion; I don't know. If material is disturbing, it could be because it is constructed around the implicit denial of some basic "truth" which humanity has formulated for itself, and without the belief in which life could seem unbearable.

JS: Of course! That's exactly what the shudder denotes. But wouldn't conversion without such an initiation be suspect? I would think that a conversion to a way of experiencing the phenomenon of existence would require of the reader a profound reaction, one that renders merely critical reaction pointless.

PB: I agree with you. Still, I don't think the word "shudder" covers the entire gamut of possible reactions.

JS: Do you feel that the initial acceptance of these basic, comforting "truths" is an individual failure of courage? Is it simply the mark of one's tribe?

PB: The initial acceptance is inevitable; it's only with time that one learns to question them; that's where invention begins.

JS: Your characters are frequently travellers or temporary residents in foreign lands. They are seldom able to assess their surroundings. To what extent have you adapted yourself to the Moroccan culture?

PB: How can I say to what extent I've adapted myself? Not very thoroughly, I should think.

JS: In your travels, have you felt yourself to be as unprepared, as vulnerable, as the characters you describe?

PB: Yes, and on innumerable occasions. If I hadn't felt "unprepared" and "vulnerable," I could not very well have made my protagonists feel that way. The difference is that after these occasions many of the protagonists were unable to recapture their previous sense of reality. This is the pretext for writing the story. "There but for the grace of God . . ."

JS: Is there some characteristic that renders such protagonists unable to recapture reality, or do they merely suffer external event to its necessarily overwhelming conclusion? (I'm assuming that the "grace of God" is more a figure of speech than an explanation for their inability.)

PB: Possibly they're too sure of their place in the world, not dubious enough about their identity; I've never thought about it. This would make them more prone to "suffer external event etc."

JS: In recent months, in separate interviews, you and William Burroughs have both cited Conrad as a favorite author. What qualities in his writing attract you? The coincidence of choice fascinates me, coming from two such stylistically distinct authors.

PB: Imagine Bill Burroughs likes Conrad for the same reason I do— because he's a pleasure to read, at least in novels like *Nostromo, Under Western Eyes, The Secret Agent* and *Victory.* I began to read Conrad seriously only when I was in my 'sixties. (The earlier books suffer from sentimentality and overwriting.)

JS: Readers often look to writers they admire for suggested reading. Is there a writer or work (perhaps less well-known) that you would care to recommend?

PB: I never feel comfortable recommending a doctor or a book. If the result isn't satisfactory, I reproach myself for not having held my tongue.

JS: Many writers aim at the unconscious (in the sense of an escape from the rational), but their prose generally reflects the effort of passage—it disintegrates into fragmentary excess, often resorting to typographical variation. You, however, are able to explore the unconscious without straining or distorting syntax. What advantage does this voice have for you that such techniques as Burroughs' "cut-up" method or other attacks on the linear lack?

PB: Since the only way of expressing an idea is through language, it follows that language should be used in the most concise and lucid manner possible; the idea is entirely at the mercy of the words used to express it. Research in innovative form is carried out in other departments of the literary laboratory, not here in my own. My principal concern is with finding sentences that will translate my ideas with the maximum accuracy.

You mention Burrough's cut-up method, which can give very impressive results when used discreetly for intensification of atmosphere. Clearly, the truncation of a sentence does violence to logical thought. The juxtaposition of morsels of material formed by random truncation "in the hands of a master," as Burroughs puts it, can achieve the desired atmospheric effect. The device is poetic and in direct opposition to the process of verbal elaboration of ideas. If I'm not using ratiocination, I prefer to write music; I can shut the door between the two chambers. (Remember that the cut-up procedure was a by-product of the *musique*

concrète movement in Paris in the late 'fifties, which in turn was a revival of surrealist techniques of the 'twenties. The technique now had
the use of the tape-recorder; the new surrealism was fundamentally
aural.)

JS: Given the two chambers of ratiocination and music, where does
your poetry lie?

PB: It lies outside both of the mentioned chambers.

JS: There are poets out there who may urge me to ask: What is the
provenance of your poetry, and how does it differ from that of your
music?

PB: When I write prose, I put words at the service of meaning. In
poetry, the words are primary, and may or may not subsequently give
rise to meaning. Save as a sort of basic training for the writing of prose,
I can think of no reason for having written my verse.

JS: The narrative voice in much of your writing is one of suspended
moral judgment (Vidal is reminded of a sharp-eyed, unblinking bird
examining the landscape more closely than it does the miniature characters who scramble across the earth). Have you been criticized for this
quality? Do you feel that it might make it difficult for some readers to
approach your work?

PB: I've been criticized at one time or another for a variety of things.
I don't know, furthermore, what "quality" is represented by Vidal's
analogy of the bird. Lack of empathy, perhaps? I'm sure that whether or
not the bird keeps people away from my work, the work wouldn't be the
same without it. And if it were not the same, it wouldn't be "better" or
"worse"; it merely wouldn't exist.

JS: The fact that Vidal's analogy suggests several possible "qualities"
is very much to the point. Lack of empathy may be one reader's reaction to what another sees as the most direct, and honest, presentation
of event. At any rate, your comment about your work suggests an
unconcern on your part with technique, or a belief that such technique
as exists emerges within the work, as part of its impulse. Is this a fair
assumption? Is it fairer in regard to your stories than your novels?

PB: Whatever the bird analogy may mean to one reader or another, to
me it evokes only the nervousness and sudden motions of a bird; it's not
surprising I fail to recognize myself.

And you're entirely correct as concerns technique, with regard to
short fiction. Novels need a certain amount of mulling over beforehand.

JS: Your answers to these questions reveal a concern for precision in language; your stories, an unusual commitment to the detail, form, and sheared-off truth of experience. Such concerns might arise if there were a threat to the language and, therefore, to our perception. Are we, as a mass media-connected people, in danger of losing sight of the truth to an extent never before witnessed?

PB: We're in danger of losing the power to imagine. That's the surest way of losing sight of "the truth," if there is such a thing. We're also in danger of losing the power to formulate our thoughts concisely, as language slips from our grasp. What is all this but a form of brainwashing on a mass scale? The quickest way to reach a totalitarian state.

JS: The marvellous, the mystical, make frequent appearances in your stories. For example, the magic stones of "You Are Not I" or the Atlajala of "The Circular Valley." Is their presence related to your desire to invent your own myths?

PB: Here I have to disagree; I don't accept your premise. The "marvellous, the mystical" don't figure in my writing. (Let us except, if you like, "The Circular Valley," admittedly a fantasy.) But the stones in "You Are Not I" are not "magical" stones; they are pieces of the crushed stone that lies along railroad tracks. There is an ellipsis in the working out of motives for the protagonist's behavior. The writer and his reader are aware that in antiquity stones were often placed in the mouths of the dead. There is no indication that the protagonist is aware of the custom; her behavior is atavistic. I imagine you assumed as much, and I go into it only in order to refute your statement containing the words "marvellous" and "mystical." My feeling is that the qualities suggested by those particular words is precisely one I've avoided. (I see I haven't taken into account the tale of "Allal"; even there I'd reject both words as inapposite. The story is presented through an omniscient observer. But to the onlookers there in the village, Allal, full of hashish, ran off naked into the palm forest. He had to be caught, subdued, and sent to a psychiatric hospital. His sensation of being inside the snake may have been a hallucinatory effect of the hashish. Being able to enter into the minds of animals is a recurrent Moroccan fantasy. A few adepts have been successful in the attempt.)

JS: This surprises me. A letter addressed to oneself is in no sense mystical, unless it is found in the street and contains a troubling message, as happens in "He of the Assembly." Then it acquires an irrational force, an obsessive significance that goes beyond intelligence. Likewise the stones. They are common material transformed by the story itself, if not by the narrator, into powerful markers for much that is buried within us. Powerful beyond logic or comprehension—these are qualities which the term "mystical" suggests to me. To you, it suggests qualities which you have avoided. What are these qualities, and why have you avoided them?

PB: To me that which is "mystical" is inexplicable save through illogic, something I find objectionable, that is, unacceptable. The word "mysticism" smells of sandalwood and regressive fanaticism. The leper's scabs, vomit and excrement for the Christian mystics. No! The mystic imagines he has a hot line to God.

JS: In your memoir, you mention a desire to invent your own myths as one impulse for writing. In what sense are your stories myths?

PB: Very few of my published stories could be counted as "myths." I discarded the myths; they served only to get me into the precinct of fiction. I myself don't consider any of my tales to be myths. "Afternoon With Antaeus" is a counter-myth, if you like.

JS: I was taken by your comments in *Without Stopping* concerning the Moroccan claim that "full participation in life demands the regular contemplation of death." Do you feel that Western civilization by and large fails to prepare its "citizens" for death, and is, therefore, robbing them of life?

PB: Yes. Since Christianity entered into its catabolic phase, no philosophy has been evolved which provides for comfortable acceptance of death. Religions always have stressed the importance of seeing death as an inseparable part of life, precisely because it's so difficult to accept.

JS: Could you explain what you mean by the "catabolic" phase Christianity has entered?

PB: Simply that its influence is in a state of progressive decline, and that the decline will continue until it reaches the point of zero, where it started.

JS: Black Sparrow Press is currently embarked on a reprinting of most, if not all, of your writing, poetry as well as prose. How did this come about? What sense do you have of the effect of this effort?

PB: When Black Sparrow Press published my collected stories, I mentioned to John Martin that it would be good to have a uniform edition of the novels. He plans to reprint them one by one. As to the "effect," you, being more or less on hand, would have a much closer view of the landscape. Here I feel as though I were on a different planet; I have no way of knowing such things.

JS: What current projects do you have, in writing, translation or music?

PB: I seldom have projects. I suddenly find something in front of me, and I work at it.

JS: This seems like a good place to thank you for having taken the time to find these questions in front of you, and to have worked on them.

Paul Bowles Interview

David Seidner/1982

From *Bomb* 4 (November 1982): 10–13. Reprinted by permission of *Bomb* and David Seidner.

The productive climate throughout Europe from about 1900 on, was based, more or less, on the promise of a new world that industry would provide. The political movements, and ensuing wars and revolutions, served both to destroy and calcify idealism in the arts. As we approach the 21st century, we can clearly see that our hopes have been dashed; we grope blindly for a new set of ideals upon which to base a new ideology. Our links to this glorious past are quickly disappearing. All us youngsters (anyone under fifty), can only dream of Paris in the twenties, the luxury of sea travel, stately old hotels in undiscovered corners of paradise, and the efficient hush of servants. In a country where underwear is still ironed, and villages spring up overnight, Paul Bowles, one of those links to the past, has chosen to make his home. Despite television, one still has the sense of being isolated in Morocco.

Bowles was born in New York City in 1910, an only child to a Unitarian dentist and his wife. As long as he can remember, he wanted to get away. But not run from, run to. At the age of 18, in 1929, he set off for Paris, with $25.00 left after paying his passage. He stayed one year in Paris where he worked for the *Herald Tribune* and cultivated a friendship with Tristan Tzara. On his return to the University of Virginia the following year, during a stint as guest editor at the University of Richmond, Bowles published Gertrude Stein's poetry and consequently, developed a correspondence with her. He returned to Paris in 1931, went straight to Stein's door, knocked on it, and was invited in. She decided Paul was not a good name for him, "it's a romantic name, and you don't look at all romantic" (which he did though, being desperately thin), so she called him "Freddie", after his middle name. Through Gertrude, Freddie met everyone. He traveled with Stein and Alice B. Toklas (another correspondent) to their country house, where from the porch, Gertrude would yell: "Run, Freddie, run, so Basket can chase you."

Basket being her standard French poodle who chased Paul
through the labyrinthian garden, jumping up from behind
and clawing his thighs (Paul wearing only lederhosen), while
Gertrude yelled: "Faster, Freddie, faster."

Paul was composing music and writing poetry. It was
through Henry Cowell that he met and studied with Aaron
Copland (and later with Nadia Boulanger). With Copland,
on Stein's insistance, Bowles went to, and fell in love with,
Tangier. Music, being his source of income, forced Bowles
back to New York, where he wrote scores for the theater,
beginning with Orson Welles, and going on to work with
William Saroyan, Philip Barry, Lillian Hellman, and Tennessee Williams. In 1937, he met Jane Auer, whom he
married one year later. They lived together in W. H. Auden's
rooming house for artists, in Gypsy Rose Lee's old rooms. It
was through Jane Bowles' novel *Two Serious Ladies* that
Paul Bowles' desire to write fiction was kindled. During the
next two decades, Paul (with or without Jane) traveled com-
pulsively throughout Europe, Asia, and Latin America. He
eventually settled in Tangier, where he lives a somewhat
Spartan existence. His home is dark and lined with books.
The canaries chirp endlessly. Visitors come and go unan-
nounced, as Bowles refuses to have a telephone.

Paul Bowles' novels include: *The Sheltering Sky, Let It
Come Down, The Spider's House*, and *Up Above the World*;
volumes of short stories: *The Delicate Prey, The Time of
Friendship, Things Gone and Things Still Here*, and *Mid-
night Mass*; travel books: *Yallah!*, and *Their Heads are
Green*; an autobiography: *Without Stopping*; translations: the
stories of Isabelle Eberhardt (published under the title: *The
Oblivion Seekers*), and many Moroccan tales translated from
the Moghrebi dialect, most notably, those of Mohammed
Mrabet. He is the founder and co-editor of *Antaeus* maga-
zine. His books have been published by Random House,
Simon & Schuster, Holt, Rinehart & Winston, Putnam, and
New Directions. They are currently available in editions by
City Lights, Echo Press, Black Sparrow Press (in the U.S.),
Peter Owen (in the U.K.), and have been translated in a
dozen languages.

His writing in general has something eerie about it; wandering characters, detached, often subjected to deception and
violence, . . . aimless. Almost black fairy tales. Bowles
claims the violence stems from the belief that our civilization
is predicated upon violence, that at any minute, we can all

disappear in a nuclear holocaust. One could call his work a
race against time in slow motion.

This interview took place during one of many unan-
nounced afternoon visits.

David Seidner: You said you could only write music in New York, and
that you always did it for the purpose of making money, that you had no
desire to write music here in Morocco . . .

Paul Bowles: Well I *have* written music here in Morocco, of course,
quite a bit. It doesn't really matter as long as I have a piano and I have
had a piano on several occasions here. But in New York I was writing
functional music and making my living doing it, which is something
else. I also wrote serious music.

DS: Do you think you could write novels in New York?

PB: I don't know; I've never tried. That's something I wouldn't be
able to say. I've written many short stories in New York. Probably if
I had a regulated life in New York, I could work on a novel, but it
would have to be a quiet house, with good food, etc. . . . .

DS: You don't like noise?

PB: Oh no, no. It bothers me very much.

DS: Have you ever crossed the Atlantic by air?

PB: Never, no.

DS: Even when you went to the States last, in 68, you went by sea?

PB: Sure. I went on the Leonardo da Vinci, and came back in '69 on
the Raffaelo. You can't go wrong on an Italian liner out of the
Mediterranean. Very good ships. Marvelous food, wonderful accommo-
dations . . . in first class. I don't know about the other accommoda-
tions, but mine were very good.

DS: You always travel first class by ship?

PB: Generally, yes . . . No, I've gone many times by freighter.

DS: What year did you first go to Ceylon?

PB: In '49.

DS: And you owned an island there?

PB: Well I didn't own it then, I bought it later, in '53. I was in
Madrid, when I got a cable from Sri Lanka, saying that the island could
be bought, giving me the price, and I immediately cabled New York
and bought it.

DS: How much was it?

PB: It was very cheap, a little over five thousand dollars, I think, with the house and all. (laughter) I think that was it, it might have been ten. Anyway it was extremely low, a fluke. It belonged to a rubber planter who lived up country in Sri Lanka, who also bred race horses and bet on them very heavily, and of course the inevitable happened, he lost, and one of his assets was this little island, which he bought as a pleasure dome, you know . . .

DS: How did you first hear about it?

PB: Through David Herbert. I was staying at Wilton and David had this pile of scrap books, photo albums really, not scrap books, and one album was almost completely devoted to this marvelous looking place called Taprobane, and I said "Oh I'd love to see that," and he said "Oh it's heavenly, just marvelous," and of course it was. He had been there with Lord and Lady Mountbatten and took pictures of them all . . . beaming . . . (laughter)

DS: Did you always feel a need to isolate yourself in somewhat paradisiac corners of the world in order to produce, to write?

PB: Well no. One doesn't know about those corners until one's visited them. Certainly in the beginning I didn't suspect they existed, but once I had seen them, I wanted to be in them, surely.

DS: And when you came to Morocco, you decided you were going to live here?

PB: No, no . . . I first came in '31. I never had any ideas about the distant future. It was a desire to come back here after the war, in '47, that I returned.

DS: Was it with the idea though that you would continue wandering as you had in the past?

PB: Without any ideas. I never had any ideas at all about what I was going to do. Because it was generally decided for me by the amount of money at my disposal.

DS: According to the music that you wrote?

PB: At that time according to the music, before that according to small inheritances, and what I was able to get, you know (laughter).

DS: Did you begin to have recognition as a composer in conjunction with Tennessee Williams' play, or was it before?

PB: Before. I didn't do anything with Tennessee until eight years

after I did the first show. I started working with Orson Welles, and that
was long before Tennessee.

DS: In the forties?

PB: In the thirties. Thirty-six.

DS: What kind of projects were they?

PB: Oh, it was called Project 891. It was marvelous. Orson was the
czar, he did everything, and at that time he also had a program in
Chicago for some reason, every Sunday night, for Bond Bread, for
which he was quite well paid. There was no money at all in '36 you
know. And with the money he made from Bond Bread, he kept his
project going, even though it was subsidized by the government, as part
of the Federal Theater. But he'd made it so much better than it could
have been without the extra money.

DS: They were projects that he wrote?

PB: Well, yes and no. The first was a project that he and Edwin
Denby wrote together. It was a translation actually, of Labiche's
"Chapeau de Paille d'Italie," the one that Cavalcanti made a film of
earlier. A marvelous, terribly funny piece. "Horse Eats Hat" it was
called. Joseph Cotton was the lead with Arlene Francis playing the hat
girl, the modiste, and Orson playing the father-in-law. It was marvelous!

DS: What theater was it performed in?

PB: Maxine Elliott.

DS: And how many projects did you do after that?

PB: Then I did the next one with him which was Marlowe's "Dr.
Faustus". That was incredible too, beautiful! He did all his magic tricks,
and the entire front of the theater was simply black velvet, all the way
up, and the lighting! . . . fantastic. He did costumes, sets, everything.
He knew exactly what he wanted. A genius. He made us *all* feel inferior, not intentionally, but he had so much energy! He could go on and
on and on, all night at times, while everyone was thoroughly exhausted.

DS: How did you two originally meet?

PB: Well, we met . . . I remember the night we met, but I don't
remember who introduced us. I don't think anyone did. He was living
on 14th Street in a basement, near Union Square. He was married to
Virginia, and I was taken down there, but I can't remember by whom. It
might have been either John Houseman or Virgil Thomson, I'm not

sure. Anyhow, I was taken down there and I met this, you know, roly-poly youth (inflating his cheeks); he was only 19! I think. Very young. He had already done a very successful negro Macbeth in Harlem, which everyone raved about. It had voodoo in it . . . just incredible. I remember going to see it before I met him.

DS: In '35?

PB: It must have been.

DS: Paid for by Bond Bread?

PB: Very likely. I've got it all in the other room, the book on the Federal Theater. Have you seen it?, it's interesting.

DS: And were you well paid as a composer?

PB: No, nobody was well paid. Everyone got the same salary 23.86.

DS: Twenty-three dollars and eighty-six cents per week?

PB: Per week. Everyone got the same. John Houseman got the same, Virgil Thomson got the same, Orson got the same. (laughter) It was, uh, democracy.

DS: And what year did you first start working with Tennessee Williams?

PB: Tennessee . . . I think it was the winter of '43-'44. He came to me with a script called "The Glass Menagerie", and left it with me. That was in New York. But we met in Acapulco. Lawrence Langner of the Theatre Guild had given him my address there, and he just arrived. I didn't know who he was. I opened the door and saw this young man wearing a huge floppy-brimmed hat and he said: "I'm Tennesseeeee Williammmmms (imitating a southern drawl), and Lawrence Langneh' told me te look u up . . ." (laughter). We went off to the beach that day and simply left him in the house. He chooses to forget that, I noticed in his memoirs. He says we were living in a pensione somewhere; far from the fact. And he lay in the hammock all day drinking rum and coke, which the servants brought him, and we came back from the beach about five and he was still there, surrounded by parrots and guaca-mayos. But he was very nice, really. He said the Guild was doing a show of his . . . what was it called . . .? "Battle of Angels", with Miriam Hopkins. But it never came in. It died at the Plymouth in Boston, I don't know why. He redid it though; I think he called it "Orpheus Descending" the second time.

DS: And later you worked together writing, for *Senso*, no?

PB: Well, we didn't exactly work together. I was here and I got a

telegram from Tennessee asking me to come to Rome. He'd been asked
to do the dialogue, adapting that is, from Boeto's novel, but he was too
busy doing something else, so I went and worked with Visconti everyday for two months. But he wasn't happy with the love scenes, and I
couldn't rewrite them, so Tennessee did, and I went off to Istanbul to
write an article for *Holiday*. It was in '53 . . . and I remember Visconti's sister taking her private plane to Stalin's funeral.

DS: So it was a whole family of arm-chair communists.

PB: Absolutely.

DS: Why do you hate Wagner?

PB: First of all, I don't like the sound it makes. (laughter) Most of
Wagner's vocal . . . I don't like vocal music. I don't like *Heldentenors,*
I don't like coloratura soprano, I don't like any voices at all, really
(more laughter). It's all these things put together, plus the insanity of
the decor and costumes. Naturally it's something to see, yes, but it's
certainly nothing to go to for pleasure.

DS: Many people do though.

PB: I know, I realize that, but it doesn't give *me* any pleasure. I
don't like the heavy sound of the music. That goes for practically all
nineteenth-century German music, as far as I'm concerned, including
Beethoven.

DS: Do you have a favorite composer?

PB: Yes, Bach, if I had to choose one. It seems a mad thing to do.
Favorite is a bad word. I love Stravinsky, and Satie.

DS: Is any of your own music available on records?

PB: Well it was, not any more though. Peggy Guggenheim produced
it and sold the albums at "Art of this Century". She was a very good
friend, we saw a great deal of each other. We met when she came to
New York at the beginning of the war and married Max Ernst, around
1940. They were living on Beekman Place. And then I went to visit her
in Venice, and she came to visit me in Sri Lanka. She said she had
come to Asia not to visit me, but to meet a Maharaja in India, and buy
some dogs, Lhasa Apsos, in Tibet. She came alone and I went to fetch
her in a Bullock cart, purposefully. It was a very primitive way of
traveling in Ceylon. It only had two wheels, and it bumped over every
cobblestone. Peggy adored it! She kept crying: "Ah! It's heaven!, ah
. . . love it!" and my teeth were being shaken out of my head. And then
another time, the three of us (with Jane Bowles) stayed together one

summer on what Peggy called the "non-Jewish lake." In Connecticut, near the New York border. I've forgotten what it was called, you know, some unheard of little place. But they didn't want any Jews.

DS: Strictly WASP.

PB: Strictly! So she got the idea of getting me to sign the rental contracts and so on, and pay out the money. I had to go down to Wall Street I remember, and this awful, you know, heavy man with glasses looking very formidable, went out of his way to tell me: "You know we don't let any Jews in, that's one of the reasons it's expensive. There's not a Jew within five miles!"

DS: It sounds like Auntie Mame.

PB: I don't know, it sounds like Germany to me, I mean Hitler's Germany. So I said: "Yes, I see, ah hah," and signed it all. And I had to smuggle Peggy in as Mrs. Bowles. (laughter)

DS: Jane Auer and Peggy Guggenheim around the non-Jewish lake!

PB: We laughed a lot. Next door to us, was, let's see, Sybille Bedford, and Kay Boyle's children by Lawrence Vail, but not Peggy's children by Lawrence Vail. Not in the house that Peggy took, but the reason she wanted to go to this lake was that on the property next door where Sybille Bedford and Jean Connolly, Cyril Connolly's first wife, were staying, Lawrence Vail was staying there too.

DS: And you never kept a diary?

PB: No, never.

DS: Do you think the fact that you never kept a diary has anything to do with your claim that your ego is practically non-existent?

PB: Possibly, could be. But I don't see the connection.

DS: Oh because often people who keep diaries feel that they're living something important, even historical; they have very high estimations of themselves.

PB: I see. Well I had a high estimation of what I was living, but I didn't think it had anything to do with anything historical. I was living in the present, there was no need to put anything down.

DS: You felt you were a man of your own time?

PB: Well how can one be anything else?

DS: Because you said once that you felt you were never of "today", that your whole life you never really felt *of* today, and that you never understood what it meant.

PB: I must have been speaking from a social point of view.

DS: Do you feel akin to any particular era more than another?

PB: No. No. Not that I can think of. I imagine all eras have had their horrors. Things get worse as we progress, obviously. The horrors today are greater than they were in the nineteenth century, and the nineteenth was worse than the eighteenth. For many reasons. Population and the spread of democratic ideals. I don't mean to sound undemocratic, that's not what I mean. But the misapprehension and misapplication of democratic ideals.

DS: Do you see yourself as being a pessimist at all? Negative?

PB: Not really, no.

DS: I ask because the characters in your stories very often seem detached, aimless, even lost. Negative in so much as, broken, in terms of spirit.

PB: Well, perhaps what you're referring to is a lack of volition. That could be. Because most of my characters are guilty of compulsive behavior.

DS: Is that autobiographical?

PB: No. *NO.* I mean one writes what one writes, one doesn't decide what to write, one writes what comes out. What ever one writes is in a sense autobiographical, of course. Not factually so, but poetically so.

DS: So you don't research your novels?

PB: No, never. They're completely intuitive. Formed organically. They just come.

DS: Do you consider yourself a romantic?

PB: What else can one be? I'm certainly not a classicist.

DS: Conrad for example, who you admire, you criticize in his early work as being too sentimental. Is there one thing that constitutes sentimentality for you besides something overworked?

PB: Well, sentimentality comes after all when the emotion expressed is not really related to the emotion which should be felt at the moment.

DS: How do you feel about your poetry?

PB: I'm a little ashamed of it.

DS: Of all of it, even the poems published by Black Sparrow?

PB: Well I went through them. You see they sent me a great big sheaf of stuff they had got together out of many many magazines from the twenties and thirties where I published. Because I sent it out like mad, cause I wrote it like mad. I typed it as fast as I could without any thought at all. And another sheet, and another . . .

DS: That for you was surrealist poetry?

PB: Right (laughter). I didn't know what I was typing.

DS: That was according to Breton's instructions?

PB: I never *met* Breton.

DS: But you said you read that book of his that told you how to do it.

PB: Oh yeah (laughter) . . . yes. What I read of Breton only emphasized what my mother taught me as a child, to exist with a completely
empty mind, not think of anything. She thought it was good for the
mind, relaxing you know. To banish all ideas, not let anything come
within your field of vision as it were. It's very difficult of course, you
always think of something, you're likely to.

DS: It's very Hindu, actually. Maybe that's where your non-existent
ego comes from.

PB: No, I don't think so. How can one attribute it to anything? It's
like having blue eyes or brown eyes. You attribute it to your genes I
suppose. And besides, I may have a great deal of ego and not know it.
Isn't that possible? Unless egoless is the man who thinks he's egoless,
I don't know. I HOPE!, I hope at least; I wouldn't want to have an ego.

DS: Yes, artists in general have enormous egos.

PB: I can only speak for myself.

DS: Was it Gertrude Stein that introduced you to Cocteau?

PB: No, I was taken there by another friend. He lived on the Rue
Vignon, I remember, behind the Madeleine. He put on a great act and
I was very much impressed by him. All that I remember I wrote in my
book, more or less. When I went back to see him another time, Jean
Desbordes answered the door, and said: *"M. Cocteau est au fond de son
lit, je regrette."* When I told my friend who had taken me there what
Jean had said, he said: "Oh, he was just smoking opium."

DS: Who else did you meet in those days? Did you know Gide at all?

PB: Well I met him, yes, but I never knew him, no. I met a lot of
people, you know, "how do you do?" I spent a lot of time with Carlo
Suares, an Egyptian banker who supported Krishnamurti. I met him in
Holland where Krishnamurti had that castle. And of course I saw a lot
of Stein, and Virgil Thomson was a great friend. He used to say that all
French perfumes could be divided into three categories: flower,
underarm, and urine (laughter).

DS: And you regularly went back to New York, no?

PB: Well, initially I went back because I didn't want to stay on any longer, working at the *Tribune* and earning so little money. I had a chance to go back before I was completely broke, so I did, naturally. And I wanted to finish the year at the University of Virginia.

DS: Do you have a diploma?

PB: No. I have no diplomas, from anywhere.

DS: And when you went back to Paris in '31, how long did you stay?

PB: Then I stayed from March until the summer, summer of '31 I came to Morocco, the winter I was back in Paris, then the spring of '32 I was in Spain, came back to Morocco, stayed here and caught typhoid, went back to Paris and was there to have typhoid, at the American Hospital, then I went to the Alps, my mother came over, and we spent the summer in Monte Carlo, then we went to Spain, and Majorca too, then I took her back to Paris, and she went to New York, then I went back to Monte Carlo.

DS: Why Monte Carlo?

PB: Because I had a friend there with whom I could stay without paying any rent, that simple. And I had a very good grand piano to play on, with no strings attached. Also I had food, everything.

DS: Where does Berlin fit in?

PB: Oh yes, I was there in '31 also, with Aaron Copland.

DS: Where did you meet?

PB: I met Aaron in New York in 1930. Yes, must have been, beginning of '30, yes. Because in the summer of '30, he was in Yaddo, an artist's colony in Saratoga Springs, and I went there then. He was writing the Piano Variations, I remember. And then I studied with him that winter until I left for Paris, and I stayed in Paris only a month, I guess, until Aaron arrived, and then we went together to Berlin. He had an apartment there that had belonged to a poet called Alfred Kreymborg, and I found a place to live and it was fine.

DS: And that's where you met Isherwood, who named Sally Bowles after you?

PB: That's right. And I had the letters to Isherwood and Spender from Edouard Roditi. And he also is the one who put me in touch with Carlo Suares.

DS: Oh you mean letters of introduction?

PB: I had letters of introduction, yes. Oh Roditi's a great one for writing them, always was.

DS: Have you kept all your letters?

PB: No, I had to sell everything when Janie was sick.

DS: The letters from Gertrude Stein too?

PB: Yes, beautiful letters. I had a beautiful one from Cocteau too that I had pasted on the inside of "Opium." I had written to ask his permission to use a collection of his poems called "Memnon" for a song-cycle I had written. He wrote back: *"Imaginez moi refusant un tel honneur!"* It's somewhere in Texas now.

An Interview with Paul Bowles

Karen LaLonde Alenier, Francine Geraci, and Ken Pottiger/1984

From *Gargoyle* 24 (Spring 1984): 5–32.

Paul Bowles was born in New York City in 1910, and has
lived for many years as an expatriate American in Tangier,
Morocco. He is a novelist (his highly acclaimed novels *The
Sheltering Sky* (1949), *Let It Come Down* (1952), *The Spider's House* (1955), and *Up Above the World* (1966) have
recently been reprinted in paperback by Black Sparrow and
Ecco Presses), short story writer (Black Sparrow published
his *Collected Stories 1939–1976* in 1979, and *Midnight Mass*
in 1981), composer (he studied music with Aaron Copland
and Virgil Thomson, and has tried his hand at operas, ballets,
incidental music for Broadway, and numerous recordings),
travel writer (*Yallah* in 1956 and *Their Heads Are Green and
Their Hands Are Blue* in 1963), and autobiographer (*Without
Stopping* in 1972), and has long been noted for translating the
work of Mohammed Mrabet, Driss ben Hamed Charhadi,
and Mohamed Choukri, as well as Roger Frison-Roche's *The
Lost Trail of the Sahara,* and Jean-Paul Sartre's *No Exit.* Paul
Bowles is also responsible for an important collection of
native North African music housed in the Library of Congress. A recording of the author reading from his City Lights
collection of stories (*One Hundred Camels in the Courtyard*)
was released by Cadmus Editions in 1981. His most recent
book is *Points In Time* (Peter Owen, 1982).

Interviewers: We were talking the other day about small presses. I was
wondering if you were aware of their proliferation in the United States.

Bowles: Well, I am aware of the proliferation of small presses.
Perhaps not to its fullest extent. But I am aware of the endless numbers
of small presses around in the United States—which I think is a good
idea, given that the big presses don't take literature seriously. . . . They
can't take it seriously, because they've got to sell. The whole thing is
a question of money. Which it didn't used to be. It was a question of
prestige, 50, 60, 70, 80 years ago. The prestige of a publishing house.

Now, nobody cares. There is no prestige. Or the one who makes the most money has the most prestige, it seems to me.

Interviewers: As far as your own work is concerned, do you have any reservations about being published by a small press?

Bowles: No, I don't. But that's because practically everything has been published before in New York. So I think I'm lucky to have it republished. Small, medium or large: it doesn't really matter.

Interviewers: What about anything you might publish in the future? . . . You have no reservations about the relatively limited resources for promotion and distribution?

Bowles: That's their business, not mine.

Interviewers: Many writers are concerned about those limitations.

Bowles: Well, those are writers who are interested in making money.

Interviewers: Have you ever received any grants or fellowships for your writing?

Bowles: Yes. Three years ago I received a grant from NEA and then two years ago I got what was called a Senior Fellowship Grant of $15,000. That was the largest I ever received; the other was $5,000 or $7,000. . . . But that's all. I had a Guggenheim, yes, years ago.

Interviewers: It's impossible, in Canada, for serious writers to make a living at it. We're heavily subsidized by various grants.

Bowles: But isn't it impossible in the States, too? . . . Pretty much so. It depends on whom you consider a serious writer. John Irving? He made some money on *Garp.* Now and then somebody who writes something fairly good can make some money. For instance, Capote has made some money, but not with his fiction. He didn't start earning money until he wrote *In Cold Blood,* and began appearing on television. But I don't count that. That's not making money from writing.

Interviewers: So you don't expect to get any money eventually (from *Midnight Mass*)?

Bowles: I'll probably get about $500, or less. They don't pay much.

Interviewers: Sometimes small presses seem to function almost as vanity presses. What's your notion on that?

Bowles: Well, it either is vanity or isn't. If it's vanity press, I'm against it. . . . I don't receive all these publications or see their brochures. But I don't think that it's possible to have too many books published. The good writers will rise to the surface. It's a natural process.

Interviewers: How do the people who are visiting you now—particularly those from the literary community—differ from those who visited you in the '50s or '60s (like Ginsberg and Burroughs)?

Bowles: I have to get impressions of the United States from the people who visit me, yes . . . Burroughs lived here. And Ginsberg came to visit Burroughs. Nobody came to visit me. . . . They were off, busy, looking after Bill Burroughs, who couldn't look after himself at that point. I don't know what he was on; he was on something. He couldn't pick up his papers. His room was full of the entire manuscript of *Naked Lunch* underfoot: hundreds of yellow pages ground into the . . . it had been there for a long time. . . . I used to ask him, "What is that?" "Ah, that's my new book." "Well, what's it doing on the floor? Do you have other copies?" "No." "But it's going to get ruined." "Well, that's the way it is." And he'd just write some more and throw it on the floor. It was all over the room. Terrible! With mouse droppings, bits of old food. How they ever managed to get the words out of it, I don't know. It was a basement apartment; a lot of dirt came in from the garden. It was not a clean room. But as far as I know, he wouldn't allow any maid to come near it.

Interviewers: Well, to get back to the original point: what are your impressions of people from the U.S. now?

Bowles: I think Americans remain Americans. I don't think they've changed. In what way would they change? You mean their ideas, the books they talk about. That changes; politics change. Many things have changed. But they haven't changed. Their reactions are the same, it seems to me. Should I say they're different? I don't know.

Interviewers: Well, the trappings have changed. We think of the '50s and the Beat generation, the '60s and the drug culture, and so on. I find, myself, that people are more conservative.

Bowles: Well, I'm not able to say that, really, I haven't seen that in the people who have been through Morocco. Compare and contrast? It seems to me people are what they've always been.

Interviewers: Of the people who do come . . . what does it seem to you they come for?

Bowles: They often bring books for me to sign. They don't have any other specific reason to come, or they don't mention it.

Interviewers: They don't come as "pilgrims"?

Bowles: I hope not.

Interviewers: I guess what we're getting at is—do you feel at all set

up as a guru, particularly with this program with the School of Visual
Arts of New York?

Bowles: God forbid. That's the last thing I want to do. A guru,
indeed: no, no. A guru is never left alone.

Interviewers: We seem to see that you're never left alone when
we're here.

Bowles: Well, that's natural. You're only here three weeks. If you
were here all year, it would be a different story. You'd find more interesting things to do. But all the people who come are people who are
only here for a short while. Possibly 1, 2, 3 days. The summer is not
like the rest of the year. Instead of every day, (in the winter people
might come) 2 or 3 times a week. They come when they come. I can't
stop them; I don't have a phone.

Interviewers: How is it that you don't have a phone?

Bowles: I hate telephones. There are many things I don't like.

Interviewers: Give us a list.

Bowles: Telephones, television, airplanes—all those things I won't
have any truck with. I don't have a television. I've never flown the
Atlantic; I never will. I don't have to. The reason is that everybody's
dead. So I don't have to go back to anybody's death bed. I'm free. It's
a nice thing.

Interviewers: Is that one reason you've chosen a country that doesn't
intrude technology into your life?

Bowles: Well, it wasn't a conscious reason, but very likely that came
into it, because I found Morocco—50 years ago, when I first came—a
pleasingly primitive country.

Interviewers: Could you speak a little bit about magic, as it pertains
to the work that you're doing? In your autobiography, you define it as
"the secret connection between the world of nature and the consciousness of man." You've also said that there's progressively less magic in
the streets of Morocco. Are you trying to preserve that magic?

Bowles: No. I wouldn't try to preserve anything. I was just remarking
on its disappearance, that is, on the modernization of the Moroccan
mind. No, how could you preserve magic? Trying to do that would be
Hitlerian, bring back the dark ages because they were nicer than today.

Interviewers: What is it that has drawn you so much to magic in
your stories?

Bowles: I think that, generally, the magic is only in the Moroccan stories. That's because it's part of the culture. Because you hear about it every day. People come, telling you what's been done to them by magic.

Interviewers: We haven't been here long enough to have experienced any of that.

Bowles: You probably haven't met the right Moroccans. You've met Moroccans who can read and write. But they're a small minority. They've learned to have other points of reference than their own memory. It makes people very different. The kind you meet at the American School would never give you any insight into the magic—in fact, they probably wouldn't want to speak of it. Or they'd speak of it with regret if you insisted: "Well, you know—ignorant people, that's the way they are."

Interviewers: Does that fall into the same category as their disdain for their own music?

Bowles: Probably. They have a feeling that their own culture is very inferior to European culture. That they haven't invented anything. So they feel slightly defensive. I suppose that's natural.

Interviewers: Something I've begun to wonder about after spending time at the S.V.A. is the plight of the creative person here, an artist or a writer. The country is so small and cannot really support the arts.

Bowles: It has no respect for it, in any case. Generally, creative people are considered slightly bonkers.

Interviewers: What do you think is going to happen to some of these (Moroccan) students?

Bowles: Well, they're either going to give it all up and do something else or they're going to emigrate, if they can, to a country where their endeavors are appreciated. They won't be appreciated here. Ever. There's no tradition for that. You're not supposed to be creative—it's evil, it's forbidden. You can't write a book because there's only one Book, the *Koran*. You can't paint pictures because that's forbidden by the *Koran*. You can't make sculptures because that's forbidden. So there's not much left. You could write poetry, I suppose, but even that would be looked on askance, I think. All this is no longer strictly true, but the popular attitude toward these things is still uninformed.

Interviewers: No one composes music?

Bowles: Well, there are some who do pop music for TV, but that's not music.

Interviewers: And melodies for folk music are not written?

Bowles: No. But folk music—that's a whole different thing. Folk music is a tradition.

Interviewers: To take you back just a wee bit on that question that no serious writer makes money. How do you live, Mr. Bowles?

Bowles: Ah. How do I live. How have I lived all my life? . . . Let's see; when I ran away from college and went to Paris I worked as a telephonist at the Paris *Herald Tribune* getting numbers. Then I worked at Banker's Trust doing foreign exchange, a comptometer. Then I went back to America and worked at Dutton's Book Shop on Fifth Avenue. Not that I've made money, but you want to know what I've done . . . Then I had some inheritances that kept me going for a few years—my grandmother, an aunt. Then, just in time, I got to do music for Orson Welles in the Federal Theater. So I joined the Federal Theater project in 1936. From then on I was writing incidental music for Broadway shows. And that went on and on for many years. I was also a music critic for some years on the *New York Herald Tribune.*

Interviewers: Did the theatre music pay well?

Bowles: Well, sure. I still get checks from those things. I just got one the other day for *Summer and Smoke.* . . . Then what happened: I wrote 4 novels, and sold 3 to films. Collected the money that I received on those three novels for the film rights. I live on the interest from that. It's not very much, with inflation, but I can squeak by here; the standard is relatively cheap. And that's what I live on. . . . Well, my father left me . . . (indistinguishable) but the main part was the movie rights.

Interviewers: When were these movies done?

Bowles: They were never made. One was bought by Twentieth Century-Fox, another by Universal, and the other by Aldritch Associates.

Interviewers: Why did they never make the films?

Bowles: Because in every case they got very poor script writers. I have all the scripts. They're unbelievably bad. I think even they themselves realized that, but by that time they had spent too much money and they shelved them all.

Interviewers: They didn't ask you to do the script writing?

Bowles: No, no one ever suggested that. Well, I'd never written a script. I think that's a very specialized form of writing. A novelist really can't do it. Just as a script writer can't write a novel.

Interviewers: So the writing you're doing at the moment is done purely for the love of your work?

Bowles: Completely from the point of view of love for my work. Not at all from the point of view of making money, because there isn't any. I know I'm not going to make any money. I don't expect to.

Interviewers: Rather a wonderful approach, that.

Bowles: I'm lucky to be able to have that point of view, yeah. If I'd been expecting to eat from my writing I think I would have cut my wrists. . . . What's the point of being hungry? I've always imagined that life works things out, somehow. Everything's always worked out and I've never made any plans. If you're ready to accept whatever life offers, it's not so bad. It's only bad if you expected something else. But if you don't expect anything, everything's great.

Interviewers: Has that always been the case with you? Have you never had particular goals in mind?

Bowles: I've never had any goals. My only goal was that I wanted to make something that people would like. I once thought it would be music, but then I decided that that would be too long a time to wait. In fact, you can wait an entire lifetime. You might spend two years writing a piece of music, orchestrating it and so on. Then it goes on the shelf. Someday, maybe, someone will contract to play it; and maybe they won't. If they do, you won't get any money for it. So how are you supposed to live? Well, most composers live by teaching, just as most writers live by teaching. It's lucky that I don't do that, because I couldn't—not really teaching.

Interviewers: How was it you were persuaded to get involved with the writing program at S.V.A.?

Bowles: Well, Silas Rhodes (Founder/President of S.V.A.) is very— what's the word . . .

Interviewers: Persuasive?

Bowles: Persuasive, yes. I said, "But, I'm not a teacher." "DOESN'T MATTER! That doesn't have anything to do with it." "But it must have!"

This was in the early Spring of 1980, when he first came and suggested it I said, "I've done that once, and I never want to have to do it again, because I can't, I'm not a teacher." I told him, "I don't believe that writing can be taught." I still don't believe it.

Interviewers: Is that off the record?

Bowles: You can say it. . . . I don't believe writing can be taught, no. I think that the writer teaches himself by reading—and writing. A writer must read many books, of course, for years and years. A writer generally starts reading books when he's 8 or 9 years old, and keeps reading all through his adolescence, and into his adulthood. By that time he's writing regularly. It should be that way. Of course, nowadays many people don't read books. Not even adults, not to speak of adolescents or children. They don't read them because they can't. *They cannot read.* I find . . . they don't really read the sentences; they scan and see what's on a page. But that isn't reading. And they write, very often, the same way, putting down the words, but not really seeing what the force of the word is in each sentence, all the words in any given sentence. They don't do it that carefully. They don't think it's necessary. I'm speaking of the bad students, of whom there are an awful lot in California. When I was there, at San Fernando State College (1968–69), they even argued about the necessity for writing good English. There were those who took definite stands against it. They said, "That's old-fashioned. English has changed. We don't use the same language any more."

Interviewers: This was the generation in the late '60s that glorified black and substandard English. There was a strenuous sociological argument at that time put forward that kids who spoke Chicano or black patois should be permitted to express themselves without any interference.

Bowles: Well, that's unfortunate. That is, for what they call underprivileged, students of underprivileged families, where English isn't really spoken. That's very hard for them. But that's no reason for lowering your standard.

Interviewers: It's also a judgment which is generally passed by romantic upper-middle class educators, who themselves don't have to live with the consequences of substandard speech.

Bowles: I know. It takes ever greater talent to use colloquial language and make a good book of it, I think. It hasn't been done very well recently. Ring Lardner used to be able to do it.

Interviewers: What do you think of the revival of the oral tradition in the form of performance? Poetry, for example.

Bowles: I don't know. It might be a good idea if people read properly, but they don't. The ones I've heard. I couldn't understand. . . .

They don't enunciate, and they don't project. They read as though they were ashamed of what they were saying.

Interviewers: What do you think of the performers who have their work memorized?

Bowles: I've never seen that.

Interviewers: It's happening more and more. . . . Have there ever been any readings here in Tangier of any consequence?

Bowles: There was a poetry society here; I don't think there is any more. Everybody died or went away. There's no English-speaking colony left here. Tangier was once very international; it isn't any more. . . . I went to one meeting (of the Poetry Society) and didn't go any more. I don't like that sort of thing.

Interviewers: You don't like organized groups of writers?

Bowles: No, no. Why should they organize? Perhaps you can tell me why. I don't know why, why they feel they must. I know there's a great deal of organization in the States.

Interviewers: Much of the organization is around the point of getting money for writers.

Bowles: Oh, getting money. Oh, really. Well, if it gets money for writers, fine. They won't get any for me.

Interviewers: Do you feel a writer should have political commitment? . . . You did have, according to your autobiography. What are your feelings at the moment?

Bowles: Politically?

Interviewers: Does a writer need to have political commitment?

Bowles: I don't think he needs to have it, no. I think that if he's a wide-awake writer, he's going to have it. But I don't think his *work* needs it. But certainly, a writer who has no idea what is going on in the world isn't going to write very useful things.

Interviewers: So you would make a big distinction between political commitment and political awareness?

Bowles: Of course. All the difference in the world. Wouldn't you? I'm not really a joiner, as I said. The only thing I ever joined was the CPUSA.

Interviewers: Is that still affecting your life?

Bowles: It has affected my life very definitely, for years and years. Of course. Oh, yes, all sorts of things happened as a result.

Interviewers: Like what?

Bowles: Well, when we were in Madeira, Mrs. Bowles' passport gave out; we had to go to Lisbon in order to get a new one for her, to the American Embassy. But then they wouldn't give her a new one, and they deported her, although she was ill. They just said, "You've got to leave tomorrow." Bang, get out! And they took the passport away from her. And they said the FBI had refused it, because she was considered a dangerous character by the FBI.

Interviewers: When was that?

Bowles: This was in '58. . . . Here, back in the early fifties, I had to go down and be fingerprinted and write a great long—pages and pages.

Interviewers: Did anybody ever ask you to take a loyalty oath?

Bowles: No. But back when I was in New York in '46 or '47 I was given a job for a year to go to South America and check through the musical libraries, the musical archives, of all the capitals. For the U.S. government. And the night before I was about to go, I got a telephone call from Washington . . . very apologetic. They said, "You will understand why it's out of the question, I'm sure. We have been making a check. You will understand. I'm sorry."

Interviewers: You once said you'd been virtually a prisoner in Morocco for the last nine years, what with problems with your papers.

Bowles: Oh, but that has nothing to do with anything, really. It might have to do with the fact that I write books.

Interviewers: And who doesn't like that?

Bowles: I don't know. Somebody here.

Interviewers: The Moroccan authorities?

Bowles: The Moroccans, yeah.

Interviewers: And it doesn't have anything to do with your previous affiliation with the Communist Party?

Bowles: I doubt it very much. Good Lord, they have plenty of professors teaching their students here who have studied in Prague and Moscow and who are Marxists, to this day. No, I think it's mostly incompetence. And some official who decides, "Now, we have to look out for this character" . . . You can get used to all sorts of things.

Interviewers: Have you any wish to leave Morocco, to be traveling, at the moment?

Bowles: No. That's why it doesn't upset me. Although it kept me from doing certain other things that I could have done.

Interviewers: Such as?

Bowles: Joseph Losey, the film director, wanted me to go to Paris a few years ago and write a score for a new film. But there was no question of it. I couldn't leave Morocco. So I didn't do that.

Interviewers: Did you make any representation (to the authorities)? Has the American Embassy been at all helpful to you here?

Bowles: All we have is a consulate here. The one American Consul was of no use whatever; the present American Consul was helpful, yes, in getting me my "Permis de Sejour" last year. Yes, he was helpful. Ordinarily they don't want to touch me. Well, because the Consulate has all the material on me there; they say, "He was a member of the Communist Party. Why should we help him?" That's the attitude. They don't say that. But they say it in their heads. They say, "Well, I'm very sorry, there's really nothing." I think there are things they could do, if they wanted. Witness the present one who did. And he's a born-again Christian!

Interviewers: Though you haven't renounced your affiliation, you have indicated that it was a passing phase; as for many people in their youths, it's something that one goes through.

Bowles: That's right.

Interviewers: And hasn't this qualification of your stand altered people's official view of you?

Bowles: It doesn't seem to, no. The attitude of the American government is, if anyone ever went so far as to become a member of the Party, then he's really beyond the pale for the rest of his life. He could have been in a front organization or something and claim he didn't realize it. But to have been in the Party itself; he knew what he was doing. So they don't feel kindly disposed to those people.

Interviewers: Did you know what you were doing?

Bowles: What, in joining the Party? Yeah.

Interviewers: You did it conscientiously and without any equivocation?

Bowles: No, I did it as a gesture of defiance, really. Whom was I defying? My family. Yeah. Because they were very anti-communist. They were anti-Semitic. And so the girl I married was Jewish. One's parents often plot one's life for one, negatively.

Interviewers: As George Ade said, "The reaction is something terrible" . . . Did you take any stand on the Vietnam War when you were teaching in California? Did you feel it necessary to take any stand?

Bowles: No. It was never mentioned. . . . As you know, I went back to the States to teach, which I'd never done. I'd been in California, Los Angeles, various times before, so I knew more or less what to expect. But it had changed a lot. Walking along Hollywood Boulevard, a Cadillac would drive up, and people would lean out and say, "Hey, man, you got a dollar for gas?" This happened to me twice. Crazy! I was walking, I didn't have a car. Little things like that impress me. . . . But I can't remember anything in particular about '68 in California. Except that I thought the culture had changed. The people seemed strange, from an alien species. But I put that down to L.A., and not the United States.

Interviewers: You said you had gone for a full year, but ended up staying only one term.

Bowles: That's right. I left at the end of January, 1969.

Interviewers: And that was your last contact with America?

Bowles: That's right.

Interviewers: And you want nothing more to do with it?

Bowles: No, it isn't that. There's no way of getting there except flying, and I don't like to fly, so I stay here. It's really that simple.

Interviewers: It isn't a rejection of the culture then.

Bowles: I think New York is impossible; you can't live there, it's dirty. It's too full of people, it's a mess. . . .

Interviewers: Excuse me, but having been in the medina here!

Bowles: Well, I don't live in the medina! Oh, Tangier is filthy now, of course, but then, the whole world is filthy, as far as I can see. I haven't seen a clean city in years. Not cleanliness the way it was in the '20s.

Interviewers: Come to Washington. It's not too bad there.

Bowles: Washington, D.C.? Well, all right, I'll remember . . . Santa Fe was pretty clean when I was there, but that was in 1965.

Interviewers: If you'd gone to Paris (two years ago) what would you have done? Taken the boat and the train?

Bowles: No, I'd have driven. It's easy. Just pile the luggage into the car.

Interviewers: You've lived here 50 years?

Bowles: I've lived here since '31, but not all the time. I went away at the end of '34 and didn't come back 'til '47, so I was away 13 years.

Interviewers: Have you felt that American culture has been passing you by?

Bowles: It doesn't worry me. I don't believe there is any such thing as "American culture." I mean, what's the difference between American culture and French or German culture? Isn't it all the same thing?

Interviewers: You mean Western civilization now functions globally? Mass media?

Bowles: I mean that Western Europe and America are really the same. Western Europe becomes America a few years later. America does it first and Western Europe becomes . . . quickly imitates it. But it's all one thing, as far as I'm concerned. France is becoming completely American. London has become American, putting up high-rise buildings and using American slang. They believe in American gadgetry—or gadgetism. Whatever we invent, they love.

Interviewers: What do you think about what the Japanese are contributing to the general world?

Bowles: I have never lived in Japan. I don't know. I like the idea of the Japanese because although they've Europeanized themselves, as soon as they get home, they take it all off, as it were, and they become Japanese again. When a businessman goes home, the first thing he does is quickly get out of the horrible clothing and get into a nice kimono.

Interviewers: What about Morocco?

Bowles: Morocco is not one country. It's like India. The culture is regional. People from one part of Morocco are not at all like people from another part. Of course, they're trying to get rid of that by relocating them . . .

Interviewers: Have you seen a change in the attitudes of the Moroccans toward themselves in national terms? Also, in recent years, the religious changes?

Bowles: Fundamentalism is something that's just barely pushed its head above the earth and is stamped out every time it shows itself. In a mosque down the street a man took the place of the Imam . . . He began praising Iran and Khomeini, and saying that was what Morocco needed. And when he finished, the entire congregation went out, and proceeded to riot, and began fighting with police, and smashed up the only liquor store in Tangier. Smashed it up; really smashed it up. But it was owned by Jews; that made it doubly easy. If they had wanted to

smash liquor, they could have gone into the Hotel Minzah, any cafe—
but they didn't; they went to the Jewish liquor store. That made it
stronger, of course—their protest. They had also, these people who
were pro-Khomeini, been studying karate for some years. And when
they had the fights with the police, they injured a lot of police. And
that was extremely bad from the official point of view, that police
should be knocked down by hooligans. And so the police went around
to every karate club to get the names of all the members, and then
they went and arrested each one, going from karate club to karate
club. That's the sort of thing that happens here! Then it turned out that
the false Imam, the replacement, had been sent by the government
purposely, as a provocation. The whole business had been run by the
government. They do strange things here, very strange. *A Thousand
and One . . .*

Interviewers: Have you ever experienced any persecution for talking
openly about the political and religious situation in Morocco?

Bowles: I never talk about religion or politics.

Interviewers: But some of your views have been published in
interviews.

Bowles: Yes, that's true. Well, I've had no troubles that I know of,
but these things may be part of the reason why I don't get my permits.
But one doesn't know; they won't tell you. I remember a few years ago
I went to the police to renew my permis de sejour, and one of the police
looked at me very coyly and said, "Are you still writing about kif?"

Interviewers: I'd like to focus a bit more on the whole question of
contemporary Islam, which the West is confronting now as a serious
force for perhaps the first time ever. I wonder if you have any sense of
what North Americans find so disturbing in Islam.

Bowles: You mean since Iran, the whole Iran thing? But we don't
even consider Iran an Islamic country; it's got nothing to do with Islam,
as far as Morocco is concerned. Most Moroccans would never admit
that they (Iranians) were Muslims. Ask (Mohammed) Mrabet, and he'll
say that they're Jews, that Khomeini is a Jew. As you know, he's gotten
a lot of arms from Israel. The Moroccans consider the Shia Muslims
heretics.

Interviewers: What is the situation between the Jews and Arabs here
in Morocco? Most of the Jews are now gone, and yet so many of the
customs are similar.

Bowles: Traditionally they're indignant with Jews for not being Muslims. They say the Jews have had every chance in the world to become Muslims for centuries, and yet they refuse. They refuse to be Muslims and yet they really are Muslims, bloodwise; they consider Jews to be the same as Arabs. But they think that Jews are headstrong, and refuse to listen to what Islam has to tell them, and go straight ahead blindly with their own false ideas. And therefore they believe that Jews are doing everything they can to destroy Islam. They're speaking of Israel; the Jews in the rest of the world don't do it violently. Since Israel started to be violent, they're absolutely quiet; and they blame the countries around. They say, "Good, I hope she destroys everything, all those stupid countries like Syria, Jordan, Iraq," and so on—who have allowed the Israelis to get all the way up to Beirut. There's only talk—that they got what they deserve.

Interviewers: As a European living in an Islamic country, what are people's reactions to you about the problems in the Middle East?

Bowles: I'm neither Nazarene or Jew to them; one or the other, it's all the same.

Interviewers: So in spite of the time you've spent here, you've not got the sense of having crossed over: you're keenly aware of the cultural barriers.

Bowles: Well, they hold the same thing against me that they do against the Jews. That is, that I've been here all these years and I haven't become a Muslim. Why haven't I? Especially since I claim that I am in agreement with Islam. Why don't I want to become a Muslim? It's impossible to explain to them. They say, "Are you a Christian, then?" and I say, "No, I'm not. I'm not Hindu, not Buddhist." "Then why can't you be a Muslim?" Then I say, "Well, I could. But I can't." (Laughs.) It would be easy if I didn't have a mind of my own. But having a mind of my own, I can't be a Muslim.

Interviewers: Do you find it an authoritarian teaching?

Bowles: No, but I find it a teaching that inhibits thought.

Interviewers: Do you feel that this culture has anything to teach to the West?

Bowles: Oh, a great deal. Of course. Ah, yes. Patience, for one thing. Living quietly, without rushing. Of course, most Americans would like to do that anyway. And acceptance of life as it comes, which I think is important. They never say, "I'm going to do this next week, next month, next year" because they're never sure they're going to be alive. They're always ready to die.

Interviewers: I've noticed that whenever anyone refers to anything that hasn't yet occurred, they always say, "Insha' Allah."

Bowles: They have to, yes. And I think that's very intelligent. How do we know what we're going to do in the future? You might as well blame your inability to do it on God as on anything else . . . I agree with them. I agree with them on many things. But I can't accept any religion. It's simple. I was taught, as a small child, that all religions were bad. And although I know that's not true, it's sort of stuck with me: never get involved with any orthodoxy of any sort.

Interviewers: What has your guiding philosophy been during your life?

Bowles: What a question!

Interviewers: We can narrow it down, if you like.

Bowles: Well, I just told it, I guess. Accept it. Accept what comes, and don't worry if it doesn't come the way you want it. Be thankful that you're still breathing. If you aren't thankful, you ought to get rid of yourself. (Laugh.) I think that's a simple way of looking at it. I've learned a lot from the Moroccans on that score. I've seen them smitten by suffering. But they're wonderful, the way they stand up, and keep saying, "Thanks to God, whatever He has given me, it's all right." I think that's good. Since you've only got one life, you might as well live it happily, rather than complain.

Interviewers: And you're happy?

Bowles: Contented. Yes. Well, I've been much happier than I am now but I don't expect to get happier and happier as I get older.

Interviewers: We've touched on how Morocco possibly drives away its young talent through lack of money and lack of appreciation. Canada is often accused of doing the same thing. I wonder if there is any sense in which you feel you were driven away from the United States.

Bowles: Driven away? Not at all. Because that is the only place I was appreciated. It was the only place I got my music played, the only place I was published.

Interviewers: You haven't published in Paris at all?

Bowles: After having been published in English in America, yes, sure. But you don't get published in Paris, obviously, unless you write in French.

Interviewers: Are there any Canadian writers who have particularly come to your attention?

Bowles: Years ago someone named Leonard Cohen began sending me his books, you know, "with appreciation . . ."

Interviewers: As one expatriate to another.

Bowles: Mmmhmm. And I thought, "Oh, he's a madman." But I don't know him. He probably isn't.

Interviewers: Do you follow any contemporary American writers?

Bowles: One or two. William Wilson, Tobias Wolfe. They're good. [*Why I Don't Write Like Franz Kafka; In the Garden of the North American Martyrs*]

Interviewers: You don't have much trouble with talking about American things. Your work has been very much . . .

Bowles: I haven't written much about America, of course, very little.

Interviewers: Where do you think the novel is going today?

Bowles: It seems to be disintegrating, falling to pieces. I don't know if it will completely, or what will come out of it. More and more books are categorized as novels, which would never have been considered novels fifty years ago: because they're not novels, not according to the traditional way of thinking. Well, a hundred years ago, would *Ulysses* have been a novel? Never. Two hundred years ago, would *Moby Dick* have been a novel? Never.

Interviewers: Are you inclined at all to experimental writing?

Bowles: Well, I've often experimented, but not with form. Because it seems to me that what I want to say would be dulled by experimental form. I want to say it as clearly as possible, in straight prose, so that everyone can understand it.

Interviewers: So where is the experiment in your writing, do you feel?

Bowles: The experimentation is in the subject matter.

Interviewers: Do you have—I hesitate to use the word 'ambition' because I've read elsewhere that you don't have any—

Bowles: You're right.

Interviewers: But artistically, is there something at the moment that you feel a need to do, something that you would like to tackle?

Bowles: No. Sorry, I have to say no. Ideas come in a flash. And they either come, or they don't come. I've never tried to push anything. I let it happen. If it doesn't happen—too bad. But I don't think that forcing anything gives good results.

Interviewers: Is that one explanation for why you haven't had a tremendous output in your life?

Bowles: Undoubtedly. I don't believe that volition helps, since writing comes out of the unconscious, in any case. You can't really force it.

Interviewers: Who was the French writer who set himself a goal to write 3 or 4 hours a day?

Bowles: Well, that's admirable. Who was that? Flaubert, probably. (Laugh.)

Interviewers: But you do have a regimen for your days?

Bowles: Well, yesterday was pretty typical . . . Writing letters, typing things, correcting proofs, going to market . . . I'm not always busy writing.

Interviewers: When it happens, then you write.

Bowles: Then I can write a lot. I may finish the whole thing very quickly.

Interviewers: What's the average time for a book?

Bowles: For a novel? Well, there's no average. The first one took eight months, the second took about 2 years, the third took another 8 or 9 months. The fourth—well, it was started one year and finished the next, and in between I was doing many other things, travel notes and so on. It took about 6 months.

Interviewers: And interrupting your work doesn't affect the flow of the idea?

Bowles: Not if I've already written part of it. If it's not written, then probably, if I traveled, I'd never write it; I'd give it up. But I can work traveling—have done, very often.

Interviewers: You find travel highly stimulating.

Bowles: Yeah. Boat travel is the best. I got on a boat in 1957, and while I was on the ship, I managed to write a long article for *Holiday* and an entire, long short story. The day I got off the ship in Sri Lanka, I mailed one off to *Holiday* and the other to *Harper's Bazaar*. They used to publish fiction. . . . Working on shipboard is easy because you know the hours of your feeding. It's like being in the hospital. It's wonderful—nothing ever happens, . . . every day is like the day before, to the minute, which is perfect for work.

Interviewers: It gives the imagination room to play.

Bowles: It leaves you free, that's right, absolutely free. You have no responsibility whatever, which is wonderful.

Interviewers: When you're trying to relax from your work, where do you go for enjoyment, peace of mind, or whatever?

Bowles: Into the other room.

Interviewers: Do you listen to music much?

Bowles: Sometimes I sit down and compose, because I do write music still.

Interviewers: But you don't have a keyboard here.

Bowles: Yes, I have. I have an electric organ in my bedroom. It's small, a Phillips. It's useful. I'd rather have a piano, but that's out of the question here. I've had a lot of pianos here in Tangier. They get pretty awful; the climate doesn't agree with them. It's dry and then suddenly very damp, and then dry . . . back and forth. It's very wet here in the winter, your shoes grow mildew on them.

Interviewers: Have you published the music you've composed in the last few years?

Bowles: No. It's not meant for that.

Interviewers: And you're not sending it to the Library of Congress?

Bowles: I've never sent anything to the Library of Congress, except recordings of Moroccan music.

Interviewers: But they have copies of some of your sheet music.

Bowles: Have they?

Interviewers: Yes.

Bowles: I didn't know. Where, in the archives?

Interviewers: Yes. They're catalogued—a piece you did—*In the Summer House,* I guess.

Bowles: They have that? They have the score to that? But I've been wondering where it was for the last 30 years. I haven't anything, you see. All my things disappeared.

Interviewers: They also have a piece you did for Gertrude Stein, some theatre music for Tennessee Wiliams, and some others.

Bowles: That's interesting to me, because I've been trying to find things for 20 or 30 years. My sheet music and my manuscripts, they've all disappeared. A lot of them turned up in Austin, Texas, in the Humanities Research Center of the University of Texas.

Interviewers: How so?

Bowles: Someone sold them to them, obviously. The closet where everything was, was opened and things were taken out, in New York. And obviously letters and certain other things were sold. Nobody gives the University of Texas anything. They pay too well. Or did.

Interviewers: Well, do you want copies of that music?

Bowles: Yeah, I'm trying to get things together; I'm going to have a volume of old songs published next year or this year in the States. And I've been rewriting and trying to get ahold of . . . Why can't you shut the door quietly?! These people bang everything. Night and day. Moroccans often annoy me considerably, from that point of view. In the old days, this building was strictly European. Since they've moved in, there's noise day and night, they leave their doors open, and they have brats who come out into the halls, and they scream from one flat to another. I don't know how anyone can accept that!

Interviewers: An awful lot seems to happen at night here. I'm used to quiet; it's anything but quiet at night here.

Bowles: You're right. And next door to me, it's anything but quiet. Because no one lives in the flat, but people rent it by the night or by the hour, and they get the key from a grocery store somewhere, they just go in and ask for the key, and pay whatever the money is, and then they come here—10, 12 people, all screaming and yelling, at 1:30 in the morning. Bang, bang, screaming. They drink, they break the elevator— that's why it's broken today—they break the windows, the front door, they smash the glass . . .

Interviewers: I thought that was part of Tangier: slamming doors and breaking windows.

Bowles: It may be part of their Tangier; it's not part of mine. I never wanted to live in close proximity to Moroccans for reasons of comfort. You can't: they're not quiet people, and they see no reason for being quiet. But at the age of 71, I can't suddenly disregard noise.

Interviewers: How's your health?

Bowles: Health? Will you give me the insurance if I tell you? . . . I think it's all right.

Interviewers: What's your notion about continuing the program with S.V.A.?

Bowles: I don't know. Each summer I say, I won't do this again. And then Mr. Rhodes comes and starts giving me pep talks. I say, "Well." It's not all that hard.

Interviewers: We are very glad that you did it this year.

Bowles: Well, I'm glad I did it this year, too. I had a good class last year. It's not easy, I mean, to have a good class. All you need is 5 or 6 bad ones and somehow the class is ruined. . . . That's why I thought this group was lucky, I was lucky . . .

Interviewers: This year they had a writer's conference in London.

Bowles: Oh, really?

Interviewers: In the United States they have a proliferation of writers conferences this summer.

Bowles: What's it all about?

Interviewers: It has to do with money.

Bowles: Whenever I ask about America the answer is money. That's nice.

Interviewers: People have more leisure time so that there are suddenly more visible writers. People in the drawers are coming out with manuscripts.

Bowles: Well, that's good. There's nothing wrong with that.

Interviewers: Apart from writing, what are your passions in life?

Bowles: Traveling. If you can call that a passion. And music, of course. Never a day goes by that I don't listen to lots of music.

Interviewers: Modern music?

Bowles: Not necessarily. I listen a lot to Bach. I've always been a great jazz fan. Not rock. Folk music in general I like but not commercial folk music. The expression is an antinomy.

Interviewers: Is there any one incident in your life that has marked you?

Bowles: More than anything else? That's very hard. . . . Well, coming here to Morocco and seeing the enormous crowds of people in Fez torturing themselves and so on, going into trances. . . . That fascinated me more than anything. Watching people leave themselves—I find that very interesting. I don't know why. I don't see a reason for it; perhaps there's a Jungian reason, or a Freudian reason; I don't know. I'm not an analyst. I've always refrained from analyzing. I don't want to know what makes it work.

Interviewers: You can't fix things?

Bowles: . . . I can't repair a radio or a car, no.

Interviewers: These people, "going out of themselves," you must have seen it in other cultures . . . Indians, for instance.

Bowles: Not to the extent that I've seen it in Morocco. I've seen Hindus rolling around the temples, hundreds of them, in piles of rice, smearing it on their bodies; their bodies were completely covered with rice. . . . But what the Indians do doesn't interest me as much as what the Moroccans do. Because, I think, we're so much farther away from that. After all, Islam is part of Judeo-Christianity, really. Both Christianity and Islam are forms of reformed Judaism. You know that. You may not believe it, but it's true. Isn't it? You don't see it as true? The Jews come first; the Christians adopted their religion. Jesus was a Jew, all the disciples were Jews. . . . But Hinduism is something so far away. Buddhism is much nearer, for me.

Interviewers: Has what you saw with these people in Fez and other places had much of an influence on your writing?

Bowles: I think it did. Certain stories. It comes into *The Spider's House*. Yes, it affected the way I thought . . . in the realization that, in order to be human, one didn't have to subscribe to any particular form of behavior, that one could lose one's self, that it was all right to froth at the mouth and fall in the street, nothing bad would happen. One could scream all day, cut oneself, hit oneself with a hatchet in the head as they do, or stick bull's horns into their intestines or their flanks, or spin round and round till they fall—it seemed to me a marvelous kind of freedom, for human beings to be able to do that, and then a few hours later, to be driving a taxi, or serving you drinks in a hotel.

Interviewers: Are you satisfied with your work, where you are?

Bowles: Yes. Well, it would be foolish not to be. . . . Not that I think it's very good! But if I were now at the age of 30, I probably wouldn't write the novels the way I wrote them, and everything would be different. But that's of no importance, really. I did what I could do at that time. That tense, "would have been," doesn't really mean anything.

Interviewers: You don't regret, for example, not having written more poetry?

Bowles: No. I rather regret having written any. It's true . . . Now that I see what poetry really is. I see that mine was "next door."

Interviewers: If you were forced to leave Morocco, where would you go?

Bowles: That's one of the worst questions. Probably to the United States.

Interviewers: And that would kill you?

Bowles: Kill me?! Well, life is going to kill me, I'm not sure when. I don't know if it would be the United States that would kill me. Morocco may kill me, who knows?

Interviewers: Have you thought about that? Can I ask you how you'd like to die, and where?

Bowles: Oh, surely; I'd like to die quickly and without any pain.

Interviewers: And in Morocco?

Bowles: Well, I don't care. . . . It's too bad that one has to have funerals and things like that. Maybe there wouldn't have to be any. But then there's the disposal of the body; that's the trouble. Why one has to have a body, I don't know. A necessary appendage to the head, I suppose. I always wished I didn't have a body. I suppose everyone does.

Paul Bowles in Exile

Jay McInerney/1985

From *Vanity Fair* [New York] 48 (September 1985):69–76, 131.
Reprinted by permission of International Creative Management, Inc.

Paul Bowles opened the world of Hip. He let in the murder, the drugs, the incest, the death of the Square . . . the call of the orgy, the end of civilization.

—Norman Mailer

As the faithful poured into the mosque for prayer, I searched for the door to a restaurant reputedly just across the street and tried to seem inconspicuous. It was my second night in Tangier. Men in dark robes huddled on the street corners, lowering their voices as I approached. The few women in evidence were upholstered in black from head to foot and looked like bandit nuns. I came upon an entrance gate at which two men in djellabas were either lounging or standing guard. I tentatively pronounced the name of my destination. They looked at each other, nodded, and ushered me inside. Even as I stepped forward I was thinking that they were too unkempt and uninviting to be doormen, and that the building before me was too dark and sinister for a public place. But I was committed. Advancing into the murky courtyard I heard the two men, both very large for Moroccans, hissing behind me. I recognized the situation immediately. It had all the ingredients of a Paul Bowles story.

I never found out what the hissing was about. The older of the two men caught up with me and led the way to the restaurant. I was relieved but vaguely disappointed, and later recalled something Bowles had said during the day: What can go wrong is always much more interesting than what goes right.

Paul Bowles's sense of what can go wrong is as acute as that of any American writer since Poe. In "A Distant Episode," one of his best-known stories, a professor of linguistics in search of new dialects ventures beyond the walls of a desert town one night and descends into a valley settlement—"an abyss"—realizing as he does that "he ought to ask himself why he was doing this irrational thing." He proceeds nonetheless, only to be set upon by nomadic tribesmen who beat him,

180

cut out his tongue, and dress him up in strings of flattened tin cans to serve as a jester, an object of amusement.

In his first and most famous novel, *The Sheltering Sky,* a husband and wife travel deeper and deeper into the Sahara, their flirtation with danger and their betrayals of each other finally consummated in madness and death. It's not simply the subject matter but the pitiless clarity, the unblinking regard in the face of human frailty and cruelty, that is so disquieting in Bowles's work. Whereas the terror in Poe seems to arise from an overheated romantic imagination suffering the torments it bodies forth, Bowles's sensibility is classical in its aloofness, his prose as hard-edged and dazzling as a desert landscape at noon.

If Paul Bowles, now seventy-four, were Japanese, he would probably be designated a Living National Treasure; if he were French, he would no doubt be besieged by television crews from the literary talk show *Apostrophes.* Given that he is American, we might expect him to be a part of the university curriculum, but his name rarely appears in a course syllabus. Perhaps because he is not representative of a particular period or school of writing, he remains something of a trade secret among writers. Of course, Bowles hasn't exerted himself in the matter of greasing the machinery of celebrity. He has never been in this country when a book of his was published, and much of his life has been spent several days' travel beyond a poste restante address. More significantly, his dark view of the species, as well as his rejection of the *Zeitgeist* of his age, may be too categorical and severe for most tastes. His estimation of human nature is like that of Calvinism without the prospect of salvation.

This month, Ecco Press is reissuing Bowles's autobiography, *Without Stopping,* which quietly disappeared shortly after its publication, in 1972, and has long been out of print. Once again available, the book should spark renewed interest in Bowles's work and a reappraisal of his career.

Lying just southwest of Gibraltar, within sight of Spain, across the famous strait, Tangier was, when Bowles first saw it, in 1931, an internationally administered city consisting of a crowded and labyrinthine native quarter—the medina—surrounded by a European community. There were only a handful of taxicabs then, Bowles recalls, and many more eucalyptus trees than there are now, but the latter-day tourist who enters the medina will feel much like the protagonist in Bowles's 1952 novel, *Let It Come Down.*

> The places through which he was passing were like the tortuous corridors in dreams. It was impossible to think of them as streets, or even as alleys. There were spaces here and there among the buildings, that was all, and some of them opened into other spaces and some did not. If he found the right series of connections he could get from one place to the next, but only by going through the buildings themselves. And the buildings seem to have come into existence like plants, chaotic, facing no way, topheavy, one growing out of the other.

Outside the medina, however, the vistas open up: the sky is brilliant; the Atlantic, mottled blue and green, about to encounter the Mediterranean, is suddenly visible as one turns the corner on a block of white stucco houses.

The day of my first visit to Bowles's apartment, a three-room flat on the top floor of a concrete edifice across from the American Consulate, a flock of sheep are grazing in the side yard. The living room has a permanent twilight aspect, and a fire always burns in the grate, regardless of the temperature outside. The sweet aroma of kif pervades the air. Although Bowles has inhabited the apartment for more than twenty-five years, it has the provisional look of a temporary encampment—the foyer is crowded with a large stack of suitcases, and framed paintings by Bowles's friend Brion Gysin lean against a wall. On a small end table lies a shiny new volume of Kafka's collected stories, one of the few objects that appear to belong exactly where they are.

"Would you like some tea?" Bowles asks after apologizing for the weather.

He rises to greet his visitors, of whom there is a steady influx, extending a hand and addressing them in whatever language is appropriate—French, Spanish, Arabic, or English. He is extremely polite and courtly in manner, giving the impression of someone who does not take social occasions for granted. His dress is rather formal for relaxing at home: a tie, a cardigan, and a tweed jacket. The black cigarette holder seems quite natural and unaffected. My first impression, of extreme delicacy, is modified over the course of the afternoon by evidence of a sinewy vigor. A friend of his wrote, "He has the beauty of a fallow deer"; my feeling is that a predator who tried to make a meal of Bowles would find his digestion unpleasantly disrupted. The craggy demeanor and laconic air seem to betray his New Hampshire roots.

On the sofa are two Moroccans: Mohammed Mrabet, one of several illiterate storytellers whose oral tales and novels Bowles has translated into English, and a young musician, who is oiling and polishing a wooden flute. "It's like cleaning a shotgun," Bowles remarks of the process, a whistle in his *s*'s, as he settles onto a cushion. The musician begins to play, filling the room with a breathy, haunting sound. Bowles nods appreciatively. When the music ends, Mrabet is eager to take center stage. He is a handsome man who appears to be in his thirties, although he claims to be fifty-four; Bowles thinks he is in his late forties. Mrabet has the sadsack aspect of Buster Keaton. He begins to complain about the difficulties of his life, speaking of several of his children who have died. *"Paul, yo he sufrido más que tú. Tú no has sufrido. Yo, yo he sufrido."* He has suffered, Paul has not. Bowles smiles. The litany is apparently familiar. But when I express my sympathy, Mrabet becomes almost indignant. *"Todo es perfecto"*—everything is perfect—he says, expressing the Islamic belief that all is as Allah wills it. It is clear that Mrabet relishes attention, that he is a born performer, and that Bowles relishes the performances, not least perhaps because he finds in Mrabet something of an alter ego. Mrabet's tales of woe are in keeping with Bowles's somewhat morbid tastes.

The conversation—about Tangier, about music and writing—proceeds in English and Spanish. Rodrigo Rey Rosa, a young Guatemalan writer whose work Bowles is translating, arrives with his girfriend. Cigarettes are emptied and refilled with kif. Bowles listens to the talk with an intensity that reminds me of a robin poised, head cocked, on a wet lawn; he dips forward suddenly to clarify a point or to dispute an opinion. Asked if he particularly admires any living American writers, Bowles taps his cigarette holder thoughtfully against the lip of an ashtray, then sits back and looks earnestly at the ceiling. Finally he asks, "Is Flannery O'Connor still alive?" When the field is expanded to include South America, he is able to endorse Jorge Luis Borges without hesitation.

When Bowles's friends wish to talk to him, they come to visit, for he has not had a phone in sixteen years. "Who can be bothered?" he says. "You'll be working, or else you're in the bathtub, and the phone rings.

You answer and a voice says, '*Allo,* Mohammed?'" One quickly gets
the sense that Bowles, having spent most of his life in undeveloped
parts of the world—North Africa, Sri Lanka, Central America—does
not have much use for high technology. He hates air travel, which is
one of the reasons he has not been to the United States since 1968, when
he taught college for a semester in California. The suitcases in the foyer
bear the yellowing tags of dry-docked steamers.

"I don't particularly like mechanization, pollution, noise—all the
things the twentieth century has brought and scattered over the world,"
he says, his voice soft, his accent patrician. "Who does, except those
who have made money by it? I can't imagine anyone embracing it."

Bowles's fiction often presents Americans in flight from civilization,
looking for escape from the bourgeois ideals of industrial progress and
teleological rationality. This is not a unique theme in Western literature,
but what makes Bowles's work so different is his tough-mindedness, his
refusal to romanticize the exotic—something that the hippies who
showed up at his door in the sixties failed to notice. "They would appear
here," he remembers, "and say, 'Hey, man, can I crash with you?' I
gather I was supposed to be a guru. But I never went in for acting."

Westerners who don djellabas and climb on camels in the hope of a
quick spiritual boost are, in Bowles's view, as naïve as Arabs who bor-
row European customs wholesale. Bowles's protagonists, seeking the
unknown, often discover the chaos that underlies the civilized mind.
Ultimately his fiction is concerned not so much with the meeting of cultures as with the peeling away of layers of acculturation, the stripping of
character and humanity to essential elements. He has more in common
with Samuel Beckett than with T. E. Lawrence.

Bowles cautions against taking his fiction to represent the actual
landscape of North Africa, and he sometimes speaks of his long
residence in Morocco as if it were purely accidental, a matter of
washing up on that shore rather than another. But one cannot help
feeling the symbiosis between the writer and his adopted environment.
Though *Without Stopping* is in general one of the most unrevealing
American autobiographies since Benjamin Franklin's, Bowles writes
frankly in it of his attachment to Tangier.

> If I am here now, it is only because I was still here when I realized to
> what an extent the world had worsened, and that I no longer wanted to
> travel. In defense of the city I can say that so far it has been touched by

fewer of the negative aspects of contemporary civilization than most cities
of its size. More important than that, I relish the idea that in the night, all
around me in my sleep, sorcery is burrowing its invisible tunnels in every
direction, from thousands of senders to thousands of unsuspecting recipients. Spells are being cast, poison is running its course; souls are being
dispossessed of parasitic pseudo-consciousnesses that lurk in the unguarded recesses of the mind.

There is drumming out there most nights. It never awakens me; I hear the
drums and incorporate them into my dream, like the nightly cries of the
muezzins. Even if in the dream I am in New York, the first *Allah akbar!*
effaces the backdrop and carries whatever comes next to North Africa,
and the dream goes on.

Bowles, a surrealist sympathizer, seems to have associated Morocco
with the anarchic forces of the unconscious. As an artist, he discovered
in North Africa a landscape and culture which are the objective
correlatives of his vision of the psyche.

The population of Tangier represents several cultures and centuries:
women in gray djellabas, only their eyes visible between wimple and
kerchief; men in business suits; country Berbers driving donkeys
along the sidewalk; cabdrivers in neo-Italian fashions piloting
twenty-year-old Mercedes *grands taxis*. It is still possible to get lost in
the medina for quite some time, and if one is obviously confused,
obviously a tourist, he will soon be set upon by "guides," hustlers,
hashish dealers, and predatory carpet sellers. For the visitor, the
combination of the almost subterranean landscape and the alien culture of the place can be very menacing, although Bowles dismisses
the likelihood of any real danger.

Paul Bowles makes his way around town in a bronze 1967 Mustang.
The day after I arrived, he picked me up at my hotel for a trip into
the hills outside of town. His driver, a tall Moroccan named Abdulwahaid, held the door for me. Life in Tangier, for an expatriate author
living largely on modest royalties, is a blend of luxury and deprivation:
the equivalent of a month's rent on a studio apartment in Manhattan
pays the annual salary of a chauffeur or cook—or buys two months'
supply of scarce firewood for heating, Bowles's biggest expense.

Abdulwahaid, whose name means "slave of the unique," stops at the
post office and picks up several airmail letters and a small package.
Bowles complains about the few stray clouds in the sky and then in-
structs Abdulwahaid to drive us up the Montaña Vieja, which winds
along a ridge overlooking Tangier and the Atlantic. Cobbles from an old

Roman highway are still visible in the roadbed. Bowles and Abdulwahaid converse in Spanish, both using the familiar form of address.

Most of the houses we pass are secluded behind white walls overhung
with bougainvillea and other flowering vines. "This is my favorite part
of town," Bowles says, leaning forward in his seat to take in the scenery
and the memories, pointing out the villa Tennessee Williams once
rented, and then the gate of the house where he and his wife, Jane, lived
in '54, and then the place he stayed in '31, when he first arrived in
Tangier.

The son of a Long Island dentist, Bowles is descended from old New
England stock. Of his odd and isolated childhood he writes in his autobiography: "At the age of five I had never yet even spoken to another
child or seen children playing together. My idea of the world was still
that of a place inhabited exclusively by adults."

When he was eighteen and already a published poet, he went, like
Poe, to the University of Virginia, but he left within a year and ran
away briefly to Paris, where he sought out the community of artists and
writers living abroad.

Bowles was twenty years old when he again traveled to Paris, this
time as Aaron Copland's student. Having established a correspondence
with Gertrude Stein, he one day appeared at her door with a sheaf of
poems. Stein, never reticent with her opinions, told him he was no poet
and suggested he stick to music. When she also suggested Tangier as a
good place to spend the summer, he and Copland decided to go. Bowles
contracted typhoid fever on his second visit, that winter, but North
Africa continued to draw him back. He spent the following winter in the
M'Zab region of the Sahara; almost fifteen years later this landscape
was to become the setting, and ultimately the protagonist, of *The
Sheltering Sky*.

Though he continued to travel in Europe and Latin America, Bowles
resided mainly in New York during the thirties and forties, becoming a
regular at Kirk and Constance Askew's legendary salon, and briefly
joining the Communist Party. He supported himself as a composer of
theater music, in which capacity he collaborated with Orson Welles,
Elia Kazan, William Saroyan, and Tennessee Williams. Bowles was
acclaimed by such peers as Virgil Thompson for his original compositions, including *The Wind Remains,* an opera that in 1943 was conducted by Leonard Bernstein and danced by Merce Cunningham at the

Museum of Modern Art. In 1937 he met Jane Auer, a young aspiring
writer. They barely knew each other when they decided to take a
trip together to Mexico, and within a year they were married.

The marriage was an eccentric one, punctuated by long separations,
dual residences, and other partners on both sides—at one point their
mutual friend Libby Holman proposed to Paul—but those who knew
them both agree that it was a remarkable romance. Bowles's sto-
icism flickers somewhat when he mentions his deceased wife, whom
he usually refers to as Mrs. Bowles. As for Jane, an old friend of
hers says, "She used to call him Fluffy and Bubbles. Can you
imagine? Paul? That prickly man? It was the most extraordinary
thing." That the austere Mr. Bowles would answer to these appella-
tions says much about the intimacy of their relationship. "She was
his muse," adds the friend. "You have to understand that."

Bowles had set writing aside when he discovered his talent for
music. He credits his wife with inspiring him to return to the
typewriter. "I never would have known that I wanted to start writing
again if I hadn't been with her when she was writing her first novel,"
Bowles acknowledges of the time Jane was at work on *Two Serious
Ladies*. "I got really interested in the whole process, and thought, I
wish I had written this book. I started writing stories about two years
after she published her novel."

The urge to write seemed inextricable from the urge to return to
North Africa. On the strength of several short stories, Bowles found an
agent. Doubleday gave him an advance against a novel, and in the
summer of 1947 he sailed to Casablanca. He had only a vague outline in
mind of the book he wanted to write, something about three Americans moving across the Sahara. "My idea was that the people would
keep moving into the desert," he says, "that one would get ill and die,
and at that point it would write itself."

Bowles traveled alone into the Algerian Sahara to work on the novel.
"I wrote in bed in hotels in the desert," he says. When he reached the
point where Port, the central character in the first half of the novel,
becomes sick, Bowles realized that he had come to his crucial juncture.
He wanted to describe Port's death from the interior of Port's mind,
and to do so he decided to take *majoun,* a potent cannabis confection.
"It gave me everything," he says. "Not that day. The day I took it I
couldn't have written anything. I was lying flat on my back. I was lying

on my back, dying. Not unhappy. Port's death became my death. That more or less broke the ice. I didn't need to take it after that."

The immense domed sky of the Sahara dominates the book. Early on, Port muses, "I often have the sensation when I look at it that it's a solid thing up there, protecting us from what's behind." As he is dying in the desert he sees the sky crack open, and in one of the most convincing and harrowing evocations of death since Tolstoy's *Ivan Ilyich* he looks into the void beyond. From there the novel follows Port's wife, Kit (who people in Tangier will assure you is a ringer for Jane), as she moves into the Sahara, fleeing the memory of her adultery with Port's friend Tunner, pursuing the primitive and the unknown, surrendering herself to a Bedouin who rapes her, finally leaving her reason behind. Bowles's desert becomes—like Conrad's jungle and Eliot's waste-land—a symbolic landscape, emblematic of a world in which individuals are radically isolated from one another.

Bowles finished *The Sheltering Sky* in nine months. "I sent it out to Doubleday," he says, "and they refused it. They said, 'We asked for a novel.' They didn't consider it a novel. I had to give back my advance. My agent told me later they called the editor on the carpet for having refused the book—only after they saw that it was selling fast. It only had to do with sales. They didn't bother to read it."

Eventually another house, New Directions, accepted the book; in the meantime Bowles sailed to New York to do the score for *Summer and Smoke*. Before he left again for Tangier, he persuaded Tennessee Williams to accompany him. "As always on a ship, I stayed in the cabin and generally in my berth, writing," he says of the journey. "It's a perfect place to write. I wrote this story and took it around to Tennessee's cabin, and he read it and said, 'Oh, I think it's wonderful, Paul, but you mustn't publish that story—people will think you're a monster.'" Bowles laughs and adds, "I was very flattered."

The piece he showed to Williams was to become "The Delicate Prey," the title story of his first collection. In it, a Moungari tribesman who commits an extremely gruesome murder is discovered by kinsmen of the victim, who take the murderer out into the desert and bury him up to his neck. The tale ends with one of the most striking images in contemporary fiction: "When they had gone the Moungari fell silent, to wait through the cold hours for the sun that would bring first warmth, then heat, thirst, fire, visions. The next night he did not know where he was, did not feel the cold. The wind blew dust along the ground into his mouth as he sang.''

Bowles expresses sympathy for the surrealist notion of shocking the bourgeoisie out of its complacency by dredging up the raw material of the unconscious and exposing it to daylight. Norman Mailer's apocalyptic assessment of Bowles's work places it in this current of literary terrorism. But like one of his characters. Bowles claims that for him writing is merely a form of personal therapy. ''I don't like the things I write about,'' he protests when asked why so much of his work deals with the dark side of human nature. ''It's a kind of exorcism. It doesn't mean that I approve of what goes on in the pages of my book—God forbid.''

After Tennessee Williams left Tangier, Truman Capote arrived and moved into the hotel in which Paul and Jane were staying. Of Capote, Bowles says dryly, ''We did not lack for entertainment at mealtimes.''

At this point, in the early fifties, Tangier was assuming the aspect of an international literary salon. The presence of Jane and Paul Bowles served as a magnetic force; then again, like the Americans who had moved to Paris in the twenties, the fashionable refugees landing in Tangier were attracted by cheap living and the atmosphere of duty-free morality. Male homosexuality was openly tolerated in Morocco. The second sons of English lords—and even first sons facing the burden of steep inheritance taxes—found that their pounds, if they could smuggle them into Tangier, went far. With life back in the States becoming increasingly puritan, Barbara Hutton, the Woolworth heiress, bought a palace in the Casbah and threw lavish parties. The Honorable David Herbert, son of the Earl of Pembroke, presided over the city's social life, as he still does today. A close friend of the Bowleses', Herbert once promised to marry Jane if anything ever happened to Paul.

Bowles, neither a joiner nor an avid partygoer, continued to travel, write, and compose. In 1955 he completed *The Spider's House,* which presciently depicted the Moroccan struggle for independence, and which remains invaluable, aside from its novelistic virtues, for its sympathetic insights into Islamic culture and postcolonial politics.

In the mid-fifties Bowles began to encounter members of the Beat movement. He first met William S. Burroughs in the spring of 1954. ''He was living down in the medina, in a brothel,'' says Bowles. ''He lay in bed all day, shot heroin, and practiced sharpshooting with a pistol against the wall of his room. I saw the wall, all pockmarked with bullet holes. I said to him, 'Why are you shooting your wall, Bill?' He said, 'It's good practice.' I didn't get to know him until '55, '56. He was writing *Naked Lunch*."

I ask Bowles about Burroughs's claim that he did not remember writing *Naked Lunch,* and he came out of a junk coma one day and it was simply there. "He ought to remember it," Bowles answers. "It was all over the floor. There were hundreds of pages of yellow foolscap all over the floor, month after month, with heel prints on them, rat droppings, bits of old sandwiches, sardines. It was filthy. I said, 'What is all that, Bill?' He said, 'That's what I'm working on.' 'Do you have a copy of it?' I asked. 'No,' he said." Bowles manages a convincing imitation of Burroughs's harsh mid-western growl. "I couldn't help myself from saying, 'Why don't you pick it up?' Candy bar in hand, he said, 'Oh, it'll get picked up someday.' As he finished a page, he'd just throw it on the floor."

Jack Kerouac was in Tangier in 1956, but Bowles, who was in Portugal at the time, did not meet him. When Allen Ginsberg arrived, Bowles was again away, this time in Sri Lanka. "Jane wrote a wonderful letter," he remembers, "telling me that Ginsberg had called up. She'd never heard of him. He said, in his brash fashion, 'Hello, this is Allen Ginsberg, the bop poet.' She said, 'The what?' He said, 'The bop poet.' And she said, 'I got the poet, but the *what* poet?' He said, *'Bop, bop, bop.'* And she said, 'All right.' Then he said, 'Do you believe in God, Jane?' And she said, 'I'm certainly not going to discuss it on the telephone. You'd better wait until Paul gets home.'"

Ginsberg was traveling with Alan Ansen and Peter Orlovsky. Soon after they arrived, Ginsberg and Ansen began sorting through the papers on Burroughs's floor. "I used to go over to Bill's apartment," says Bowles, "and they would all be sitting there, and Allen, who hasn't got a good reading voice, would be reading out loud. Bill wouldn't read it out loud. Hearing Allen Ginsberg read it, it wasn't very impressive. Have you heard him?" Bowles begins to drone a nasal Buddhist raga. "Anyway, Bill is wonderful reading his own stuff, but he wouldn't— I don't know why. He didn't think it existed yet. It was on the floor. So they put it together, and it spelled *mother*. Once it was published and I was able to read it cover to cover, I liked it. I read it three times. I think

Bills' the greatest American humorist. I wish he'd concentrate on humor."

Bowles is frequently lumped in with the Beats in surveys of American literature, but his relation to the movement is a little like that of Manet to the Impressionists; Bowles stood between the European modernists and the Beats, an elder patron with an affinity for Beat ideals. "I was never part of a group," Bowles says, "but I felt sympathy for the Beats. I approved of their existence as a group. It seemed a new thing. I thought it was careless, though. There's a certain amount of carelessness in the writing of all those people." The fastidious craftsman shakes his head and smiles ruefully. "Jane said, 'I think they've all *just* read Céline.' "

When asked if he and others in the Tangier literary community ever discussed their work together, Bowles replies emphatically, "No. Bill and I talked about the dollar and what it was worth, or who had invaded whom with what justification. Nobody ever talks about his work except a few maniac writers, some that shouldn't even write. They're generally the ones who talk about their writing." Clearly, Bowles has not spent much time on campus recently, and I don't want to be the one to tell him that talking about writing is the growth industry of publishing and the humanities.

I ask Bowles if he and Jane ever talked about their work with each other. "When it was finished we did," he says. "Sometimes Jane discussed it in the middle of writing. It wasn't really a discussion—she would call me from the next room and say. 'What genus is the canary?' or 'Exactly how do you build a cantilever bridge?' I said, 'Does it matter how it was built? The word *cantilever* tells the whole story.' She said, 'I've got to know how it was made.' In the end she simply spoke of a bridge going across the gorge. She had to build the bridge before she could talk about it.

"We would work in hotels when we were traveling. We would have adjoining rooms. She'd be in her bed working, and I'd be in my bed working. She'd call out, 'Is it *i-e* or *e-i*?' " Bowles smiles at the memory.

In 1957 Jane Bowles suffered a stroke from which she was never to recover. Until her death, in 1973 at a clinic in Spain, she was afflicted with impaired vision, aphasia, seizures, and depression. In the sixties

Paul Bowles turned increasingly to translation, virtually inventing a new genre when he began to transcribe and translate the tales of Moroccan storytellers, among them—in addition to Mrabet—Larbi Layachi and Ahmed Yacoubi. "The real reason I started translating," Bowles explains, "was that Mrs. Bowles was ill and I couldn't write, because I would only have twenty minutes and then I would be called downstairs. One needs solitude and privacy and more or less unlimited time to write novels. Solitude seems an unlikely prospect for Bowles these days. In the morning he works on his translations, his correspondence, and his own short stories, but in the afternoon the visitors—a Danish architect, a French journalist, a British novelist, the semi-resident Mrabet—come and stay to chat, drink tea, and smoke kif. Though Bowles no longer goes out at night, he is a vivid presence in the English-speaking community, which gathers at Guita's, the restaurant across from the mosque. They argue about his work, which has for better or worse put a version of their experience on the map, and about his marriage, as if Jane and Paul had just left the room. But Bowles is a private man, with a reserved, almost impersonal interest in his neighbors. As the titles of his novels—*The Sheltering Sky, Let It Come Down, Up Above the World*—suggest, his is an aerial, cosmic point of view, that of an observer looking down from a great height.

When asked if there is a specific message in his fiction, Bowles snorts derisively and examines his cigarette holder as if reading an inscription. Three days later, on an expedition some thirty miles south of Tangier, he surveys the new cinder-block suburbs of a fishing village in which he once lived. "Here's my message," he says, then pauses and smiles. "Everything gets worse."

Conversation with Paul Bowles

Gena Dagel Caponi/1986

I went to Tangier in 1986 to interview Paul Bowles for a book I was writing, a series of essays that became an interpretive biography (*Paul Bowles: Romantic Savage,* Carbondale and Edwardsville: Southern Illinois University Press, 1994). Actually, I first went in late December of 1985, but a tall and sinister Berber in a hooded woolen robe whom we had refused as a guide frightened my husband and me at the bus station in Ceuta, so we returned to Spain. "I saw your passport," he whispered with menace. "I know where you're going, and when you get there, I'll be there waiting for you."

In February we tried again, this time flying into the airport in Tangier. Nothing of note happened, and when I told Paul Bowles about our encounter with the stranger in the bus station, he seemed skeptical. "Threatened you? But I've never heard of such a thing. At any rate, he wouldn't be dangerous, unless, of course, he was crazy."

Over the next week, I met with Bowles for five afternoons, arriving at times I could only hope would be agreeable, since Bowles has no telephone, preferring inconvenience to anxiety. "Talking on the telephone is very much like flying," he says. "One always wishes it were over. The nervous tension is terrible. One is definitely out of contact in both cases, and nothing brings one back to reality except hanging up or landing."

He was generous with his time, and during the cold wet days of February had fewer visitors than in other months. Most of my questions were tiresome requests for clarification of things he'd said and written elsewhere, and although I never felt I had penetrated through these stories to something less deliberately constructed, never did Bowles express impatience, exasperation, or even disdain. He could not have been more charming. He asked about friends of his with whom I had spoken in New York. He showed us an old camel's hair *djellaba,* played tapes of his music, and complained about not being able to find so much of what he had put away in suitcases in his apartment.

Bowles's apartment is in a modern international-style

concrete building on a wide paved street across from the
American consulate just outside the older section of Tangier.
Coming to it from the conjested medieval city feels erie, as if
one had turned a corner in Brooklyn and arrived in Kansas.
The hallways inside are dark and deserted, and there is no
one to ask for directions. Bowles answers the door himself,
quizzical, wondering, "Should I have been expecting you?" I
apologize for not having made this exact date of our belated
arrival more clear, and we step into the famous suitcase-
filled hallway.

The living room is small and dark, with red and yellow
Moroccan rugs on the floor and black and grey cushions
below the bookcases lining the wall. A sofa faces the doorway, and the only other furniture consists of two round
tables, one in front of the sofa and one in the corner piled with
books, and a trunk. The fireplace mantel holds small ex-
quisite art objects, and the fire is usually lit. "One must have
a fire," Bowles insists. (At some point during each evening
we were there, he stood in front of the fire and carefully
rolled five cigarettes between his fingers until all the tobacco
had fallen out into the flames. Then he refilled each with *kif,*
placed them side-by-side on the mantel, and slowly smoked
them in succession over the course of the interview).

He greets his visitors cordially, shakes hands with a
squeeze. He dresses casually, a turtleneck sweater or shirt
and tie under a pullover, Wrangler corduroy jeans, brown
hush-puppies. He wears two rings on his right hand. His eyes
are clear blue, and he does not wear glasses. His chauffeur
has just returned from the market. "For once he got everything he wanted," Bowles says, as he prepares tea. "I've
noticed Americans don't take sugar these days. I suppose it's
bad for you. Of course, eating is bad for you. It will kill you.
You can eat for seventy-five, eighty years, and then suddenly
one day you're dead."

After years of problems with digestion and his liver,
Bowles eats plain food: first a clear soup of chicken broth,
tapioca, and soy sauce, over which he shrugs, "It's good if
you like it." A small steak, asparagus, and a green salad
make up his dinner, "if you call this dinner," he says. "Paul
complains about everything, always," said Virgil Thomson.
"It's part of his charm." Yet as he chats with visitors, one
feels this is not complaining, just amused exasperation that
the world can be so much the way it is. He sits at a low table,
crossing his legs underneath him.

Paul Bowles: I can't sit at this table without taking off my shoes. I suppose that's why I usually eat in the kitchen. But the maid hasn't come to clean the kitchen. She's in court, suing her husband. He left her and eight children for another woman. Actually, he moved her and her children out and moved another woman in.

Gena Caponi: Will she get satisfaction in the courts?

PB: No, not unless she has a lawyer, which she can't afford. He left her to starve with eight children. She has no money. Even a lawyer wouldn't help much.

GC: I want to tell you how much I like your recent work. I think *Points in Time* is as fine as anything you've written.

PB: Thank you. So do I. It's not a long book. It's not a novel. They put that on it. "First novel in so many years." I was shocked. Astonished.

GC: It's almost anti-novelistic, isn't it?

PB: I call it a lyrical history.

GC: How historical is it?

PB: Somewhat. I hate doing research. I can't think of anything more difficult. I read, and then I go on long walks with a tape-recorder. I find invention that way.

GC: Did you have to go looking for the historical material in the book or did you send away for it?

PB: No, I had it all here. Things that were of interest to me, naturally.

GC: You haven't always used a tape-recorder.

PB: I never saw a tape-recorder until 1956 or '55. They were clumsier then. You couldn't walk around with them. The difficulty in using one is forming sentences from thoughts. I used a notebook before that. I wrote three-quarters of *Up Above the World* while walking. I'm a peripatetic writer.

GC: Would you say *Points in Time* is more along the lines of your previous travel essays?

PB: I rather think of it as reportage, not travel essays.

GC: Did you deliberately break from using a narrative thread?

PB: No, there's no narrative thread. It's something like a necklace with charms hung on it. Pearls if you prefer.

GC: I've always thought there was a great similarity between "In the Red Room" and *Points in Time*.

PB: You've got something there. I can't tell you what. They were written at the same time, but printed separately for financial reasons.

GC: I know you've said "In the Red Room" was based on an incident you heard about. Someone gone berserk. A few of your stories are about schizophrenia.

PB: "You Are Not I" is. "If I Should Open My Mouth."

GC: What about Grove in *Up Above the World*?

PB: He was just plain nuts.

GC: Kitty?

PB: No, that was a fantasy. A children's story, really.

GC: "Doña Faustina"?

PB: That was based on fact. A woman in Mexico who killed 28 children. It was in the papers every day. The Mexicans have a thing about blood. There's a ritual for bathing a baby boy in bull's blood.

GC: Many of your characters seem to stand on the edges of what we know or can know. On the edge peering into what lies beyond. I suppose this is why critics like to stress the element of madness in some of your work.

PB: Most critics don't understand the first thing about my work. There was one book by Wayne Pounds. Have you read that? He got most of it right. It's quite psychological, but a lot of it is on target. I have no objection to psychology. Particularly Jung. Not so much Freud. But Jung is interesting.

GC: Do you discover insights into your work when you read criticism? Things that you might have understood at an unconscious level but hadn't consciously articulated?

PB: Of course, all my work comes from the unconscious. I suppose what makes the criticism accurate is the critic's understanding at that level.

GC: The unconscious level, you mean? As if the unconscious communicated to another unconscious?

PB: I don't know that it's about communication. More of a feeling.

GC: There's much of Poe in your work. Beyond the fact, of course, that you read Poe as a child. What you are saying now sounds very much like Poe to me—representations not of reality but of states of mind.

PB: It would please me if it had that effect.

GC: In that sense, your fiction is the truth.

PB: Yes, it's all true. The truth comes out in fiction. The truth about a person, if one knows how to read between the lines. Rilke, for instance *The Notebooks of Malte Laurids Brigge* is simply an *autobiographie a clef.*

GC: And a good critic reads between the lines?

PB: He has to have the proper spectacles. I'm not a good critic. I've only written about Durrell and *The Alleys of Marrakech* [by Peter Maynes].

GC: When you began writing music reviews for the *Herald Tribune,* did Virgil Thomson coach you?

PB: He chastized me once. "Just tell 'em what happened, baby. That's all they want to know. Nobody cares about your opinion. Who are you?"

GC: Did you ever think you might have continued writing criticism?

PB: I didn't have the training for it like Virgil. And I found the editors quite tyrannical.

GC: It isn't as if you had no training in music. What kind of teacher was Copland?

PB: Very patient. Although he was pleased if you got things quickly.

GC: Did you ever regret not having studied with Boulanger?

PB: No, not really. I found her rather worrying. She was very severe, rather like a crochety maiden aunt. Everyone says she was a magnificent teacher. I'm sure she was. For me, she was a bit formidable.

GC: Roger Sessions?

PB: Yes, one winter. That was enough. He wasn't what you would call personable.

GC: I imagine your process in writing music would be quite different from that in writing fiction.

PB: If you're writing music, sometimes you tend to drown in it. It's more physically exhausting. That's one of the reasons I gave it up.

GC: I would think orchestration would be demanding.

PB: Orchestration? No, that's just drudgery. In writing music one has to be much more conscious of form than in fiction. Every note. I don't know anything about music since I left in 1946. I'm very old-fashioned. I never experimented with notation, like Cage. Most of them are absurd.

GC: You used to improvise.

PB: I did?

GC: Virgil Thomson says in his autobiography that you played lovely improvisations that reminded him very much of Ravel.

PB: Virgil says I did it in front of him? Extraordinary. I never took improvisation seriously. It isn't composition. It isn't sequential sound. It isn't structured, anyway.

GC: Which of your music are you most fond of?

PB: I suppose the Latin American pieces. The Two Piano Concerto. *A Picnic Cantata.*

GC: And other composers?

PB: The big three: Bach, Scarlatti, Satie.

GC: Earlier you mentioned Cage. Did you enjoy his music?

PB: He was more amusing in writing than in his music. And most amusing of all in person. He found his music amusing. I've seen him rolling on the floor in delight with his own music. That's hardly the mark of a serious composer.

GC: What about Thomson? He enjoyed his musical jokes.

PB: Well, of course, Virgil is obviously perverse. He generally had a point to make.

GC: Did you find Stein tyrannical?

PB: Yes, but she was such a full person, you didn't mind. She was a theater of one. Her on stage, you watching as the audience.

GC: She ordered you around. She made you wear lederhosen and had her dog chase you.

PB: She was playing a game. I was too. I could have sat down and said I didn't want to.

GC: Did you ever know Nabokov?

PB: I knew Nicholas Nabokov, the younger brother of Vladimir.

GC: Did you read him?

PB: As much as I could. What he said about Borges, that was awful. He put it in his wife's mouth—my wife remembered that. He said Borges was a landscape with marvelous façades, beautiful architecture. But when you go there, there's nothing there. It's like movie sets. And then it's never very engaging and sympathetic in a writer to let you know he thinks he's great.

GC: You've done so much translation. What do you think about when you begin a translation?

PB: It's important to pick the style. Then you must have a sense of the voice of narrator, the rhythm and inflection.

GC: I heard someone talk about seeing the word "translador" on moving vans and realizing that a translator transports things from one place to another, from one country to another.

PB: In some sense, he's a traitor. I want to carry it over the border intact, but of course, that's impossible.

GC: What is it that's missing?

PB: I don't think it's possible for a Westerner to understand what goes on in an illiterate Moroccan's head. You've heard Mrabet telling stories. I don't know if he knows the difference between fantasy and fact. I don't think he cares much.

GC: Have you ever thought of joining a formal religion such as Islam?

PB: No. I suppose if I were to choose anything, it would be Buddhism. That's about as close to atheism as you can get and still call it a religion.

GC: To hear you mention Buddhism makes me think of the different kinds of nothingness in your work—what's beyond the sheltering sky, and the abyss in "The Echo."

PB: Since this life is all we can know, by definition anything beyond can be only nothingness.

GC: You once said in a letter to your editor at Random House that all your stories were mysteries, with the mystery being the motivation for the characters' behavior. Do you begin with that mystery, the motivation, in mind?

PB: I often have no idea what I'm going to write when I sit down. I never plan ahead of time, so how could I know the motivation? Writing isn't about an idea. It comes more from a kind of feeling.

GC: From the unconscious.

PB: Exactly. And if it comes from the unconscious, how can it be wrong?

GC: The integrity of the unconscious.

PB: It's all I've got.

GC: But so much of the unconscious is affected by other people, formed by unpleasant experiences.

PB: Yes, but what else have you got to rely on?

"It isn't much, this life, but it's all we've got," he says, smiling. "It's not such a wonderful thing. Considering the inevitables, I don't know which is worse: the taxes or the dying that gets you out of paying them."

Bowles has always claimed that he returned to Morocco in 1947 because of a dream. I ask him whether he still dreams at night, and he affirms that he does, but he doesn't record his dreams or use them for his fiction. "I'm purely hedonistic about dreaming. It doesn't give me anything, but it's the pleasantest part of the day," he says. "What I dream about is places. I very seldom dream about anybody I know. There are people, but they are only passersby, people I met traveling. I dream about landscapes. Or New York. Most of the time I'm in New York."

When we get ready to leave this apartment for the last time, Bowles asks us where we are headed. We tell him that we are planning a trip to Fez. He looks pleased and asks whether we have a map. We hadn't thought about one. He asks us to wait a minute, goes around the corner into his bedroom, and returns with a map, one that has been used for a long time, but with care. The paper is soft but not torn. I imagine the journeys Paul Bowles must have taken with this map and ask him whether he remembers the first time he saw Fez.

"Of course I do," he smiles. "We came on it from the hills, and it was like a diamond in a field of emeralds. In those days the city was completely enclosed by walls."

I sigh and say, "We'll never see it the way you did then, will we?"

He smiles again. "No, of course not. No one will."

We take the stairs outside and find we have gotten turned around. Somehow we have come out the back entrance. A tall hooded figure stands guard outside the door and seems little aware of our exiting. In the nearly deserted carport is Mr. Bowles's copper-colored late-'60s vintage Mustang. We look up to his apartment window. There is no light. Later that evening, I replay one of the many tapes from our discussions. I hear a faint hissing as I imagine Paul Bowles speaking, but there is no voice other than my own.

Interview with Paul Bowles

Allen Hibbard/1988

Allen Hibbard: What is the motive for writing a story? Why do you bother to sit down and work out a story that has been told, or work out an idea that has just popped into your head?

Paul Bowles: I suppose a lot of it is the desire to make a pattern, an order out of what is more chaotic than it should be—to give it form.

AH: Do you imagine a kind of audience out there?

PB: No. I'm my own audience. I assume that something that satisfies me will satisfy the audience that I write for—whoever that is. I don't think that it will satisfy the great public, but that is something else. They have other books to satisfy them.

AH: Indeed, they do! You do the same thing, I bet, with your music. Simply listening and seeing what works, and when you were content with the sound you got, that was it.

PB: Yes. In music it's the form and the sound, of course.

AH: Sometimes I get a strong sense in the stories that they were formed, fashioned, almost as though they were miniature musical compositions. There's a real sense of counterpoint, of balance; a sense of when to bring in background, when to introduce dialogue. Again, the analogy which springs to mind is music.

PB: It could be. I'm not conscious of it. People have said it, so therefore it is probably true.

AH: What in your mind stands out as being a major difference between the novel and the story? What can the story do that novel can't? It seems as though you have been writing more stories recently. . . . They do, of course, take less time to write.

PB: Well, yes, of course. But I enjoy them more.

201

AH: You don't have to keep up such a sustained effort, and stay with characters so long.

PB: It seems as though the writing of a novel isn't over for such a long time.

AH: There seem to be similarities between the internal progress of your characters in stories and those in your novels. Take Port in *The Sheltering Sky,* and Dyar in *Let It Come Down,* for example, and compare them to the protagonists in earlier stories such as "Tapiama" and "Pastor Dowe at Tacaté." They are all characters who enter the unknown, move about in it a while, become uncomfortable, then set out in another direction. The stories seem to be based on some kind of journey—like the novels.

PB: You're simply contrasting some of the stories with novels . . . I don't know what the connections are. I don't see any. I'm not a critic. I don't analyse these kinds of things. . . . It's all right to pull things apart, to see what the strands are, the fibers.

AH: What kind of sensation did you have upon finishing "Tea on the Mountain," the first story in *The Collected Stories*?

PB: Nostalgia. I was in New York, in Brooklyn Heights, that's where I was writing, in 1939. I wished I was back there to relive what Tangier was like in those days.

AH: You often write about places other than where you are when you are writing.

PB: Uhm, yes. Well it's natural.

AH: Does it sometimes take a little distance before we can absorb the place?

PB: I never like writing about the place I'm in. I can do it sometimes, if I have to. When I was in my traveling days I would always write about other places I had been. That's because one has to invent the atmosphere. That is, remember. When writing about the place one is in, it becomes journalism.

AH: There are too many details. They don't have a chance to filter out. When you remember you leave a lot out.

PB: Also, you remember that which is important for the atmosphere, and that which isn't is forgotten.

AH: In a story like "At Paso Rojo," for example, you wrote at Oche Rios in Jamaica . . . and yet it seems to be set somewhere in Costa Rica. Do sometimes likenesses of the places you are in creep in, even though you may be writing about a place other than [that which] you are in, such as in that story?

PB: No, it doesn't do that in that story. It DID in *The Sheltering Sky,* but that was because it was part of the aesthetic, but it doesn't happen by itself. I made it happen. I made lists of things I saw on my walks, then put them in. I never did it after that.

AH: It's been interesting to look at the various collections of your stories which have come out, and what stories are included in each. One of the stories which caught my eye in *Call at Corazón* (Peter Owen, 1988) which I hadn't seen before was "Sylvie Ann, The Boogie Man."

PB: That wasn't in any other collection. Oh, yes, it was. Years ago. '59. It came out and was published by Heinemann in London, but nowhere else.

AH: Why was it left out of the *Collected*?

PB: It came just at the time there was a lot of trouble with blacks, and I thought I don't know what to write. Whatever you write they won't like it; so I thought I'd better not write anything. . . . I don't know if blacks would object to it or not. It does show the black as being illiterate and a laundress.

AH: Also in the *Call at Corazón* collection we have "An Inopportune Visit," not found elsewhere. The conceit there is marvelous—to have a saint come back so that you can show a unique perspective on the modern world . . . Where did the idea come from?

PB: I don't know. I have no idea. I think I was sitting one day thinking what a shame it was that nobody was singing Gregorian chants, and that's because they don't do anything in Latin anymore. And I thought, "What would it be like if someone came back and realized what was going on?" They'd be horrified!

AH: It of course comes out in the end that Santa Rosenda rushes to the altar and begins to attack the priest. . . . I realize that my Black Sparrow edition of *Midnight Mass* doesn't have "In the Red Room."

PB: The reason for that is that a publisher in L.A. wrote me sometime in the late seventies, asking me for a story. They wanted to publish it by itself, and they did. But there was a proviso in the contract saying that I couldn't sell it to anyone else or have it published for a year after the original publication, so the first edition of *Midnight Mass* was just coming out and I couldn't send it to them. Once the year was over I sent it and they put out a second edition, with the story in it.

AH: In the story, "Midnight Mass" you always have the suspicion that Madame Dervaux had something to do with the appropriation of the house, and the artist moving in, but there is never any proof of that.

PB: No, probably not. I imagine the Moroccan family did that by themselves and she knowing that would immediately say, "Ah, then. I want the tower." She was probably willing to pay a good price.

AH: That leads to suspicions in the end, when she is there entrenched in the house.

PB: Yah, but I don't know.

AH: Well, there is no way of telling in the story.

PB: It doesn't matter, really.

AH: One of my favorite stories in that volume is "Here To Learn." You said that you liked it, too. Is it your favorite, or do you have any favorites?

PB: Not really.

AH: Not any that you like more than others?

PB: Some I like less than others.

AH: One thing which is evident in a story like "Ahmed and Madame" is that, like so many of your stories, it involves a chain of deception.

PB: Ah!

AH: I suppose the first deception is the bringing of the plants by the gardener under false pretenses.

PB: And the second one was the real gardener cutting them and ruining them.

AH: Right.

PB: Killing them.

AH: And then the . . .

PB: . . . third big deception was when the ones who had originally supplied the hot plants come back and he goes to the door and tells them that she is going to get the police. Then when he comes back, Madame says, "Oh, what did you tell them?" and he said, "No Moslem would take advantage of a woman without a husband." . . . Then he says, "You can't trust anyone."

AH: I suppose the reader of "Kitty" is apt to draw a connection to Kafka's "Metamorphosis." I'm sure that you didn't have that in mind when you wrote it.

PB: It's a well-known story of metamorphosis.

AH: You have a number of other stories which involve metamorphosis. "Allal," for instance.

PB: Yes . . . but he didn't mean to. He didn't start out wanting to become a snake, but Kitty started out wanting to be a cat. A woman was here last week from London, a woman with a difficult name. I've known her for many years. She has a daughter, about eight or so, and her mother read her "Kitty" a year or so ago and she decided that she was going to become a cat, and her mother would say, "Where are your hands?" and the daughter would say, "I have no hands. I have claws."

AH: So, life does imitate art.

PB: Then her mother wrote and asked, "Couldn't you publish it by itself?" But I said, "No. No. Because I don't think it is really a child's story." . . . I wrote it as a child's story.

AH: You did?

PB: For a collection called *Wonders,* put out by Simon & Schuster. It is supposed to be a child's story, by adults. But, someone else had the same idea of publishing it in a book by itself. She got in touch with one or two publishers and they said, "Oh, no. It's much too gruesome for small children." The Americans thought it was too gruesome, so I wrote this back to . . . you know who and she wrote me that she had read my letter to her little girl and the little girl, when she heard what the Americans had said, she stamped her foot and said, "Rubbish!" It's very funny. I can't imagine any other small child saying "Rubbish."

AH: A lot of these later stories seem to have a little more wit or slyness.

PB: They're not so . . . Gothic.

AH: Then, too, you seem to get a little more involved in some of these later stories. In "Unwelcome Words" you even appear as the writer of these letters.

PB: The protagonist.

AH: The reader's never really sure about how many of the attitudes expressed in the letters coincide with your own.

PB: Oh, no. It's not about me at all.

AH: It's interesting to come across the story of Valeska, because last summer when I was here you told it in its real form, using her real name . . . and now it pops up in the story.

PB: More or less as it happened . . . *exactly* as it happened!

AH: I wonder how appropriate it would be when writing about them to talk about them to mention the real names.

PB: It doesn't seem important one way or the other. I mean it had nothing to do with the story. It was based on episodes. That's all.

AH: In that story and some of these other later ones you get a sense of being cramped in more. The man the narrator is writing to is immobile, but the person who is writing the letter also seems to be feeling hemmed in by Tangier, talking about the villas around, and the increasing crowds and Tangier being a less liveable kind of city. I suppose it does seem a lot less exotic than it did.

PB: Well, it is.

AH: A lot of memory comes through in these stories, too. It seems as though the narrators are continually delving back into the past and pulling up little bits and pieces of things. There's that story about the mosquito netting that the writer tells, becoming drunker and drunker. . . . It seems to have taken place in Latin America or somewhere. Is that something out of an imagined past? Or a real one?

PB: No. It was out of a real past. Absolutely.

AH: In Mexico?

PB: In Mexico. It's all in the story. I took a train and the train went as far as the railroad had been built down into the state of Guerrero. There's nothing there. I don't know why they built it that far. But they came to an arroyo above which they couldn't build a decent bridge so the railroad just stopped on the side of the arroyo. . . . There's no reason for it to go anywhere.

AH: And that's where you stopped?

PB: Yes! That's where I stopped.

AH: You like places at the end of the tracks, don't you?

PB: Well, yes, they're more interesting.

AH: At the end of "Unwelcome Words" there's this bit about rewriting the end of *Huckleberry Finn*. There's a suggestion that you think in some way Twain's ending was twisted to make it acceptable to the American public. Do you think that a muzzle has been placed on a lot of American writers, even unconsciously?

PB: I don't think any muzzle was placed on Mark Twain . . . except by himself. I think that he was afraid he had written such a lyrical novel. . . . He had wanted it to be popular, so he had to make a farce.

. . . I never did understand just what he was aiming at. . . . You didn't have tea?

AH: I did have tea. Mrabet kindly fixed me a cup when I first came in. . . . The first story in *Unwelcome Words*—"Julian Vreden"—that's a recent story as well?

PB: That was written in 1984.

AH: I presume that it happened as it was told. You begin by noting there was a newspaper account, and this is what had happened.

PB: I read it in a paper in New York.

AH: In *Unwelcome Words,* too, one of the things which is rather obvious, is the shift in style, not only the epistolary, but the monologue. Why the monologue, especially the monologue with no punctuation? You do it "Afternoon with Antaeus" . . .

PB: . . . but not without punctuation.

AH: Yes. Without punctuation you get a lot of enjambments which carry one from one sentence to another.

PB: You think so? You think they could apply to one sentence as well as to another?

AH: Sometimes you go a little further and you get the beginning of the next before you stop, then you go back and you stop and you begin again. . . . In "New York 1965" neither of these women, the one telling nor the one being told about, is very likeable. You get these two positions. The one is a moralist commenting on how awful the other's life is—how she's taking care of her son and living her life in Tangier. They're both equally as repulsive.

PB: Yes, I think they are. The poetess isn't very likeable.

AH: When you first begin, you think that the storyteller might have some redeeming virtue, but as you move through you get a sense that her words are motivated by jealousy and a whole lot of other emotions. After all, her friend has become a rather famous poet.

PB: Yes, and Kathleen thinks that's a lot of nonsense.

AH: And she hasn't read any of the poetry!

PB: NO! Of course she hasn't. She says, "Thank God, I don't have to read it." When the poet says "I've been writing a lot of poetry," she says, "I'll *bet* you have!"

AH: What takes you back to the New England setting in "Massachusetts 1932"?

PB: What takes me back anywhere?

AH: The difference between that one and the New York monologue—at least a key difference—is that the man whom the narrator is talking to is right there in the room, apparently, and in the first one you don't have a sense of exactly to whom it is being told. The other person never surfaces and she isn't being offered drinks or anything.

PB: No. And the last one also . . .

AH: Although in the last one, the one set in Tangier, you get more of a sense of the motive of the telling. . . . The place I had in mind as I was reading the story was somewhere up on the hill just between the Marshan and the Old Mountain.

PB: Well, that's where it was.

AH: Of course, what seems to happen in that story is that as one moves through the story it becomes less and less obvious who is to blame for what has gone wrong. It seems as though the motive for telling the story is some kind of guilt.

PB: Well, partially. She's not sure . . . No, I don't think she really believes that the woman was screaming and she heard her. She kept thinking it might have been so. She didn't do anything. She couldn't really have.

AH: You also get the piece of information right here at the end that the people who have come in and beaten her while her boyfriend's been away came in the first time when they had left their guardpost.

PB: Except that you feel they were justified in leaving, because the Countess had told them two hours and it had been five hours. So they had done more than their share.

AH: But it is one of those situations where you just can't determine who is to blame.

PB: No. . . . She couldn't help thinking maybe it would have been different if she had stayed on another half hour. Who knows?

AH: What pulled you in the direction of using monologue in the later stories, or why you decided to use that means of telling?

PB: Well, it's hard to say. I don't know. I heard the voice of the woman telling about the peacocks [in "Tangier 1975"], and heard it very strongly in my ear and so I started writing what she would say, and what she did say, in her kind of speech. Once I had written one, I found it fun to become someone else and write what words I heard in my head—rather like writing music.

AH: You stick with one voice.

PB: Yes, all are in one voice.

AH: If you begin with the sound of the peacocks, that would have been toward the end.

PB: Well, they're there, in the woods. . . . They sound like lost souls (sound) . . . and then it come down (continues sound) in a long arch of sound, coming down.

AH: The other few stories in *Unwelcome Words* seem to have been based on reminiscences of particular character—"Hugh Harper," "Dinner at Sir Nigel's." I remember you told me once that Hugh Harper was based upon a real character. Was Sir Nigel as well?

PB: Oh, yes! The whole business.

AH: Who was the person on which it was based?

PB: I don't see any point in connecting up fiction with fact. It doesn't tell anything about the fiction, just to recount the facts, does it? It might have come from many different sources. In that one, though, it didn't. It all came from one source, the dinner I had with him—Sir Cyril.

AH: Things change of course, in the writing. You can never get it down the way it happened.

PB: No.

AH: Nor do you want to.

PB: No, because it isn't journalism. You're inventing. There's less invention in that [story] than in most.

Paul Bowles: The Complete Outsider

Catherine Warnow and Regina Weinreich/1988

From the film, "Paul Bowles: The Complete Outsider" (Waterfall Productions, 1993), with permission of Catherine Warnow and Regina Weinreich.

The following interview is extracted from a documentary film on Paul Bowles by Catherine Warnow and Regina Weinreich, whose questions here are noted "Q." The conversations took place during November of 1988 and were conducted at various sites about Tangier and in Paul Bowles's home, beginning at a Tangier Mosque.

Paul Bowles: This is the mosque nearest my house. I come by here every day for a walk. But this is Friday, the holy day. The women outside are there waiting to be given alms. In Fez, I've seen them sit in the antechamber of the Moulay Idress, but they don't go inside where the men are praying. They touch their face to the ground.

Q: What does Islam mean?

PB: It's a submission. It means giving yourself to Allah, a surrender to the greater power. Often I see them outside my window any time of day. They pray five times a day. But Friday is a special time. Saturday is the Jewish Sabbath, and when that's all over, then the Christians' begin. Friday, Saturday, Sunday—all Sabbaths. You have to know who's what if you're going to a shop. The big places observe European weekend.

The daily life is built around the concept of the religion. A good Christian must be a Christian at all moments, and the same applies here. It's more or less like any other religion: no lying, no stealing. Not so different from Christianity. From centuries ago, Christians have colonized them and mistreated them. It began with the Crusades, so they felt a certain solidarity, which perhaps Christians don't feel because they haven't been picked on.

The actual interpretation of Islamic law is very different among those who study as opposed to the man in the street who has all sorts of prejudices. One has to distinguish between what is said in the street and what is part of the religion itself. The average Moroccan does not know the Koran, or just knows a little of it.

Q: What about the holy wars against the infidel?

PB: When has the *Jihad* actually been practiced?

Q: Why do you eat in bed?

PB: It was something my doctor suggested. I digest my food better in bed under normal circumstances. I find it takes longer, and of course the more slowly you eat the better you digest. Whereas someone else might take one-half hour to eat, it takes me one and a quarter. Mrabet makes breakfast. Abdelwahab comes and makes me lunch. Mrabet comes and he serves me my dinner, so that I eat all three meals in bed. All my life, I've had breakfast in bed.

Q: What else do you do in bed?

PB: I write in bed. It's a good idea in this country and Algeria, where I wrote *The Sheltering Sky*. The only place to get warm is in bed. If I had to get up at a chair and a table, I'd freeze to death. In the desert, if you leave a glass of water on your night table, it freezes. You can see your breath until about noon.

Q: Where did you write *The Sheltering Sky*?

PB: I wrote most of *The Sheltering Sky* in Algeria. I began it and ended it in Fez. All the action takes place in Algeria. There's no Moroccan scene, although critics think it's about Morocco. I wanted it to be about the desert, because I had been there before in '31, and now it was '47. I remembered everything and wrote it from memory, and at the same time I wanted to go back and refresh that memory and also find small details of everyday life which I could sprinkle over that memory in the writing.

Q: Why don't you plan more? Does it come from living in Morocco?

PB: It's an arbitrary idea of mine. I didn't learn it here, I'm sure. I still have that—never try to plan anything. Generally you're disappointed. It doesn't turn out the way you thought it would. If you don't plan anything, whatever turns out is gravy.

I remember Virgil Thomson's remark about *monument publique*. He said, *si on devient un monument publique, le peuple pisse dessus*.

Q: When we asked Virgil about interviewing you for this film, he said, "No, I'm not going to do your homework for you."

PB: Paul will do your homework for you. I remember he wrote a

long letter to Aaron Copland, telling him not to worry. Aaron was
worried that I was not behaving like a serious music student should in
Paris.

Q: Why not?

PB: I was going off to Spain, to Morocco, not keeping appointments
with Boulanger. Aaron felt responsible for me, because I was his pupil,
and it was his idea that I should go to Paris. I wasn't serious.

Q: Virgil Thomson said you were the freest spirit he's ever known.
What did he mean by that?

PB: The freest? I feel no obligation. If you feel no sense of obligation, then it's all a big zero.

Q: What's in it for you?

PB: What is in it? The ability to move around when I felt like and
where I felt like without telling anyone. I had an appointment with
Prokofiev. Instead of keeping the date, I went to Gare de l'Est. I went
to Germany.

Q: But that's very rude!

PB: Very rude. Terrible. Unheard of. When a very important person
like Prokofiev agrees to give you lessons and you never get in touch
with him, it's unheard of.

Q: Why did you do that?

PB: Compulsive, I don't know.

Q: But we know you as reliable, not rude.

PB: I'll tell you. I was eighteen years old, that explains it. Once I
came of age, I began to feel embarrassed about such behavior. I was
older. I was already married, so naturally one changes. I was no longer
a fly-by-night, crazy young man. I was pretty crazy when I was in my
teens. But teenagers are likely to be crazy, aren't they? You can't say
that whatever's unconventional is crazy, can you? It depends upon what
one means by the word "crazy." I misbehaved rather when I was
younger.

Q: How?

PB: By going off to Europe without telling my family. And having
them look for my body in the East River. I think my tastes have remained the same. What I like to eat. I've always hated noise. Personal
tastes remain the same.

Q: Did you have pets?

PB: I had canaries, but Mrabet took them away, and the last one died a month ago. What I used to have were parrots, which I liked a lot. I had two in Tangier, but they both died. Occasionally they sell them here.

We had coatamundi, wonderful animals, very amusing, with very sharp teeth. One of them slept in Jane's hair every night where he made himself a nest. She let him sleep there every night. We had all sorts of birds. We had a lot of trouble with them. A policeman lived next door, and we had a macaw, who made a terrific sound. He came one day, as Mexicans will, with a pistol, and he said, "That bird's going to die." And Jane said, "Won't you have a rum and coke?" and he did, and put his gun away.

Q: What is your favorite of the stories you have written?

PB: There is one story which I feel is better than the others. It's actually one that entails no violence, because people think of me as a violent writer, which is not true at all. I've written over fifty stories, only five of which are violent, which leaves forty-five which are not violent.

This piece is called "The Time of Friendship," and nothing happens in it. I like it because to me it's a faithful picture of a place and a fairly faithful facsimile of a person who's in it, an old Swiss teacher, who's name is Weisling, which I changed to Windling, so she shouldn't recognize herself. But she died anyway. It's a good picture of a place, which is the desert. As far as the novels go, what I like best is *Up Above the World* because it's the best written. After all, what one writes for is to write well, to use the language well, to make the words tell the most they can, in the smallest number. Therefore, I think *Up Above the World* is my best book. And Grove, the hero of that book, is intelligent. And it's the best written. What's *in* a novel is not important to me. It's how it's told, how the words go together, what makes a good sentence. After all, there's nothing in writing except words, patterns of words.

Q: Are you more famous now than you used to be?

PB: To be more famous you have to be famous originally, which I'm not.

Q: Well, why are you getting all this attention today?

PB: I suppose people are just discovering the books. They could have read them thirty years ago, most of them, but they didn't have circulation, they weren't going around. Now is the first time they're all in print. And that's good, especially in Europe. Because in America people are not very aware of the books. But in France, Italy, Spain, Japan—yes.

People pay too much attention to what's in the book and to my characters. People disapprove of them. The invention of sympathetic characters, fascinating plots—I don't think that counts. It may count with the big public, but it doesn't count with me. I'm just one person, but I write these books. And what counts with me is the language. That's why I've never understood the praise given to *The Sheltering Sky*. It's not the best written. It's the first, how could it be? They're not reading for the language at all; they don't really care whether a sentence is well expressed or not. Naturally they don't. Well, we don't agree, that's all.

Q: What advice would you give a young writer?

PB: I'd advise him never to talk about what he's writing to anyone. Be absolutely silent. Never to reread it himself unless he's finished writing it, because that's how you get blocked. Never talk about it, never show it to anyone, be absolutely still about it until it's published. Then he doesn't have to talk about it.

Write what occurs to you and just start in. Don't make plans beforehand, don't make first drafts, nonsense. Just write it. I never made a first draft. What I wrote I sent to the publisher.

I recently wrote a piece for [the Japanese journal] *Shinshosha,* and I think they were horrified, but they printed it. They came and began asking me the typical questions that people ask. "Why do you live in Morocco? Is it a good place to work? Have you became a Moslem?" Things that have nothing to do with anyone. Just superficial gossip.

I don't want anyone to know about me. In the first place "I" don't exist. I disapprove very much of the tendency in America and everywhere to make an individual out of the writer to such an extent that the writer's life and his choices and his taste are more important than what he writes.

If he's a writer, the only thing that counts is what he writes.

I was asked three times by someone in Paris to respond to a questionnaire. I threw it away. It had one question: Why do you write? I replied in one sentence: "*J'ecris parce que j'habite le pays des vivants.*" I write because I'm still alive, which is a perfectly good answer, and they printed it.

I thought it was a rude answer.

I was a composer for as long as I've been a writer. I came here because I wanted to write a novel. I had a commission to do it. I was sick of writing music for other people—Joseph Losey, Orson Welles, a whole lot of other people, endless. Tennessee Williams, José Ferrer, a ballet with Salvador Dalí, and many other things. An opera with Federico García Lorca, but he was already shot, so I had to work with his brother Francisco.

All these things were very interesting, and I kept alive by doing them, but they didn't keep my imagination alive.

So I got this commission from Doubleday and came over here, where I'd been before, of course. Little by little the words took over from the notes, the musical notes, and now I haven't written music in four years.

I don't make plans. They make themselves. I dislike the words "stimulus" or "inspiration," because they imply consciousness. I write unconsciously, without knowing what I am writing.

I think of myself as an existentialist. My mind works like that. I live in the present. I don't think about the future. Whatever happens is what happens.

Q: Do you see yourself as part of an expatriate tradition?

PB: Is there an expatriate tradition? What is it?

Q: Edith Wharton, Stein, Hemingway, Henry James, J. F. Cooper.

PB: I don't think they liked the U.S. I don't think it pleased them. For someone else, Greece might have been as interesting. Or Italy. For me, it was Morocco. Again it was chance. It was chance that Gertrude Stein suggested it. She might have said Spain, and I would have gone there.

It takes two to tango. Morocco is there, and I'm here, and we got on together.

I find the desert very exciting, because there's nothing there. You won't find a tree or a rock or a bush. You won't find anything at all, except sand dunes. You can pretend you're lost in there. You can get lost in there. It's very beautiful. Even Jane thought it very beautiful, the most beautiful place you ever saw.

I don't try to analyze the emotions of any of my characters. I don't give them emotions. Thoughts are the most important. You can explain a thought but not an emotion. You can't use emotions. There's nothing you can do with them.

Q: Many people would wonder what could be more important than emotions.

PB: Ideas. What one decides. What one decides life means. It isn't people. Life is about oneself against the world, other people, against that backdrop of other people.

This applies to me and the way I treat my characters. My characters are the product of my thoughts. Emotions can't give you protagonists, can't give you anything, it seems to me.

Q: What is your idea of a good time?

PB: Forgetting myself, laughing. It requires the presence of other people to forget oneself. Man is gregarious. I don't want to be gregarious. I don't even want to be human. But what can I do? I'm in the land of the living!

Q: What were your happiest years?

PB: There were plenty of happy years when I was young, let us say in my early twenties. Those were the happiest times, although there were always problems. There always are. Illness, lack of money, annoying parents. Parents are always a great problem it seems to me. When I was older, they weren't a problem. I just never saw them.

Q: You seem more interested in illiterate Moroccans than in educated ones.

PB: I've always found that illiterate people have far better memories. The illiterate has to remember every detail. He has no way of knowing what happened in the past, unless he remembers details. In fact, in order to write "10," they make 10 little marks, so it shows how differently their minds work.

And they invent better. They're free to remember, to invent—as they would put it, to lie. They're much better at lying because they remember their lies. They don't get them mixed up. They're easier to work with. Much. The literate are less interesting. They have generally absorbed French ideas from their professors. The illiterates are much, much better.

Q: Do you type your novels?

PB: No. I write my novels or anything else, lying in bed. I've written everything in longhand, which is much more satisfactory for me, because I change every word as I write it. To write a sentence may involve many rewrites before I go on to the next. Sometimes to get started it helps to hear the final sentences that you wrote the last time.

Q: How many hours a day do you write?

PB: I was always very lazy. I just worked until I didn't want to work any more, and then I forgot about it. Possibly two hours a day.

Each novel had a different routine. With *The Sheltering Sky* I was wandering around the desert, so I wrote it in bed in one hotel after another. *Let It Come Down* I wrote in India and Sri Lanka, sweating. It was very hot. I often wrote at night, using a lantern, which also attracts many insects, thousands of them. For *Spider's House,* I used to get up early in the morning on Taprobane, my island in Ceylon, between early tea and breakfast. So by nine I was hungry, because I'd been working all the time. *Up Above the World* I wrote wandering about on the mountain, because that's where I was, above the world.

I always worked when I felt like it, never when I didn't.

Q: What is your social life like?

PB: I don't know what a social life is. People sometimes drop in. They know that I can always be found at five o'clock, because at six I go to bed and have dinner. I've cut all connection with everybody. My social life is restricted to those who serve me and give me meals, and those who want to interview me.

Now someone in Austria wants to come, and this goes on all over the place. They want interviews. I don't know.

The man who wrote the books didn't exist. No writer exists. He exists in his books, and that's all. What he does is of no interest except to him and his family.

Q: How would you summarize your achievement?

PB: I've written some books and some music. That's what I've achieved.

Paul Bowles: Touched by Magic

Soledad Alameda/1990

From *El País Setional* [Madrid, Spain] (15 February 1990): 26–29.
Copyright © *El País* 1993. Reprinted by permission of *El País*.

The legend of an American writer in Tangier is that he lives
in a lovely house no doubt surrounded by trees, perhaps high
above a steep cliff, from which he hears the noise of the
waves during his tormented nights. Paul Bowles lives in a
small apartment too incommodious to merit description.
Two piles of suitcases in the entryway, a light bulb covered
with red paper, cushions on the floor, the disorder and dust of
a lifetime, grime. This is what we see when a young Moroccan opens the door, signaling us that "Paul" is sick. The
porter had advised the same, as had a neighbor with her face
half covered by a veil. The writer is "Paul" to everyone. We
wait a few minutes, until from another room, an older man
appears, walking at a right angle, in socks and a robe. He has
gotten out of bed to receive us and, so we assume, to let us
know that he cannot grant the agreed upon interview. But he
begs us to accompany him into his room; he lies down on the
little bed, we cover him up, we arrange the pillows, he
searches with his feet for the hot water bottle and, smiling,
says we may begin to talk.

Q: At this point in your life, do you have any strong desire to return to
the United States?

A: I have no such desire. Perhaps if it were possible to travel by ship
I would do it; but I don't like planes. Furthermore, I don't know anybody there. Everyone has died; I have no family, no friends. What
would I do with myself? Nothing. My agent is there, yes, but I have
agents in other places. No, no. If I had heard wonderful things about the
United States . . . I would be curious. But everyone has told me such
awful things that I have no interest in seeing it: that it is a completely
criminal country, dirty, extremely expensive. Why go?

Q: Do you still feel you're an American?

A: I am an American.

Q: It's just that it caught my attention while reading your autobiography and also a biography about you that one of your countrymen wrote . . .

A: I hate it. He wrote it maliciously. He came five times from America so that I could help him. I told him, "I don't want for you or anybody to write my biography." He answered that more things needed to be told and when I refused to reply to his questions, each time he became more offended. He ended up writing the book, and he has the legal right to do that. But it was immoral, and his book is defamatory. They paid him a fortune. The publisher was a friend of Anne Getty, and I do mean friend, and she gave him $2.5 million to start this enterprise. Later they quarreled and Anne took back the money. The only thing I regret is that they didn't quarrel before publishing that garbage.

Q: What stories did the author want to tell and how much did he hurt you?

A: He wrote scandalous lies about my wife Jane. He talks, for example, about the time when she was already sick and we were in Lisbon, and I was going to the American Embassy every day for them to give us a passport. They told me that they couldn't do it, that beforehand they had to get in touch with the FBI. Finally they told us no and demanded that we leave Portugal immediately. This problem was due to our former activities in the Communist party for a few short months many years ago. But that made no difference. That which had been true was still true. They're like that. Well, now this man writes that all this is a lie, that it's my imagination, a manipulation to get Jane off my hands, to get her away from me. I will never forgive him.

Q: The story about your wife's illness, her being poisoned by a Moroccan woman, do you believe it, or is it a story that has circulated, yours notwithstanding?

A: It's possible, but unlikely. When Jane got sick for the first time the doctor who tended her, who was a good doctor, told me that she thought poisoning was a possibility and when I said to her, "How can you believe in a thing like that?" she replied, "Look, I've been a doctor in Morocco for 18 years, and during this time I've seen so many similar cases that I can believe it. This country is terrible. You have to see it to believe it."

Q: In the last of your books published in Spain, *Midnight Mass,* two of the stories involve poisonings.

A: Yes. The story about the American who was poisoned by his servant was taken from an actual event that I didn't experience first hand, but which some friends of mine know a great deal about. That man died just as I recounted here, in Morocco. The other story, the one about the woman who puts poison in a plate of food in order to kill the in-laws of her son so that he can inherit their house, is a commonplace thing, something that happens here. People are like this, not all of them, but enough of them that one has to be careful.

Q: Did you become interested in these themes before your wife got sick?

A: Definitely. When I first came to Morocco 60 years ago, these things were normal, much more than now. I was fascinated and I asked questions to find out more. Thus I was able to recognize that the practice of black magic was commonplace, that it was literally in the fabric of this society. And that it animated it. Black magic and white magic, which is not so serious. And it is so extensive, so common, that the enchantments, the routine spells, over issues of little value, are common knowledge. I myself have found under my pillowcase a small bag of powders that turned out to be arsenic mixed with lead, which acts upon the skin, penetrating and eventually poisoning. Women in particular possess this knowledge; the men are really the victims. Then there are the great sorcerers and true witches to whom one appeals for important matters, for deaths. This idea interested me a great deal for a time; then I backed off from it. I got scared.

Q: Did you start to believe in it?

A: I don't believe in it. But if they believe, and have faith, it can turn out that they succeed. As it happens, at a specific moment of my life I looked for it and it found me.

Q: When the doctor spoke about the possibility that your wife had been poisoned, what did you do? Did you tell her?

A: The doctor said that we had to get that woman out of the house. But Jane neither agreed nor wanted to hear any talk about that. Everyone was telling her so, but Jane stood firm: "I brought her into the house and I will turn her out when I've a mind to, and you will keep out of this." Finally I intervened but it was too late, she'd already been here for 20 years.

Q: A man who follows reason, an intellectual, who finds himself in such a situation must feel very helpless.

A: The worst part was that there was nothing I could do. Jane didn't believe that this woman would have been poisoning her even though everyone was telling her so, the Europeans and the Moroccans. "You just don't know her," was her reply.

Q: It would seem to be a case of possession.

A: Yes, at night when Jane was asleep she would go to her bedside and talk to her in whispers. I saw it. She told her, "Tomorrow you are going to give me 50,000 francs. I need 50,000 francs." Over and over. And in the morning when Jane awoke the first thing that she would say was that she had to give 50,000 francs to her friend. It seems unbelievable, doesn't it? When I had finally sent her to hell I wanted to go get a plant that was on the lower floor which Jane had occupied. It was a philodendron which nobody was taking care of and was there on the terrace. This woman stood herself in the doorway and told me, "That plant stays here." "I'm going to take it with me," I protested. And then she took a small dagger which she always carried out of the belt of her pants and told me that she was going to kill me. No plant is worth dying for so I departed. But I told my writer friend Mohammed Mrabet, and he decided to go get the pot. She threatened him, but he brought the plant up and set about transplanting it because the pot was small and the plant couldn't grow in it. Upon breaking the clay, we were horrified. Among the roots there was a big wad of very dirty cloth. My own Moroccan servant shouted, "Don't touch it!" and Mrabet was also frightened. I replied that I was not Muslim and that their spells couldn't affect me. At least, this is what they tell me and I believe it. So I picked up this thing and opened it. It was disgusting. A mass of hair and rotted unrecognizable stuff.

Q: Did you know what the charm was for?

A: Yes. I asked my Moroccan friends. The plant served as an assistant to this woman; while she was out of the house, it kept Jane under her influence. It had specific instructions that my wife not escape the possession.

Q: Do you believe in such things or not?

A: I experienced it in this case, but it is something others believe in. It worked as it did because that woman wanted it to and believed that she could do it. But this does not oblige me to take it seriously. However it is true that in Morocco poisons are used and the killers remain anonymous because in this country there is no chance of an autopsy.

They believe that when a person dies, it is because God has taken him. They say, "If they're already dead, what difference does it make who did it?"

Q: Were you afraid? Did you feel threatened?

A: Yes. All the Moroccans told me, "Be careful. She's going to kill you." And she had threatened me: "I will kill you." But I knew that she didn't have any particular power. I considered her a criminal, nothing more. She was no witch, even though she would have liked to be one. It went on like that, even though I refused to see her. For years, she sent me threatening letters which she did not write, because she's illiterate. But I never believed her.

Q: How did she succeed in fascinating your wife to the point of enslaving her?

A: I've never understood that. I took her to court. Imagine the irony. An Algerian friend had told me that he knew a wonderful girl, and one day we went to the place where she sold wheat. There she was, in the big straw hat with ribbons that the farm women wear, in a red and white striped apron. She had very wild eyes. The only thing that attracted one's attention were her strange eyes. She said that she was a saint, a virgin, that she had certificates to prove it. She had gone to several doctors to get them.

Q: It has been said that the protagonist couple in your best-known book, *The Sheltering Sky*, tells of the relationship of you and your wife. Writers always deny things like this. But was it actually true?

A: Jane was not with me on that trip. The male protagonist is a self-portrait. As for the female character, let us say that I used Jane as a model the same way that a painter would.

Q: Bertolucci, on becoming interested in this book . . .

A: Yes, Bertolucci also believes that the characters are us, he told me personally. I've tried to convince him to the contrary, but he's told me in no uncertain terms he wants this story to be true and he intends to make the movie with this idea in mind.

Q: Bertolucci is probably more fascinated with you two than with the book.

A: Yes, I know. I'm glad that Bertolucci is making the film because he is a man of refined intelligence and sensitivity. It would not have pleased me at all if an American director from Hollywood had bought the rights. Of course, there is a Spanish director who has bought the rights for another of my books. His name is Pedro Almodóvar.

Q: For many years you were a composer; then you turned to literature and ended up abandoning music for good. Do you know why this happened?

A: There are things that cannot be said with music, many things; for example, relationships among people. At one point that was what I became interested in describing. Music is abstract and I wanted to be very specific in describing these things. I had spent many years in the abstract, too many years.

Q: And you felt the need to descend . . .

A: Literature is beneath music?

Q: I'm referring to the need to descend to the most everyday things, to people's whims.

A: Exactly. And music wouldn't let me do that. Even though, perhaps, I concentrated sufficiently on technique to achieve it. Writing words is less painful for me; writing music makes me very anxious. But I don't know why this happened to me.

Q: In one of your biographies written by a French author, it says that the only thing that has really ever interested you has been writing.

A: I would never put it that way. I always say that I don't know; an answer that is certain and true. Many people come up to me and ask me why I came to Morocco and why I stayed . . . These are questions that I cannot answer because the answer is very complex. These are things that stand outside of me, that come upon me, like Jane's illness.

Q: Commenting on this period of time, you say that you've been happy without trying almost all your life, and that from the time Jane became ill you lived in hell until the point that you got used to it. Did you mean to protect yourself from suffering, or did you abandon yourself to the situation?

A: It wasn't easy to protect one's self. She could not write, and this made her suffer tremendously. She called to me every second, for me to come talk to her, and I couldn't do any writing, either. So I gave up trying and devoted myself to translations. During this time I translated ten of Mrabet's books, including *Love With a Few Hairs,* which was published in his country.

Q: After reading your autobiography, I came to the conclusion that you are a very cold person, that you have passed through cities and people without anything leaving the slightest mark.

A: But it was done on purpose. That is what I wanted, a relationship with facts, nothing more. Look, I accepted writing my life story for one single reason: because I needed money to take care of Jane. At the beginning I said no, until the publishers raised the offer to a large sum, but no one has understood that I never wanted in any way to talk about real people; I only like to talk about the people I invent. My publisher would call me once a month to tell me, "Write about everyone you've known. You need to talk about sexuality, about drugs." That is what I was not ready to give. I didn't want to tell how at any particular moment Max Ernst had a French mistress with whom he was living and his wife was furious.

Q: It also caught my attention that you say that you've never believed in love, that the sexual act disgusts you because its only purpose is procreation.

A: I've been asked if I've ever been in love in my life, and I've had to say no. To be in love is something else. I don't know if it has any-thing to do with sex. I don't know. Who knows. Maybe love exists.

Q: What importance has it had in your life?

A: Not much importance. I don't remember it having any. How does love express itself? I believe that I've been able to express it better with music than in words, because to me love is something abstract. Maybe because of that I wanted to abandon music. Those are rare things for me, and I don't know what to think about them. I've always thought about love as something prohibited by society, by the world. I suppose that that's the result of having a family from New England. Religion and love were obscene topics that didn't come up at home.

Q: On leaving your homeland and starting to live your life, did love cease being obscene?

A: I've always hung on to that idea; that idea has had a hold on me. In what I did and what I thought, I knew it was coloring my perceptions.

Q: Do you mean that you've never freed yourself from that repressive upbringing, that you continued to be a little boy in New England?

A: Exactly that. One can't throw everything in the trash. That's not an option. One remains as one was as a child, on into adolescence. One becomes a man and still preserves the rules that one's parents taught.

Q: All of the traveling that you have done. Was it guided by a need to know yourself, to escape?

A: I say that I wanted to come to know the world.

Q: And come to know yourself?

A: It's difficult to answer that now. I believed that I was motivated by my eagerness to know the world.

Q: In *The Sheltering Sky* the story is told about a trip through the desert, but that trip is also the initiation of one of the characters. Perhaps, as is wont to happen, you are using fiction to describe reality.

A: I was writing in an obsessive manner, everything I do I do obsessively. I mean that generally I don't know what I'm doing. I know that I have to write and write, and afterward, if someone asks me what I wanted to say, then I tell them I don't know.

Q: Something else that you say is that someone who has been in the desert is never the same again. What do you mean by that?

A: It's true that one changes. But I can't explain it exactly. I realized that I loved all those things: the sun, the silence, the nothingness. I had never been sure whether I liked those things. But in order to feel all that you have to be completely alone, far from the natives and the colonials. I now think it's an esthetic consideration more than anything else.

Q: Your wife was a writer before you were. What influence did she have on your decision to write?

A: While she was writing her second novel, since she had destroyed the first one in French, I looked it over chapter by chapter, discussing it with her. And this made me want to be a writer, I thought that I would have liked to write her novel; that it would be good to be a writer, better than making music. But the odd thing is that she destroyed her work, that no sooner did she finish it than she tossed it in the trash. So if there remains anything of hers it's because I've kept it.

Q: Why would she want to destroy her work? Do you think that she was a self-destructive woman?

A: I don't know. I never managed to grasp her viewpoint. Never.

Q: Was she crazy?

A: Oh, no. She was neurotic, changing from hour to hour, like mercury. She was an odd bird; but she was a woman, she wasn't a man, and I arrived at the conclusion that a woman can change from one minute to the next without anyone saying anything about it. All she has to say is, "This is how I feel right now."

Q: And you consider men to be more clearheaded?

A: If they aren't, they hide what they feel. Showing yourself to be emotional and ever-changing seems embarrassing to them.

Q: You've now lived most of your lifetime. When you take account of it all, are you satisfied?

A: Yes, I'm happy with the way in which things have transpired. I have no regrets, everything happened as it had to happen, because everything is written.

Q: Do you believe in predestination?

A: Yes. Because I've lived here many years, where everyone believes in it. Yes, the only thing that you can do is to follow your destiny.

Q: Have you ended up thinking like a Muslim?

A: No. But perhaps I'm more Muslim than Christian. I've never understood what Christianity was about. When I've asked, no one has been able to explain it to me. I understand Islam much better, and maybe for this reason certain of my beliefs have been corrupted.

Bowles's friend, Mrabet, author of *Love With a Few Hairs,* smokes a pipe of *kif* in front of the fireplace in the small living room and waits while we finish with photographs of the writer. He has been asked to take me to the balcony to see the "secretary plant." Its branches, as big around as fingers, like claws, have grown so much in the past twenty years that they take up the entire space and are beginning to invade the house. Mrabet remarks that he is going to write the Bowleses' history. He knows him well; since he came into his life fifteen years ago, to stay.

"It wasn't the Moroccan woman who poisoned Jane. Perhaps she tried to kill herself some other way."

"What? What do you mean?" I ask.

"Well, it's complicated to explain, it's something that I'll have to tell in my book."

At present, he takes care of Bowles, who has transcribed the stories that he, an illiterate, dictates to a tape recorder. "It's the Jews who practice magic in Morocco, not the Arabs."

Perhaps he has forgotten the secret he told us earlier: he has visited a man in the country who, with the roots of a certain small plant, can cure his American friend of this recent illness.

Mercury at 80

Stephen Davis/1990

From *The Boston Globe Magazine* (4 March 1990): 14–20, 24–25. Copyright © 1990 Stephen Davis. Reprinted by permission of Stephen Davis.

On a cerulean blue autumn evening in Morocco, in the jasmine-scented gardens of Tangier's El Minzeh Hotel, Italian film director Bernardo Bertolucci is hosting a glittering cocktail party. Guests include select members of Tangier's diplomatic and expatriate community plus the cast and crew of Bertolucci's new movie, whose interiors are being shot in and around the city before the production moves to points deeper into the Sahara.

Bertolucci's current epic, his first since *The Last Emperor*, a multiple Oscar winner, is an adaptation of an almost-forgotten 1949 novel set in the desert, *The Sheltering Sky*. His two Hollywood stars, the glamorous and garrulous Debra Winger and the soft-spoken, faintly sinister John Malkovich, hold court in separate corners of the oasislike garden, obviously relieved that another day's shooting in the oppressive heat is finished.

And over by the pool, in the shade of a giant palm, sits the guest of honor: the impeccably tailored white-haired American author of *The Sheltering Sky*, Paul Bowles. Eighty years old, resident of Tangier since 1947, the slender and elegant Bowles sips a glass of sweet mint tea, chats with the friends and admirers who surround him, and signs copies of his books. After four decades of self-imposed exile, Paul Bowles is clearly relishing his time in the spotlight. Smiling, magisterial, Bowles looks like an old god: Mercury at 80.

Since 1947 Bowles has lived on the other fringe of Western Civ., an appropriate address for the dean of American expatriate writers. He is an authentic literary cult hero, an author who often depicts his country-men losing themselves to the mysteries of worlds beyond experience and comprehension.

Among more famous writers Bowles' technical skills are considered legendary and alchemical. A few years ago Gore Vidal wrote of

227

Bowles: "He cooly creates nightmare visions in which his specimens drown in fantasy, in madness, in death. His short stories with their plain lines of monochromatic prose exploit extreme situations with a chilling resourcefulness. He says, in short, 'Let us sink. Let us drown.' His stories are among the best ever written by an American." Bowles' influence on Mod. US Lit. is even more succinctly defined by Norman Mailer: "Paul Bowles opened the world of Hip. He let in the murder, the drugs, the incest, the death of the Square . . . the call of the orgy, the end of civilization."

Bowles' protean career as composer, writer, and translator spans almost every major artistic movement of our century. He is the last of the Lost Generation of writers who knew Paris in the '20s. He participated in the radical art of the '30s and the New York vanguard of the '40s. In the '50s he was the patron saint of the Beats—Kerouac, Ginsberg, Burroughs—who flocked to Tangier, and he served the same role for many of the so-called underground writers of the '60s. Even in the '70s he was proclaimed the first of the minimalists. In the '80s Sting and other rock stars wrote songs in homage to Paul Bowles.

But in the United States, his native land, Bowles is barely known except among academics and rare-book collectors. One senses that, like his own hero Edgar Allan Poe, Paul Bowles will be considered a "great" writer only after he dies. That is, unless Signore Bertolucci rehabilitates him first.

A quick study of Paul Bowles' career is almost impossible, since the scope of his achievement extends so far back. He was born in New York in 1910, the descendant of two old New England families. Early music lessons blossomed into operettas written before he was 10. He enrolled at the University of Virginia because Poe had gone there, but quickly ran away to Paris after his first poems were published in the avant-garde literary magazine *transition.*

In Paris, his blond good looks and precocity won him a place in the household of Gertrude Stein and Alice B. Toklas in 1928. Eventually Miss Stein, the arbiter of good taste in expat Lost Generation artistic circles, bluntly told the young Bowles to forget poetry—"Your work is all false!" she complained—and advised him to concentrate on music instead, so he might earn a living.

Thus Bowles took up composition lessons with another expat, Aaron Copland. Together, teacher and pupil voyaged through Europe and, again at Stein's suggestion, North Africa. Observing the coast of

Morocco for the first time from ship deck in 1931, Bowles later wrote, "I felt that some interior mechanism had been set in motion by the sight of the approaching land. . . . Like any Romantic, I had been certain that sometime in my life I should come into a magic place which in disclosing its secrets would give me wisdom and ecstasy—perhaps even death."

During the '30s Bowles continued his musical studies with Virgil Thomson and Nadia Boulanger. In 1937 he met and married a young New Yorker named Jane Auer, who as Jane Bowles would attract a fiercely loyal literary cult of her own. The Bowleses were a notorious couple even back then, "famous among the famous," in the words of Gore Vidal. Bowles was assumed to be homosexual, and she was openly lesbian. They spent long periods sojourning in Central America, often with traveling companions. Bowles would collect local folk melodies, which back in New York would be transformed into the operas, songs, piano music, and ballet and film scores he produced.

By 1938 Bowles was composing incidental stage music for Orson Welles' Mercury Theater; this occupation would sustain him in the New York of the war years. Bowles composed music for plays by Lillian Hellman, William Saroyan, and George Abbott, and for most of Tennessee Williams' early triumphs. By night he also served as a music critic for the old *Herald Tribune*.

Tiring of that life, Bowles changed careers again in 1947, when it was safe to travel after the tumult of the war. Leaving New York, he returned to Morocco and began to write fiction, later that year publishing a landmark short story, "A Distant Episode," in *Partisan Review*. The story concerns a distinguished European professor of linguistics who visits the Sahara to study tribal dialects but who instead wanders down the wrong alley and is kidnapped by nomads. They cut out his tongue and enslave him, quite willingly in the end. This shocking, viscerachurning clash of civilization and savagery became the fulcrum of Paul Bowles' new career as a writer.

He spent 1948 wandering through Saharan towns, working on his first novel, *The Sheltering Sky*, which had been commissioned on the strength of "A Distant Episode." The story of the desert journey of two skittishly married Americans, Kit and Port Moresby, and their companion, Tunner, *The Sheltering Sky* pitches its drifting, soul-sick characters into various fatal agonies of alienation and despair.

When published in 1949, the novel caused a furor, with Bowles denounced as the archbishop of paranoid expatriation. He was accused of the sins of postwar French existentialism: moving his cast of spiritual misfits through Godforsaken wastelands in search of Everything and Nothing. Why not, his supporters argued. Look at the times! Tennessee Williams, reviewing the book for *The New York Times,* observed *The Sheltering Sky* to be "one of the few books to bear the spiritual imprint of recent history in the western world."

The Sheltering Sky was a bestseller in 1950, and Bowles has been crafting prose ever since: three more novels, several collections of lapidary short stories and poetry, and more than 20 volumes of English translations of Moroccan stories from Maghrebi Arabic.

Only 10 years ago, few of Bowles' books were in print. Critics complained that, in anticipating literary modernism, Bowles' style seemed dated. Others were put off by Bowles' championing of kif and *majoun* (both age-old Moroccan cannabis preparations) as aids to writerly insight and technique. After Jane Bowles died in 1973, having gone mad, Bowles' output dwindled. But he always had champions on both sides of the Atlantic, and his cult was sustained by small presses— Black Sparrow, City Lights, and Tombouctou in California, Peter Owen in London—and magazines from *Rolling Stone* to *Antaeus,* the respected literary quarterly Bowles cofounded in Tangier in 1970.

But the years of obscurity and neglect are safely in the past. Bertolucci, auteur of *Last Tango in Paris, The Conformist, 1900,* and *The Last Emperor,* is busy converting *The Sheltering Sky* into the hottest movie of 1991. Random House is paying Bowles in the low six figures for reprint rights to the novel, and he is now shadowed around Tangier by TV crews from the BBC and the French channel Antenne 2, who are intent on documenting his daily routine.

The amazing thing, for anyone familiar with Bowles' work turns out to be the writer's epochal stamina and patience. All those years, he stayed in remote Morocco and never sold out. Paul Bowles simply waited, and now the world has come to him.

With no phone and only a post office box for an address, Bowles is not an easy man to find. To know him, one must know Tangier.

Like its most famous resident, Tangier has braved some hard times and is now back in the limelight. A 5,000-year-old white-walled Mediterranean city overlooking the Strait of Gibraltar, Tangier was Tingis to the seafaring Phoenicians and Tingitana Mauretania to the

Romans. When Paul Bowles first arrived, it wasn't part of Morocco but a wide-open International Zone run by its foreign legations.

After World War II Tangier flourished as an offshore banking parlor whose generous exchange rates and permissive moral code attracted members of the Euro-American Hipoisie—the Bowleses, Truman Capote, Cecil Beaton, minor British royalty, and literary artists such as Jean Genet, William Burroughs, and Brion Gysin. Bowles recalls that it was Tangier's golden era, when the streets were full of flowers and one could have anything for almost nothing.

But Tangier quickly lost its allure when it was absorbed into newly independent Morocco in 1956. Tangier became shabby. The efficient colonial postal system collapsed, making life more difficult. Beggars filled the streets of the medina, or native quarter, and the boulevards of the newer European city farther up the hill. Due to a lifelong grudge, Morocco's autocratic king, Hassan II, never visits Tangier; for years the old city of cats and whores has been economically bypassed by Morocco's other cities—Fez and Marrakesh, Casablanca and Rabat. Recently it took a Saudi prince rather than the king to build an imposing new mosque whose minaret is now properly taller than the spire of the Catholic *eglise* across town.

This is a sign of better times for Tangier. With the destruction of Beirut, Tangier has become a new playground for the Arab petrocracy from the Middle East. Property values have skyrocketed since the Kuwaitis and rich young sports from the Emirates began wheeling their enormous white BMWs through the Socco Grande at nightfall. And they're not the only ones. Malcolm Forbes has a huge palace in Tangier (though Bowles says Forbes rarely visits); last year's mammoth birthday party for Forbes, starring Elizabeth Taylor and a cast of thousands, put raffish Tangier back on the social map for the first time since heiress Barbara Hutton occupied her own sultanic palace in the Casbah, back in the '50s.

And now here's Bernardo Bertolucci, transforming Tangier into a meticulous re-creation of its 1948 self for *The Sheltering Sky,* which in turn was being chronicled in October by an editorial team from *Vogue.* Tangier, it would seem, might be the new In Spot of the Gay Nineties.

A few days after the cocktail party I knock on the door of Paul Bowles' fourth-floor apartment on the outskirts of town. Though rather reclusive ("Bowles doesn't mix much," an old Tangerine at the party had said), Bowles usually offers a cup of tea and an hour of chat to whomever turns up at his doorstep after lunch. I had visited him a few times in the '70s and found him to be hospitable, attentive, and insightful about my own research in Morocco's hill country. Now I'm curious to see how the sudden bustle around him has changed his life.

His door, No. 20, is opened by another Tangier legend, Mohammed Mrabet. Señor Bowles is still working on the film, Mrabet says, but I'm welcome to come in and wait. We sit in a living room stuffed with books, correspondence, paintings, and cassettes. Red-eyed as a Rastafarian, about 50, Mrabet smokes kif in a long pipe called a *sebsi* and complains about his publisher. Since 1967 Bowles has recorded and translated a dozen volumes of this Riffian's tall tales and pipe dreams, which have been reprinted all over the world. Mrabet can neither read nor write, yet here he is, moaning that all publishers are bastards and thieves possessed by evil djinn.

Just then, Bowles arrives from a blistering day on the set. He's nattily attired in a three-piece English tweed suit and matching brown suede shoes, a silk tie knotted at his neck. Despite two recent operations, he looks octogenarically healthy, if somewhat exhausted and startled to find a visitor. I apologize profusely and move toward the door, but Bowles says, "No, please don't go. Good to see you again. How long has it been since you were here? Well, let's sit because I'm all in, as the British say." Speaking gruffly in Spanish, he tells the wasted Mrabet to get in the kitchen and put the kettle on.

"Oh, I'm very tired," Bowles says, as he slumps into a nest of pillows propped against a bookcase. "When they first told me about this movie, they didn't inform me I was expected to work on it. Now Bertolucci has got me on the set as an advisor and recording voice-overs like a narrator. I'm also appearing in several scenes—just, you know, walking through. But he shoots them over and again and just informed me—Mrabet? are you listening?—that they want me back on the set *at 8:45 in the morning!*"

Spoken as if the hour were unthinkable, uncivilized. Nothing happens in the morning in Tangier.

Mrabet comes in with deep amber cups of tea and talks about how sick he was at the party. "After one drink I go out to a cafe and throw-up vomit two, three liters," he says with pride. "It's my liver," he confides. A doctor gives him medication, but Mrabet prefers the folk-loric treatment, honey and olive oil.

Stimulated by the strong black tea, Bowles is recalled to life, his blue eyes alert and searching. I ask if Winger and Malkovich remind him of the characters he created 40 years ago and remark that to me they seem old for the roles. "Oh no," Bowles retorts, eyebrows raised. "You're mistaken. The text states that they've been married a dozen years. They're in their 30s, the characters, which is right for these actors." (Bertolucci's first choices for the roles were William Hurt and Melanie Griffith; both declined due to the imminent arrival of babies.)

"And yes," he goes on, "they do remind me of the Moresbys, espe-cially when they're made up and in costume. People have always asked whether the characters represent me and Mrs. Bowles, but of course they don't really. No. It's more like a story about a journey we *might* have gone on, but we didn't."

Bowles says he was amused to see that Bertolucci's crew spent the day laying tracks near the bottom of the Casbah so an old trolley could rumble through a scene. "As far as I know, no streetcar ever operated in Morocco," he says. "But then, I don't really see why they're filming here in the first place since the actual story is set entirely in Algeria." Bowles is less amused that the director has summoned a band of Moroc-can musicians from the village of Jahjouka to play music for the sound-track. "I'm against it," he fumes. "The music they hear on their travels should be Algerian! It's ridiculous, the whole thing. There aren't even any dunes in Morocco!"

Then I make the mistake of mentioning *The Invisible Spectator,* the unauthorized biography published last year by Christopher Sawyer-Laucanno, who teaches at MIT. I can see by Bowles' pained expression that this subject is touchy. Though Bowles refused to cooperate, his biographer showed up anyway for tea and Bowles, with characteristic hospitality, did not turn him away. Even before the book came out last summer, Bowles publicly complained, in a journal entry published in *Antaeus:* "Conversation with [Sawyer-Laucanno] is like talking with the doctor immediately after he tells you: 'Yes, you have cancer,' and then goes on: 'But let's speak about something else.' I wonder if he knows how deeply I resent his flouting my wishes."

"To add insult to injury," Bowles now says, *"The New York Times* reviewed his book prominently, called me a bore almost in passing, and said my apartment house looks like a corner in Queens." He laughs without humor. His voice is sad and heavy, bitter. "They also said one tends to get the biographer one deserves. But I think I ought to deserve better than Christopher Sawyer-Laucanno."

Asked whom he would have chosen, he responds, "No one, because I didn't want a biography in my lifetime. But if I *had* to choose, it would have been Millicent Dillon, just out of loyalty." Dillon wrote *A Little Original Sin,* a biography of Jane Bowles. "No," he says, "I don't like his book at all."

There is a silence. I tell Bowles that the last time I'd seen him, he said he felt isolated and cut off from the Western world, and now, at an advanced age, he is reaping a harvest of recognition and cash. How is he coping?

He laughs. "I don't know. How should I be coping?"

Well, I say, you could refuse Bertolucci the way you rejected the biography.

"I see what you mean," he says. "You're right. I can tell you that all this is not what I'm used to."

At 5 o'clock, the apartment begins to fill up with friends: a 40-ish American couple and an older Englishwoman who has a house in Tangier and an art gallery in Paris. She gives Bowles a copy of Bertolucci's screenplay, a hot black-market item in Tangier these days. Somehow, she gloats, one of her servants had gotten one. One of the visitors takes out a joint and lights it. "Mrabet's finest," he says.

"We're filming at the Hotel Continental tomorrow," Bowles tells me when I leave. "If we don't see you there, come back before you leave Tangier. Don't fail."

"Ah, you're back," Paul Bowles says when I knock on his door a week later. He shakes hands warmly. "Tell me, how was it up in Jahjouka?"

I explain that it was a bit of an ordeal: spending several days battling heat, thirst, Moroccan officialdom, long uphill hikes, and a feuding mountain tribe in order to visit the musicians in their village. "But at least it was an *ecstatic* ordeal," I report, "once the music started."

"Of course it was an ordeal," Bowles snorts. "That's why I don't go up there. But when they came down here last summer to play with the Rolling Stones [a group of Jahjouka musicians played on one of the

Steel Wheels tracks], I visited the recording session and quite liked the music I heard." (Bowles is a longtime connoisseur of Moroccan folk music; an album of his field recordings had been issued by the Library of Congress.)

Mohammad Mrabet breaks in to proclaim he doesn't understand why anyone—Bowles, the Stones, Bertolucci, me—likes that music. "It's just peep, peep, peep," he says, laughing. "Look at me. I'm Moroccan, and I don't like it." He nods toward Bowles and says in Spanish that Bowles has lived here for 60 years and even *he* doesn't understand Morocco. He adds, "No Nazarene can understand Morocco. Not possible."

When Mrabet is finished, Bowles mentions that he had dinner with Debra Winger the night before. Winger is installed with her family in a rented villa on the Old Mountain, overlooking the town. "And she was quite upset. Bertolucci was making her play her big mad scene out of sequence because all the interior scenes are being done here. She said she told him that she didn't want to go mad before she 'experienced' the events in the story that drive her insane."

Which is understandable, he says with a sigh, since still to be filmed are an affair with Tunner (played in the movie by Campbell Scott, son of George C.), the death of her husband, and her rape and abduction into a harem. "One can sympathize," Bowles says, "but Bertolucci was firm. She has to go mad, for continuity's sake, before any of this happens. I suppose it's one of the hazards of the trade."

Mrabet looks at his watch, conspicuously. "I'm afraid I must go to bed at 6 o'clock," Bowles says. "My health has been fragile, and Mrabet has me on a regimen. Come back tomorrow and we can talk." Later, in the Gran Café Paris, where the day's gossip is retailed every night, an old friend of Bowles' laments that the writer is too dependent on Mrabet, who feeds him and puts him to bed as well as controls access to Bowles and prevents him from making new friendships. It is rumored that Bowles has made Mrabet his heir, the friend says, and recalls the old Tangier expat legend that Jane Bowles went mad only after being poisoned by her Moroccan maid. I think of the hours I have spent with Bowles and Mrabet, and wonder if I will ever see them again.

Two months later, Bertolucci and his crew have reached Ouarzazate, an old caravan terminus in the extreme south of Morocco. The project is on schedule despite occasional days lost to the ravages of intestinal microbes, which induce a diarrhea so awesome that, after a few days, a traveler questions his or her sanity and prospects for the future. In their darkened hotel rooms, the members of the company are drinking 100 cases of mineral water a day. Sidi Ali and Sidi Harazem seem to be the favorite brands.

Spirits remain high. The cast senses that *The Sheltering Sky* is going to be a big hit that is also an artistic success. So one evening there's another gathering for the crew after supper, with penetrating dance rhythms pumped out by the Jahjouka musicians, whom Bertolucci has imported from their northern lair so they can be filmed in the undulating Ouarzazate desert hillscape. The musicians have a violin and a half-dozen hand drummers working, and the beat is irresistible. When Tair the fiddler and Bashir Attar begin to sing, Debra Winger gets up to dance, eyes closed, swinging her hips. Soon everybody's doing it, and the dancers spill onto the terrace and gasp when they look up at the blazing canopy of stars that illumines the black cobalt of the enormous Saharan sky.

Paul Bowles, meanwhile, remains in Tangier. He told Bertolucci that he didn't enjoy traveling in Morocco anymore. For Bowles, Tangier is like a lover or a wife. "There is drumming out there most nights," he has written. "It never awakens me. I hear the drums and incorporate them into my dream, like the nightly call of the muezzins. Even if in the dream I'm in New York, the first *Allah akbar!* effaces the backdrop and carries whatever comes next to North Africa, and the dream goes on."

Paul Bowles: A Nomad Stranded in Tangier

Josep Massot/1990

From *La Vanguardia Magazine* [Madrid, Spain] (15 April 1990).

Paul Bowles will be 80 in December and after having created all possible maps of our internal and external geography, he has settled for good in his small and unglamorous apartment in Tangier. In the narrow, short hallway are stacked forgotten trunks and leather suitcases with exotic cargo tickets, gathering dust like vestiges of a shipwreck in time. The living room, as well, seems to exist in a realm outside time, halfway between day and night. Bowles always has the shades drawn, and the mixture of filtered sunlight and electric light creates an atmosphere the color of sand. The fire is blazing, in spite of the fact that the temperature outside is springlike. More than a hundred books line the bookshelves, major editions of his own works and those of his friends, like James Purdy. Next to the sofa, covered with pillows, are tapes of Bach and Arabian music, a tea tray, and in the corner opposite, more books. Between them is a French essay on sorcery.

Paul Bowles and Jane Auer had a strange marriage. Mythmakers compare them to Zelda and Scott Fitzgerald from the desperate postwar years, without specifying who is Zelda and who Scott. Jane exercised a strange fascination over many, often becoming the center around which pivoted those celebrities near the Bowleses. They were like Lewis Carroll and Alice in the maze of the Casbah, or King Arthur and Guinevere in an artificial kingdom, with the difference that it was she who held a court of knights bewitched while he rode off in search of the Grail—to South America, Africa, Asia, and the dark side of the spirit, that vast unexplored continent, dwelling place of monsters, labyrinth of the mind. "As a child I was afraid that a monster lived inside me, or that I myself was a monster, or that my mother was a monster who had come into my room in the middle of the night," said Paul Bowles. In Ceylon he would hear a rumor of flocks of enormous vampire bats, and his blood would run cold at the thought of the dangers all around. In Morocco he would see men taking the shape of animals and would know the essence

of solitude in the desert that, they say, changes people. In his
tales of hermetic worlds, as intense as legends, nothing
happens, but through his narrative he creates a countryside,
the interior world of fear and fatality, of death and of people
persecuted by the macabre breath of calamity arriving at the
end of their journey.

Bowles is an affable and entertaining man, with a good
sense of humor that leaves him only when he is talking about
his wife. He has transferred his own existential fears to his
characters, translated the anguishing descent into hell of
Sartre's *Huis Clos* into the English *No Exit* for a production
by John Huston. He considered this task a therapeutic exer-
cise, freeing him of an obsession with such anxieties. This
terror as powerful as a drug—the "miserable miracle," as the
great traveler Henri Michaux called it—Bowles transformed
in quiet dreams, cruel stories that reflect a tripart universe:
the mind, the body, and the spirit, three realms in which man
wanders, occasionally catching a glimpse of himself as if in a
mirror. He writes of a world without love, often frustrating,
full of guilt rather than joy, and of a "sheltering sky," solid
and opaque, that hides space devastated by constellations
and clouds, whose meaning one can never know, because it
is wrapped up with the mystery of his own existence.

Q: In your autobiography, which is now being published for the first
time in Castilian, you say that the men of the maternal side of your
family would break their noses with a hammer according to custom. Is
that right?

A: I have never understood this and it remains a mystery for me.
I don't know why. My great grandfather must have had some kind of
obsession with his nose. I suppose that someone had broken his when he
was young, and he said, from now on I'm going to break the noses of
my children. It's sadistic to be sure, and as a small child I was afraid
that they were going to make me do the same thing.

Q: You also say that you learned to pretend that what gave you
pleasure disgusted you, and to express enthusiasm for that which you
found distasteful so that your father wouldn't notice and forbid it.

A: I suppose all children fear their fathers, especially if that father is
cruel. But no one in my family was religious, in fact quite the contrary.
They were intolerant of any form of religion or of sexual pleasure. The

Bowleses are from New England. That is where all of the fanatical religions were born. From childhood my mother was a Unitarian, something frowned upon in the United States; it was the religion of Emerson
and of Thoreau; they ridiculed Catholics because the Catholics say that
Jesus Christ was the son of God and they found that absurd: no one is
the son of God, that is impossible.

Q: You spoke with no other children until the age of 5 years, and
already at this age you were inventing countries and writing stories that
you hid from your father. Later, as soon as you could, you fled the
United States.

A: I didn't like the United States. When I was 5 years old, what I
wanted was to escape from my family, to go to another home with other
people, and later when I was older what I wanted was to escape from
the country entirely. It seems normal to me that a young man should
want to escape from his family and country. I suppose that because one
knows his city and his culture, is used to it, has lived always inside of
it, he would want to know the opposite. No more than that. Just like the
cat or the dog that you have in your house: if you leave the door open
one minute it's off and running.

Q: And yet in your writing there appears to be a certain vengeance
of non-Western cultures towards the Western ones. You have a story in
which there is a European linguist who wants to be friends with the
Berbers, is captured by them, and they cut out his tongue and turn him
into a musical toy to serve as an object of ridicule.

A: That thing about cutting out the tongue is a little bit exaggerated
but it serves for the purposes of fiction. I don't know of anybody who's
had his tongue cut out. Other things, yes.

Q: In your books—as well as in a novel by one of your favorite
authors, Gide—there appears every kind of physical mutilation. Are
you embracing the primitive, the irrational, in rejection of the rational
culture of the West?

A: It's an emotional issue which gives me satisfaction. Emotional,
not personal. It is not an idea. I don't have ideas. Nor do I use alle-
gories or metaphors.

Q: Despite all the years you've been living in Tangier, they still
consider you a foreigner.

A: Certainly. I am a foreigner. It makes no difference that I've lived
here 59 years. You can live your whole life and always be a foreigner.

I am not a Muslim, and if you're not a Muslim, they don't accept you. They don't accept Christians and they call me a Christian (nesrani, nazareno). "Why don't you want to become a Muslim?" they always say to me. And I reply that I cannot. "Why not?" they insist. And I can't tell them it's because I don't believe in God. They don't like Christians, but they hate atheists. They think that it is a poison very dangerous for the world.

Q: You reject the United States but in Tangier many Moroccans surely wonder what you're doing here when what to them would seem most pleasing would be, no doubt, to live in New York.

A: Yes. For them, New York means money. But I never wanted to become rich. The small countries replace what they destroy with imitations of things from the United States. But that's also happening in Europe. They don't want to leave any traces of the past. They all feel embarrassment. It is painful and incurable. They want to erase any memory.

Q: You studied music with Nadia Boulanger and were close friends with Copland and Bernstein. You say that you admire Satie and Stravinsky, but your music explores no new territory like Cage.

A: Cage was a comedian. One time he came to my house with a record, put it on, and started to writhe around on the floor moaning with pleasure. No serious composer writhes around on the floor making such noises.

The first time Bowles came to Tangier was in 1931, on the advice of Gertrude Stein, who had just told him that he wasn't a poet. Much later he returned with Jane. She had published *Two Serious Ladies,* and he alternated writing and composing music. By then, they had established a code of sexual tolerance, by which Jane had turned away sexually from men and Paul, more and more, from women. The permissive nature of Tangier, the easy access to drugs, the inexpensive and exotic life, had attracted many of their wandering friends, like Tennessee Williams, Truman Capote, Gore Vidal, Brion Gysin, Cecil Beaton, and years later, Brian Jones. William Burroughs came as well, and thus drew to Tangier Allen Ginsberg and Jack Kerouac, who helped type *Naked Lunch.* Behind him Bowles had left the companionship of the surrealists (Ernst, Duchamp) or poets like Auden. He has been considered a minor writer, protagonist in a life more interesting than his novels (few great novelists had passionate lives). Bertolucci, Almodóvar, Sting or King Crimson having launched him into celebrity.

Q: The title of your autobiography, *Without Stopping,* has been parodied under the title "Without Telling."

A: Yes, it was Bill Burroughs. He had a reason for saying that, but on the other hand critics said that it was an autobiography that said nothing. I don't understand it. People want to know what I eat for lunch and above all, why this thing, why that. I never answer a question that starts with a why.

Q: Is it true that Burroughs killed his wife in Mexico?

A: He said that he didn't mean to do it but Brion Gysin said to him, "Are you sure?" and Bill answered, "Well, I really couldn't say for sure."

Q: In one of his exhibits he painted pictures by shooting paint from a gun onto the canvas.

A: Yes, he has a unique manner of painting. Bill has always had a great affection for firearms. I remember that here in Tangier he used to plop down on his bed, grab a gun and start firing at everything, at the wall and at the photographs he had hung on the walls.

Q: To get inside the death of the protagonist in *The Sheltering Sky*, you tried *majoun* (hashish paste). Do you usually write under the effects of drugs?

A: I haven't used *majoun* since 1964, and no, I can't write under the effects of drugs.

Q: Burroughs does.

A: Yes, but he doesn't care whether he finishes a sentence or not. I am limited to writing, never explaining what I write. I don't know what I write. I am very traditional.

Q: Not very. A critic called those American writers who talked about America "redskins" and those who looked to Europe "palefaces." Gore Vidal on the other hand said that you are the only one who writes as if Melville had never existed.

A: Oh, surely, because traditional does not necessarily mean that which follows what came before. The content of my writings is untraditional but their form must be; if not, no one could understand me.

Q: Stevenson said that the important thing is to tell stories. Did he influence your style of telling stories about the Arabs?

A: Yes, yes, that affected my style quite a bit. Now my style is much simpler. I'm used to working with illiterate people. They have hardly any vocabulary and their manner of storytelling is very simple. It is pure narrative. There is no thought behind it.

Q: What do you think of the biography that Dillon wrote about Jane?

A: She managed to do exhaustive research. She never knew Jane, and I think that she never understood that the most important thing about Jane was her sense of humor. She makes the book a tragedy. She talks a lot about her illness, and this is not very interesting. Other people's illness is dreadful. Who wants to hear about such things?

Q: In every way, the two of you had a marriage that was somewhat atypical, and one wonders why you got married at all.

A: Why? We got married in 1938 and it would not have been possible for us to travel together if we were not married. She was a virgin and couldn't consider living with a man out of wedlock. Today everything would be different. But all that took place more than half a century ago.

Q: Is it true that Dillon wrote about Cherifa, the Arab woman that Jane fell in love with? Did she practice witchcraft?

A: Who knows? She wanted to. She did all kinds of awful things. There's a large plant over there, on the terrace, behind the *cortinas*. It was in the downstairs apartment where Jane lived. When my wife died, she wanted it brought up to my floor, but Cherifa threw a fit. "The plant stays here," she said. She placed herself in the doorway so that I couldn't carry it through, and took out the knife that she always carried under her djebella in her jeans, and she was so proud of it because she was always talking about killing men while making threatening gestures like slitting throats. She had a very criminal instinct. I went on up because I didn't want to lose an eye. Later the plant grew until it got too big for its pot so that we had to break the clay to put it into a bigger one, and discovered that among the roots there was a rag. When Mrabet and my servant saw it, they drew back. "Don't touch it," they said. Certainly, because black magic terrified them. I unwrapped it and saw there was inside pubic hair, coagulated menstrual blood and antimony, all very nasty. I flushed it down the toilet. Afterward I found out that Cherifa talked with her plant. She would whisper to it, "When I am away you must talk to Jane and tell her that I'm in charge here and that I need more money," and the plant, according to her, listened and talked to Jane. It was her spy plant.

Q: Are there magic formulas by which one person can possess another?

A: Yes, there are many. There are substances to give to the victim, and this is more dangerous. This is what people said she did to Jane and that for this reason she was ill and had a stroke. I wasn't there, I was in Kenya, in East Africa, and I didn't know about it. When I arrived two months later she was very sick. She didn't know what I was saying, she had aphasia, she would use antonyms, she would say "cold" for "hot," "up" for "down," "he" for "she." People thought that this was very entertaining but it was not amusing in the least and I couldn't go away again. They would say to her, "Jane, you are marvelous." In reality she became very aggressive. She suffered a lot. She was a writer and could neither see nor write. She had to go to classes in New York so they could teach her to talk again. She was never happy again after the accident. Not one moment. She wanted to die. She said that every minute. She asked me to give her some kind of poison and I told her that that was impossible, that no one can kill another person and she answered, "If one wants the other to do it, he does it." She tried to take her own life.

Q: Do you believe that Cherifa killed her?

A: I've never been able to accept that, because if Jane were to die, she would lose everything. The most likely cause of everything was that she drank too much.

Q: How has your life been since Jane's death?

A: My life changed utterly. I've remained here, not bored, but rather static. I could continue traveling, but there are no longer ships. The great ships have died, and I hate airplanes. What's more, I have neither the energy nor the need to stir myself. I no longer know anybody. Outside of living here, I have cut off relations with almost everybody. They have been cut off. Here I also have no friends. I have only a Moroccan chauffeur who comes every morning, makes me a meal, and in the afternoon prepares dinner.

Q: Don't you even perhaps want to go have tea at one of the cafés in the city?

A: No, no, how can I go? The Café de Paris is full of police and spies.

Index

Index